TRANSFORMING THEOLOGY

STUDENT EXPERIENCE AND
TRANSFORMATIVE LEARNING
IN UNDERGRADUATE
THEOLOGICAL EDUCATION

Les Ball

Transforming Theology
Les Ball

SCD Press
PO Box 6110,
Norwest NSW 2153
scdpress@scd.edu.au

First published 2012
Reprinted with new preface in 2023

© Les Ball 2023

Cataloguing-in-Publication entry is available for the National Library of Australia http:/ catalogue.nla.gov.au/.

ISBN-13: 978-1-925730-47-0 (Paperback)
ISBN-13: 978-1-925730-48-7 (E-book)

Key words: curriculum; integrated learning; life experience; student-centred learning

Cover design and internal layout and design: Lankshear Design Pty Ltd.

TRANSFORMING THEOLOGY

STUDENT EXPERIENCE AND
TRANSFORMATIVE LEARNING
IN UNDERGRADUATE
THEOLOGICAL EDUCATION

Les Ball

SCD Press
2023

Publications associated with SCD Learning & Teaching Theology Conferences

1. Les Ball, *Transforming Theology. Student Experience and Transformative Learning in Undergraduate Theological Education* (Preston, Vic.: Mosaic, 2012). Second edition: Norwest, NSW, SCD Press, 2023.
2. Les Ball & James R. Harrison (eds.), *Learning & Teaching Theology. Some Ways Ahead* (Northcote, Vic: Morning Star, 2014). Second edition: Macquarie Park, SCD Press, 2024.
3. Yvette Debergue & James R. Harrison (eds.), *Teaching Theology in a Technological Age* (Cambridge: Cambridge Scholars Publishing, 2015).
4. Les Ball & Peter G. Bolt (eds.), *Wondering About God Together. Research-Led Learning & Teaching in Theological Education* (Macquarie Park, NSW: SCD Press, 2018).
5. Peter G. Bolt & Peter Laughlin (eds.), *God's Exemplary Graduates: Character-Oriented Graduate Attributes in Theological Education* (Macquarie Park, NSW: SCD Press, 2021).
6. Les Ball, *Learning to be Learners: A Mathegenical Approach to Theological Education* (Macquarie Park, NSW: SCD Press, 2022).
7. Peter G. Bolt & Peter Laughlin (eds.), *Testing Us Testing God. Assessment and Theological Competency* (Macquarie Park, NSW: SCD Press, 2022).
8. Peter G. Bolt & Peter Laughlin (eds.), *Thinking for Ourselves for God's Sake* (Norwest, NSW: SCD Press, 2024).

CONTENTS

Acknowledgements	vii
Author's Preface to the Second Edition	ix
Executive Summary	xvii
1 *Genesis of the Project*	1
2 *What are They Saying about Transformative Education?*	9
3 *Curriculum Design and Developments: Learning from History*	39
4 *A Continuing Journey: Life Experience and Learning*	61
5 *A Challenging Journey: Transformation through Learning*	83
6 *Where Does Curriculum Fit into the Journey?*	113
7 *The Current State of Play: Some Good Examples*	137
8 *Where to Next? Recommendations for Principles, Practices and Curriculum Design*	159
Postscript: My Personal Research Journey	194
Appendix A: Data Sources	198
Appendix B: Denominational Variations	203
Appendix C: Analysis of Graduate Surveys	208
Appendix D: Focus Groups Analysis	211
Appendix E: Stakeholder Interviews Synthesis	219
Appendix F: NCLS Leaders Survey 2011 Analysis	228
Index	232

ACKNOWLEDGEMENTS

While there are far too many people to acknowledge individually, the research would not have been possible without the expert facilitation of a number of key people and the process would not have been as rewarding without the personal encouragement of many others. I wish to acknowledge both my professional indebtedness and my personal appreciation with respect to the following people who have contributed so much to the whole undertaking.

The project was conceived, initiated and constantly supported by the Council of Deans of Theology, with special encouragement provided by the Council Chair, Professor Anne Hunt. ANZATS has provided opportunities for the sharing of the research at its conferences, thanks largely to the Rev Dr Charles Sherlock. Professor Paul Beirne's project leadership has been both facilitative and encouraging at all times, a style maintained by Associate Professor Gerard Moore when he assumed the leadership role late in the project. I have been immensely helped by the expertise, enthusiasm and commitment of all team members: the Rev Dr Mark Harding, Dr Neil Holm, Associate Professor Robert McIver, Professor Neil Ormerod and Professor Peter Sherlock. Without their preliminary work, the project would never have started; without their ongoing commitment, it would not have been so fruitful. Several expert consultants – Dr Alex Nelson, Shane Hoy, Dr Paul Chesterton – have also provided valuable assistance in preparing, processing and evaluating research instruments.

As the lead institution, MCD University of Divinity provided excellent administrative support, especially from Tricia Lewis in managing finances,

Hazel Hughes in organizing the workshop, and Mark Lindsay in facilitating ethics clearances – all services performed with diligence, efficiency and friendliness. Malyon College was always ready to help at no notice in the tasks of typing, photocopying and other emergency secretarial services, so my heartfelt thanks go to Susan Pottinger and Nancy Connell for that. The various school principals, secretaries, registrars and personal assistants who organized all my campus visits and supplied much information are too numerous to list, but their efforts and their hospitality have alwaysbeen appreciated.

A special word of appreciation goes to the Australian Learning and Teaching Council (and its successor the Office for Learning and Teaching). This body has been much more than a funding agency. Its facilitation of the project, its equipping of our team leadership, its adaptability in processes, and its very personal encouragement of our work have been often noted and endorsed by the whole team.

Finally, I want to thank sincerely all those who gave of their time to provide input into the research. The hundreds of students, faculty, graduates, committee members and church personnel who provided such candid and insightful data have given a dynamic and contemporary edge to the entire project.

Les Ball
Project Manager

AUTHOR'S PREFACE TO THE SECOND EDITION

TRANSFORMING THEOLOGY: TEN YEARS ON

Prior to the early years of the twenty-first century, there had been a dearth of scholarly attention given to theological education in Australia. What little had been published consisted mainly of individual institutions' memoirs detailing their origins and successive periods of development. There had been no credible research or literature on the processes or quality of theological education in Australia and very little cooperative critique of the overall provision of educational programs. Theological education was generally a quite insular affair. The detailed research of Charles Foster et al. was published in 2004 as *Educating Clergy: Teaching Practices and Pastoral Imagination*, but this was a book on American seminary programs preparing candidates for ordained clergy which, while presenting worthwhile principles for pastoral preparation, had limited direct application to the general delivery of theological education in the Australian context.

With the formation of the Australian Council of Deans of Theology, there arose a mood for more cooperative and direct self-examination of the Australian provision of theological education. The Council, with financial support from the Australian Government Office for Learning and Teaching, sponsored two seminal research and publication projects, *Uncovering Theology* (2008) and *Transforming Theology* (2010-2012). In the first of these publications, Charles Sherlock produced a thoroughly researched empirical snapshot of the state of theological education in Australia. The study involved was essentially quantitative, but Sherlock extrapolated from the data a number of emergent themes that warranted further examination. One of these was the common claim by theological providers that studying theology was inherently transformative. While commonly claimed, there was no tangible data to support the claim. The Council of Deans resolved to test this claim and so the Transforming Theology project was launched as a qualitative study of transformative learning in theological degrees. This book, *Transforming Theology*, was first issued in 2012, with the results and recommendations emerging from that national research. Together, these two projects and publications provided a researched platform that served as a base for the next decade of pedagogical creativity and scholarly research in Australian theological education.

Since 2012, there has been a surge of national learning and teaching conferences and publications, which have focused on the processes and quality of theological learning. Conferences such as those sponsored by Sydney College of Divinity with the associated publications in this *Learning and Teaching Theology* series have brought together theological educators from Australia and abroad in a sharing of research and innovative thinking on the qualitative aspects of teaching and student development. The conversation has grown from 'what should we teach?' to 'how can we teach best to meet the needs of our students?' There has been an increasing focus on the quality of the student produced by theological education as distinct from the traditional focus on the effectual transmission of theological knowledge. Titles in the series – *Teaching Theology in a Technological Age*, *Wondering about God Together*, *God's Exemplary Graduates* – are indicative of the tenor of this burgeoning interest. Other theological bodies, such as Australian College of Theology, University of Divinity, Christian Heritage College, and many more, have sponsored similar conferences and scholarly publications in educational areas. The past decade has produced a spate of such high quality pedagogically focused work in which the Australian theological community can be seen as among the global leaders in such critical and creative self-examination and professional development.

A key finding of *Transforming Theology* is that the claim to transformative learning was, as at 2012, more aspirational than demonstrable. The recommendation flowing from this finding was that 'aspirational' needed to become more 'intentional' and, ultimately, 'strategic' in implementation, with demonstrable outcomes. Since 2012, the networking of scholars mentioned above has made significant progress in this direction, with a far more concentrated effort to define what graduate attributes are sought rather than simply setting goals in terms of content exposure. I have keenly devoured the scholarship from this period, and I have been excited at the creativity and determination of teachers to ensure the personal development of students as well as their content competence. The intentionality to transform people that was desired in 2012 has certainly progressed significantly in the past decade.

When the Transforming Theology project was in progress, there was considerable tension between the two concepts of 'formation' and 'transformation'. 'Formation' was generally conceived as shaping a student to become fit for purpose, especially the purpose of ordained clergy or comparable accredited vocational ministry. Accordingly, the role of theological education was to equip a candidate for ministry with sound and proven theology and the necessary formal and personal skills to perform ministerial duties. 'Formation', then, began from a reasonably pre-determined understanding of the requisites of ministerial office and so the training was shaped by such a concept. This was essentially a seminary approach, but it is the approach that has framed theological education for most of Australia's history. 'Transformation', however, was largely coloured by the work of Jack Mezirow who, in the 1970-1990s, popularized the concept of transformative learning as a part of the general move towards andragogical teaching of adults, who should be responsible for their own development rather than being moulded into an externally determined pattern. Mezirow's classic statement of transformative learning rested on the student's encounter with a disorienting event that led to critical reflection and revaluation of perspectives, leading ultimately to a changed perspective with concomitant action. Such radical open-ended and unpredictable transformation was seen as inherently incompatible with the notion of formation, with its known – and safer - structures and parameters. While both emphases had their strengths and virtues, they also had their weaknesses and inappropriateness. Formation developed a skilled minister, but it was too narrow and restrictive; transformation was liberating and individual, but it was potentially dangerous to theological orthodoxy and tended towards anarchism in theology and practice. This tension was palpable in 2012. However, there has been a noticeable development in the nuancing of such terminology, as a result of more mature thinking and of other movements within the broader church.

One such movement, which was in progress earlier than 2012 but which has intensified since then, is the progressive laicising of the church. Once the preserve of Nonconformity (such as Methodists, Baptists, and Congregationalists), the involvement of laity in an increasingly wide range of ministry functions now pervades most church strands, including the conservative established churches where priestly roles are distinctively defined. Reasons for this are varied, but they include the modern social aversion to institutionalism, the reluctance to commit to 'permanent' vocations, and the contemporary difficulty of recruitment to structured clergy. This reduced demarcation of ministry functions in the churches with its greater lay involvement has had a marked impact on the nature of those presenting for theological education. Theological education has experienced a comparable laicising evolution. Only the minority of students are focused on heading to permanent ordained vocations. Most students enrol for personal growth or interest, generally with a view to more effectual lay involvement, but not necessarily as a lifetime, or even a full-time, commitment. The operational assumption that teaching within a vocational ministry preparation environment is suited to all theological students is no longer tenable. Few students are full-time, residential, or ordination-bound. Most are part-time, rarely found on campus outside of class hours (if indeed they attend physical classes), and maintain a secular career, with their ministry involvement seen as an adjunct to that primary occupation.

This laicising trend within Australian theological education has had a clear impact on the understanding of the terms 'formation' and 'transformation'. The previous focus on vocational priestly formation has moved towards formation as personal and spiritual growth and practices rather than professional and vocational preparation *per se*. Vocational skills are taught more generically than sacramentally, with such formal development that is needed left to denominational agencies such as dedicated seminaries or other in-house accreditation programs. At the same time, transformation has come to be seen as the understanding, articulation, refinement, and expansion of world-view rather than (necessarily) radical change. True, the student's already partially formed world-view may ultimately be so refined as to be fundamentally changed, but that is not the essential thrust of transformation. The transformation sought is more that of the personal appropriation of a theological framework that 'makes sense' of all that a graduate will encounter in personal, public, and professional life. Consequently, the two terms have tended to merge into 'wholistic' or 'integrative', which allows for personal determination of resultant roles while selecting the areas of development to be undertaken. The personhood of the learner has become the focus of formation rather than (just) the role. The learner's world-view has become something to be grown, expanded, and clarified to become an articulate platform for life action and mores rather than a definite break from, let alone the demolition of, that perspective that had brought the student to theological education in the first place. The ideal of integration of a theologically formed world-view and lived personal and professional practice is emerging as an articulated and desired attribute of theological graduates. This is not a debasement of classical theology; it is rather an elevation of theology from a learned corpus to a lived *habitus*.

At the present time (2023), we cannot ignore the significance of the global pandemic that has captured the world of late. One effect on education caused by the pandemic is that remote, especially online learning has become a new reality, with even the most dogged resistance to the medium having been forced to engage with it. Consequently, learning management systems have of necessity become more sophisticated, with much progress in technology-based communication now being a norm. There has been the need to adapt pedagogies from a classroom environment to a virtual screen-based medium, which has presented many challenges for traditional classroom-based teachers. However, it is noteworthy that such virtual-world pedagogical challenges are being well met – and mastered – by a new wave of young digital natives, both teachers and students. The main challenge remaining in the online medium is that of formative development, as described above. In this milieu, the learner is remote and often almost anonymous, so how can we grow the person of such an enrolment? There is clearly much still to be done in this area, but one thing needs to be front and centre. Online learning can never be effective in developing a person if it is run on a 'set and forget' basis, where simply providing and encountering learning content on a website is effectively the totality of the teaching and learning experience. In all cases, whether concrete or virtual, there needs to be a conscious, caring, and effective establishment of a community of learning wherein the formative integration of the learner is a central plank. Regardless of medium, there is always the need to focus on personhood as well as pedagogy.

While we can confidently say that the decade of scholarly activity has clearly articulated the intention to develop well-formed graduates, there remains an equally clear lack of development in another crucial area. Attention to pedagogic processes and personal growth will always fall short if equal attention is not given to curriculum itself. A review of current course structures reveals the largely static nature of curriculum design. Despite the articulation of learner-focused goals and pedagogies, course structures remain largely tied to a system of compartmentalized content-driven blocks and majors, designed to produce discrete discipline-based content expertise but failing to incorporate strategies for consistent and coherent integration, of either content or personhood. Even when an integrative unit is present in an award, it is typically a concluding supplement to study that takes the form of a personalized application to a ministry context. Such an application, though clearly of value, is not a fully developed concept of integration, which needs to be incorporated as a modus operandi from the beginning of study and maintained consistently throughout the course. The Executive Summary of *Transforming Theology* draws attention to the 'high degree of (curriculum) commonality and very limited development of basic content, aims and structures over the past thirty-five years'. It is fair to say that curriculum has been barely touched since 2012, with the only change to that Executive comment being the change of 'thirty-five' to 'forty-five'. The final statement of the Executive Summary is, 'The culminating recommendation … is the recasting of curriculum structure based on content-focused fields of study to a structure based on learner-focused levels of learning'. That recommendation is yet to be addressed. Without a fundamental shift in curriculum architecture, it is hard to see how authentic integration will become the norm of theological education.

An ancillary to all the above discussion is the emergent need for further teacher education among theological educators. As in virtually all Australian Higher Education fields, lecturers are typically appointed on the basis of their profound content expertise, with little if any focus on educational qualifications or demonstrated teaching expertise or awareness. Accreditation bodies are increasingly calling for educational (that is, learning and teaching) development of theological teachers, but even beyond such external impetus, there is a clear need for teachers to undergo further training and professional development as teachers if they are to develop clear understanding of the processes of authentic integrative learning and teaching. The recent emergence of specialized postgraduate Certificates in Theological Education designed for theological teachers (such as those developed by University of Divinity, Sydney College of Divinity, and Christian Heritage College) is evidence of an awareness of the need for teachers themselves to develop their own integrative approach to integrative teaching. To date, the take-up of such programs has been limited, so this needs to be a priority in the near future.

Transforming Theology is an exploration of transformative learning, which has evolved into a quest for integrative learning. The aspirations of 2012 have been further articulated into clear statements of intention in the ensuing decade. What remains is the strategic implementation of those intentions. Another of the recent books in this series, *Learning to Be Learners*, with its subtitle 'A Mathegenical Approach to Theological Education', is effectively my sequel to *Transforming Theology*, as it takes the decade of progress in intentionality to the next step of strategy for implementation. *Learning to Be Learners* attempts to address the need for a cohesive approach that holds the inculturation of a theologically informed world-view, the scaffolded architecture of curriculum design, and learner-developing pedagogical practices in a symbiotic unity at all points of any award. The book itself is designed as a tool for the sort of professional teacher development envisaged above, with a view to promoting that learner-focused learning recommended in *Transforming Theology*. As *Transforming Theology* set out aspirations, and ensuing scholarship has articulated intentions, *Learning to Be Learners* sets out a strategy for integrative learner-focused learning. The two works embrace research and progressive development; both will benefit from a reading of the other, as literal bookends of a decade.

EXECUTIVE SUMMARY

The book is the outcome of research undertaken by Melbourne College of Divinity (now University of Divinity) as the lead institution on behalf of the Council of Deans of Theology into the area of transformative learning in theology in the Australian context. The research flows out of a previous study commissioned by the Council under the title of *Uncovering Theology* (2008). Its starting point is the claims made by various theological colleges that they provide a transformative educational experience, claims that had not previously been analysed or tested in any strategic way. Thus the research set out to test such claims against the actual experience and aspirations of students, educators and stakeholders, especially in view of the increasingly diverse backgrounds and experiences of contemporary students. The ultimate aim of the research is to make recommendations for the strategic incorporation of student experience and effective transformative learning into the curriculum of undergraduate theological degrees.

There is an extensive literature that has emerged since the 1970s in the area of transformative learning, with a recent application of such principles to theological education. A review of this literature affirms the creedal bases of traditional theological teaching and the development of practical skills as legitimate components of contemporary theological education in the service of the churches. At the same time, it throws up significant challenges in the key areas of Course Aims, Curriculum, Methods and Outcomes, all of which stand in need of close scrutiny and prudent revision in the quest for the authentic transformative learning so widely expressed as a desirable outcome of theological education.

A comprehensive analysis of historical curriculum documents from major providers focused on the design of curriculum. This review revealed a high degree of commonality and very limited development of basic content, aims and structures over the past thirty-five years, despite the varying philosophical and institutional bases of the teaching bodies. Some key issues that militate against transformative experience were identified as the seemingly inherent compartmentalisation of theological courses, the widespread but variable notion of foundationalism in introductory units, and the heavy workload imposed on students, especially in the early stages of a course.

Wide ranging field research was undertaken in the areas of the engagement of courses with students' life experience and the opportunities for transformative learning experiences. A fundamental premise of transformative learning is that it connects with and forms part of the stage of life of the learner, who comes to the educative program with significant life experience and established character and learning styles. While this implies a dynamic connection between curriculum and life, the research showed that, despite recent developments in experiential learning in field placements or other practical learning exercises, connection with a student's prior or concurrent life experience was generally not strategically structured within a curriculum. The general disconnection between theological studies and life experience is seen as a limiting feature of the programs.

Inquiry into transformative learning focused on input from students, recent graduates, current faculty, church leaders and other stakeholders, to discover the extent to which the concept of transformative learning is currently incorporated in degree programs, and someways in which the concept may be enhanced in future developments of curriculum. While most parties strongly desire it as an aspirational outcome, great variability exists in its implementation. There are few deliberately structured transformative elements within the formal degree program, with most relying on the relatively unstructured extra-curricular life of campuses to provide this dimension. A few recent curriculum developments have incorporated transformative learning strategically in the degree, especially by placing intentionally transformative units within the degree curriculum at strategic points and the use of integrating exit projects. There is a high level of consensus that theological education needs to incorporate the whole life of the student while anchoring theology in the faith tradition which has given rise to it, that is, to make theological education transformative rather than merely cognitive.

The mission of theological providers is largely to safeguard and to perpetuate the sacred knowledge and wisdom of the Christian tradition and so curricula have been traditionally organised around the systematic content bases of that tradition. However, in the interest of more transformative learning, curriculum needs to be developed in ways that will be more effectively engaged by the learners. This approach requires a collaborative review of curriculum, especially by faculty as the chief agents in the design and delivery of programs, with effective dialogue amongst all parties and balance amongst competing requirements. It also means designing curriculum on the basis of articulated graduate attributes, which should drive the whole process, and with specified learning outcomes being explicitly linked to the desired attributes. A student-centred curriculum structure and delivery instead of a content-centred structure will be more likely to achieve the personal goal of transformation. This does not necessitate a reduction of content, but it re-fashions the delivery and appropriation of that content in ways that are more coherently integrated and more personally transformative.

The research identified a number of good examples of transformative practices based on effective operational principles. These principles involve the clear articulation of philosophical coherence and institutional purpose, locating theological education in the context of community engagement and intentionally connecting with the students' life experience, incorporating the principles of deep learning, and proactive consultation with stakeholders and the expansion of faculty horizons. Good practices include curriculum design that de-emphasises content in the early stage in order to promote learning skills and to establish a platform for personal development; that strategically sequences learning units throughout the degree; and that includes specifically transformative units throughout the course, with opportunity for personal integration in the final stages. They also include learning methods which maximise learner activity and discovery rather than teacher delivery and which promote relational integrity rather than individualism.

The book concludes by offering a number of recommendations for embedding certain elements into undergraduate theological curriculum design that will incorporate student experience and transformative learning. As an acknowledgement of various contexts and variability in terminology, the recommendations are expressed in general terms with the aim of being readily applicable to active implementation in a number of varied contexts. Four overarching governing principles are educed, namely, the primacy of biblical and theological knowledge; contemporary engagement of theology with society and culture; holistic integration of learning and life; and intentionality and strategicality of a transformative agenda expressed in curriculum design and development. There follows a set of suggestions as to how such principles maybe effectively be implemented in classroom practices. The culminating recommendation, in terms of the research project title, is the recasting of curriculum structure based on content-focused fields of study to a structure based on learner-focused levels of learning.

1 | GENESIS OF THE PROJECT

INCORPORATING STUDENT EXPERIENCE AND TRANSFORMATIVE LEARNING INTO CURRICULUM DESIGN AND PLANNING OF UNDERGRADUATE THEOLOGICAL DEGREES

1. Origin of the Project

The genesis of the project is located in the initial scoping study into theological education undertaken by the Council of Deans of Theology in 2008, whose results were published as *Uncovering Theology: The Depth, Reach and Utility of Australian Theological Education*.[1] This study revealed a number of significant features of the theological landscape, with two aspects being of particular interest to the large majority of theological educators. One major feature is the *diversity in clientele* amongst those who choose to study theology. Over the past thirty years the clientele of theological programs has shifted from predominantly students oriented to ordained ministry (generally male, Anglo-celtic and young) to persons who are undertaking theological studies for diverse reasons, often for their own sake, out of personal interest or to enrich their current professional activity through increased theological and ethical reflection. This has led to greater diversity in the gender, age range, ethnic and cultural background and previous educational background of students.[2] The

---

1   Charles Sherlock, *Uncovering Theology: The Depth, Reach and Utility of Australian Theological Education* (Adelaide: ATF Press, 2009).
2   This has been documented in Sherlock, *Uncovering Theology*.

other feature of note is the repeated claims of theological colleges *to provide transformative, holistic and integrative learning experiences.*[3] Although these terms can be distinguished, scholars such as Cranton and Roy[4] argue for a holistic view of transformative learning that incorporates all three. To some extent the sector assumes that the study of theology involves a significant experience of personal transformation, but there has been little actual evidence produced to support such an assumption.

Such claims, then, need to be tested both against the expectations and aspirations of the students and against the actual performance of the colleges involved. They also need testing against theories of transformative learning current in the educational sector. On the other hand, church constituencies (the major stakeholders in the provision of theological education) are increasingly looking to theological colleges to provide more than academic skills, with an increasing demand for genuine human "formation" for their students who are undertaking ministerial training.

The Council of Deans resolved to address this new context and this common claim of theological education to develop a more strategic approach to the issues of diverse student experience and transformative learning within a theological context. This research sought to consider the extent to which the needs of the increasingly diverse clientele are met through the undergraduate theological curriculum and the extent to which transformative education assists in meeting these needs. The project was thus designed to take into account the diversity of goals and aspirations present within the student body and to develop a more educationally professional and evidence-based approach to claims made about transformative learning.

The initial scoping study of 2008 was funded by a grant from the Australian Learning and Teaching Council (ALTC), an initiative of the Australian Government Department of Education, Employment and Workplace Relations. The current project, a more extensive two-year study, was similarly funded by an ALTC grant awarded to the project team working under the banner of

---

3   Charles Sherlock notes that "a sector-wide swing has taken place towards 'integrated', 'holistic' or 'transformative' learning – words appearing time and time again in college websites, promotional materials and handbooks." Sherlock, *Uncovering Theology*, 58.
4   Patricia Cranton and Merv Roy, "When the Bottom Falls Out of the Bucket: Toward A Holistic Perspective on Transformative Learning." *Journal of Transformative Education* 1:2 (2003): 86-98.

Melbourne College of Divinity (now University of Divinity) as the lead institution on behalf of the Council of Deans.[5]

2. Aims of the Project

The project set out to identify the strengths and weaknesses of the undergraduate theological education curriculum in providing an increasingly diverse population of theological students with a transformative education. Thus the project sought to undertake a comprehensive analysis of the current student profile and expectations; an examination of curriculum development to identify best practice in learning and teaching approaches and curriculum design to match the expectations and needs of increased student diversity; a review of the expectations of those major stakeholders whose primary interest is in the training of ordained ministers; an analysis and evaluation of claims made in relation to transformative learning through a consideration of student experience of learning and teaching; and importantly, the identification of curriculum factors and learning and teaching methods which contribute to or hinder transformative learning in theology.

Essentially, the research aimed at addressing the following topical questions. How can the diverse background and experiences of theological students be effectively recognised and engaged in theological education? How can transformative learning be appropriately defined within the Australian theological context? How can transformative learning as so defined be integrated into curriculum design? How can transformative learning be incorporated into and improve the teaching and learning dimensions of theological education?

In addressing these questions, the project sought to deliver a number of specific outcomes. First of these was a description of the variety of institutional settings and an analysis of their responsiveness to student experience and their degree of incorporation of transformative learning within their program. Following this, it sought to utilise accurate research data on student experience and transformative learning to provide guidelines for the sector in

---

5 In 2011, the Australian Government amended its structures with the closure of ALTC and the transfer of its relevant role to the Office for Learning and Teaching. While support for this project has been provided by the Australian Government Office for Learning and Teaching, the views in this project do not necessarily reflect the views of the Australian Government Office for Learning and Teaching.

curriculum design and planning and the development of effective teaching and learning processes. Within this, it sought also to identify and disseminate best practice within the sector in terms of incorporating student experience into curriculum design.

3. Scope of the Project

The project has drawn together a wide array of theological education providers in a remarkable exercise in cooperative research. Through the facilitation of the Council of Deans, there were fifteen major tertiary institutions joined as research partners in the project, under the lead institution of Melbourne College of Divinity (now University of Divinity). These partners were Adelaide College of Divinity, Australian & New Zealand Association of Theological Schools, Australian Catholic University, Australian College of Theology, Australian Lutheran College (now a member of University of Divinity), Avondale College of Higher Education, Brisbane College of Theology (since closed), Harvest West Bible College, Melbourne College of Divinity, Moore Theological College, Sydney College of Divinity, Tabor Adelaide, Tabor Victoria, University of Otago (NZ), and Wesley Institute. This partnership thus incorporated all institutional types – universities, State-based and national teaching consortia, and independent colleges – and a diversity of ecclesiastical traditions in an unprecedented collaboration. The Council of Deans appointed a team of seven theological leaders to conduct the research, namely, Professor Paul Beirne (Dean, Melbourne College of Divinity, Project Team Leader to February 2012), Associate Professor Gerard Moore (Charles Sturt University, Project Team Leader from February 2012), Dr Les Ball (former Dean, Brisbane College of Theology, Project Manager), the Rev Dr Mark Harding (Dean, Australian College of Theology), Dr Neil Holm (Director of Coursework, Sydney College of Divinity), Associate Professor Robert McIver (Head of School of Ministry and Theology, Avondale College of Higher Education), and Professor Neil Ormerod (Australian Catholic University). Professor Peter Sherlock (Vice-Chancellor, University of Divinity) joined the team in February 2012.

Yet the scope of the research extended beyond this partnership to encompass all higher education providers of undergraduate theological degrees in Australia. This included those Council of Deans members who were not part of the original partnership and others who are not Council members.

Thus, the number of institutions who participated in the study was in excess of fifty teaching campuses across all Australian States. Individual participants in the various surveys, interviews, workshops and dialogues totalled in excess of 700, including current students and recent graduates, teaching faculty and administrators, academic heads of schools and faculties, church leaders and other employers. The project was thus enabled to compile a comprehensive picture of currency in undergraduate theological education in Australia.

4. Methods of the Project

A variety of research strategies were used in the project, commencing with an analysis of pertinent literature. First, there was an extensive survey of secondary and other scholarly literature on transformative learning, with particular reference to its utilization in theological programs, to reach an understanding of the concepts of transformative learning and to arrive at a legitimate definition of this concept for Australian theological education. Then, there was a documentary comparison of the past and present curricula of numerous Australian Higher Education Providers, including the six universities which offer theology degrees (Australian Catholic University, Charles Sturt University, Flinders University, Murdoch University, University of Newcastle, University of Notre Dame Australia), five major theological consortia with their numerous constituent campuses (Adelaide College of Divinity, Australian College of Theology, Brisbane College of Theology, Melbourne College of Divinity, Sydney College of Divinity), and a wide range of independent theological colleges (including Alphacrucis College, Christian Heritage College, Harvest Bible College, Harvest West Bible College, Moore Theological College, Perth Bible College, Tabor Adelaide, Tabor Victoria). This documentary comparison served to develop a longitudinal account of shifts in curricula and to identify currently emergent practices. Current curriculum documents from the undergraduate programs in education and nursing of thirteen Australian universities were analysed to discern what developments are occurring in other human service-oriented educational programs.

The literary and documentary analysis was supplemented by extensive field research. Student expectations and experience were explored in depth. In 2010, focus groups of twenty current students were held in three States and an initial student survey of another twenty students was conducted as a companion exercise. In 2011, a series of three more extensive student surveys was conducted across Australia involving 237 first year students, 141 final year students, and a continuing cohort of 187 students followed across a twelve month interval, finishing with the second part of the survey in 2012. These student-based instruments sought to correlate age, expectations/faith/spirituality, career possibilities (ordained/non-ordained), previous educational level and identification of current practice with various student expectations and experiences and to identify whether transformation as defined has occurred in their theological education. Other standard student surveys such as Course Experience Questionnaires and Graduate Surveys were also examined, with responses received from 646 recent graduates of major universities and consortia. The project also used a section of the National Church Life Survey *Leaders Survey 2011* to gather further perspectives on historical ministry training from a wide range of current church practitioners, with 2235 responses received to a specific project module within the leaders' survey.

Teaching faculty and other key stakeholders were involved in series of one-to-one interviews and a national colloquium and workshop which investigated the culture, matters of curriculum design and development, and delivery practices of the various colleges and universities in the areas of engaging students' experience and transformative learning. Other major stakeholders were identified as Deans and Heads of Schools or Academic Chairs, significant church leaders with responsibility for training and placement of ministers and other typical employers of theological graduates as well as graduates from the past five years.

A preliminary round of unstructured interviews with nineteen Principals and Deans of colleges and university departments was conducted in early 2011 to establish parameters of inquiry for later instruments. This was followed in late 2011 by a set of more in-depth and structured interviews with ninety key stakeholders from fifteen institutions across all mainland States. This representative sample of stakeholders was interviewed individually and their input was correlated with the returns from other interview and survey data. The national workshop held in 2012 involved seventy-three delegates, mainly senior teaching personnel, representing forty institutions associated with fifteen denominational traditions. Processing of all the data compiled was led by the project manager and the research team, assisted by several expert consultants (Dr Alex Nelson, Consultant Psychologist, Sydney; Mr Shane Hoy, Head of Curriculum, Education Queensland; Dr Paul Chesterton,

Evaluation Consultant, Sydney). Together, these strategies provided a vast store of data and perspectives on both actual achievements and current processes as well as a wide range of aspirations for enhancement.

There were two significant methodological differences between the *Uncovering Theology* and the *Transforming Theology* projects. The earlier project was by design a scoping study, which concentrated on discovering what is actually (and factually) happening across the theological education sector in Australia. Consequently, it had a quantitative focus which provided a clear and comprehensive picture of the overall scene and it identified a number of emergent issues which could warrant further analysis. The current study is by nature a sequel to that study, which therefore takes a qualitative approach to probing how effectively certain claims are being implemented and how the value of educational delivery may be enhanced. Thus it is less descriptive and more evaluative. The other main difference is the scope of input agents. *Uncovering Theology* relied almost exclusively on the extensive official documentation supplied by the teaching institutions and a key one-day national workshop of theological faculty and college personnel which provided significant input in response to key focus topics. Since *Transforming Theology* had a much longer time frame in which to work, the scope of research input was expanded considerably to include large numbers of current students, recent graduates, church leaders and other employers of theological graduates, who were engaged in various surveys, focus groups and intensive individual interviews. Consequently, the earlier limits of institutional perspectives were expanded to embrace a wider ambit of users of the programs, not just the providers. In many cases, this extended research reach has resulted in a significantly more varied assessment of what is being provided.

5. Value of the Project

The tertiary theological education sector makes a significant contribution to Australian society through its education of ministers, chaplains, counsellors, educators (primary, secondary and tertiary) and employees for the not-for-profit sector, adding to the overall social capital. In the present tertiary environment, however, it is facing many challenges. The project recognises that in Australia we have a new context where much of the education within theological colleges is not directed to students training for ministry. This shift towards a more diverse student body is a trend which warrants significant investigation, since theological education now serves a market which has greater volatility than most educational settings. Consequently, the sector needs to understand better its student body, their needs and desired outcomes. To date there has been little analysis of the student experience of theological education. In terms of student experience and expectations, claims advancing the transformative nature of theology programs require empirical verification if they are to be upheld. By providing a sound understanding of underlying principles and an evidence-based review of stakeholder requirements, successful teaching and learning practices and aspirational proposals, this research has the potential to enrich the quality of theological education in Australia for those who are arguably the most significant stakeholders: future students.

2 | WHAT ARE THEY SAYING ABOUT TRANSFORMATIVE EDUCATION?

THOUGHTS EMERGING FROM A REVIEW OF SOME PERTINENT RECENT LITERATURE IN THE FIELD.

1. What are They Saying about Transformative Education in General?

Jack Mezirow: a brief introduction

The field of transformative learning has achieved great prominence in educational literatureover the past thirty years. Since Jack Mezirow's origination of the term (even if not the concept) in the 1970s, it has flourished as a fertile ground of exploration intertiary education. Mezirow himself has been involved in the gradual evolution of his thinking, producing a number of variations and refinements in his constructs.[1] While it is beyond thescope of this work to analyse Mezirow's contribution, no account of the field can start without taking his workas a launching pad.

Mezirow's original input in 1978 was inspired by his desire to enhance the learning experience and quality of mature women returning to education after

---

[1] Mezirow's thinking has under gone a process of evolution from the 1970s to the 2000s.Some key expressions of the development of his thought may be found in his following works:
Transformative dimensions of adult learning (San Francisco: Jossey-Bass, 1991).
"Understanding Transformation Theory," Adult Education Quarterly, 44:4 (1994): 222-232.
Learning as Transformation: Critical Perspectives on a Theory in Progress (San Francisco: Jossey-Bass, 2000).
"An Overview of transformative learning," in P Sutherland and J Crowther, eds, *Lifelong Learning: Concepts and Contexts* (New York: Routledge, 2006), 24-38.
For a lucid analysis of the development and current state of Mezirow's thought, see the article by Andrew Kitchenham,"The Evolution of John Mezirow's Transformative Learning Theory," *Journal of Transformative Education* (2008), 6:104-123.

an extended period away from work or education. Over the following years, he progressively developed his schema of what he termed "transformative learning," identifying ten phases of such learningas it applied to adult learners who brought significant life experience, but not necessarily traditional educational skills, with them into their learning programs. These phases stem from an initial disorienting event, which leads on to critical reflection on previously held core assumptions, accompanied by reflective discourse to test the validity of both the assumptions and the critique of them, and ultimately ensuing in some active outcome.[2] Mezirow suggested that the most significant learning for adults arises from perspective transformation, which occurs when people examine their values, beliefs and presuppositions through such a processes of critical reflection and rational discourse. This process causes people to modify their meaning schemes and ideally transform their meaning perspectives.[3] He defined perspective transformation as:

> The process of becoming critically aware of how and why our assumptions have come to constrain the way we perceive, understand, and feel about our world; changing these structures or habitual expectation to make possible a more inclusive, discriminating, and integrative perspective; and finally making choices or otherwise acting on these new understandings.[4]

Such transformation of meaning perspectives is seen as the most important learning for an adult. While typically initiated by a confrontational or disorienting event, it may be associated not only with traumatic events in a person's life but also with the accretion of events as a person grows and develops. Such developmental learning is thus also a process of perspective transformations towards meaning perspectives which are more inclusive, discriminating, and integrative.[5]

Many have found Mezirow's work a good way of understanding adult learning. Edward Taylor confirmed through his review of empirical studies that adults in many stages and in many situations experience perspective transformations.[6] However, his research did indicate that a more holistic and

---

2   Mezirow, "Understanding Transformation Theory," 224.
3   Ibid, 223.
4   Mezirow, *Transformative dimensions of adult learning*, 167.
5   Ibid, 167.
6   Edward Taylor, "Building Upon the Theoretical Debate: A Critical Review of the Empirical Studies of Mezirow's Transformative Learning Theory," *Adult Education Quarterly*, 48:1 (1997): 51.

grounded view of transformative learning in adulthood was required to explain all the dimensions of learning that were at work. He concluded that Mezirow's theory is "only a beginning and there is still much to be learned about the complex nature of adult learning."[7] Mezirow's theory has continued to gain wide acceptance and has been used by many as a tool to understand adult learning, to evaluate adult learning programs and to foster adult learning. Principal advocates have been such people as Taylor and Patricia Cranton, with recent insights being collected in a 2009 volume.[8] The establishment of the *Journal of Transformative Education* in 2003 provided a scholarly vehicle for the dissemination of transformative ideals.

Further Development
Although the dominant theory, Mezirow's constructivist approach, especially its emphasis on rationality and cognition, has been subject to critical analysis that has laid the foundations for other perspectives on transformational learning. These perspectives include those of Boyd and Dirkx (emotional and spiritual dimensions of learning); Daloz (response to experience); Newman (social action); O'Sullivan (cosmology); and Robinson (integrative learning).[9] Taking the lead from Taylor's critical review, this research adopts a broad, inclusive, integrated, or holistic view of transformative learning. This broader scope has allowed greater opportunity to consider the spiritual dimensions that resonate with traditional theological interests in the spiritual formation of ordination students and practices of spiritual direction and discipleship training.

While transformative theory was widely accepted with very little criticism being raised within the first decade of Mezirow's introducing his theory, since the 1990s some concerns have been raised. At first, these mainly involved aspects of the theory that Mezirow had not fully developed. In large part they did not challenge the fundamental principles of the theory but provided avenues in which the theory could be expanded and further developed. The main criticism stemmed from Mezirow's over-emphasis on both individual transformation and rational discourse with too little (if any) regard afforded

---

7   Ibid, 56.
8   J Mezirow, E Taylor and Associates, *Transformative learning in practice: Insights from community, workplace and higher education* (San Francisco: Jossey-Bass, 2009).
9   Olen Gunnlaugson, "Toward Integrally Informed Theories of Transformative Learning," *Journal of Transformative Education* 3: 4 (2005): 331-353;
    John M Dirkx, "Transformative Learning and the Journey of Individuation," *ERIC Digest* No 223. ERIC Clearinghouse on Adult Career and Vocational Education, 2000.

to social transformation and the non-rational or affective elements in educational development.

More recently, there has been more trenchant criticism of the whole notion of transformative learning. Critics have focused on the increasingly convoluted and variable expressions of transformative learning and its still insistent holding to critical disorientation, reflective processing and identity formation as mandatory elements of authentic adult education. The criticism has noted its neglect (or even exclusion) of the attainment of specific and necessary knowledge as a legitimate goal, or the attainment of conventional vocational and social skills, as well as its insistence on changed identity rather than progressive personal growth. At the same time, its accommodation of values and emotive or spiritual qualities is seen as intangible and peripheral if not illegitimate. Some critics have gone so far as to say that transformative learning does not actually exist and, if it does, its good qualities are indistinguishable from any other kind of effectual learning which is simply a matter of developing a person who will inevitably grow and change in knowledge, understanding and perceptions. Newman berates the whole notion of transformative learning as "only existing in the realm of theory" and proposes that "we strike the phrase *transformative learning* from the educational lexicon altogether," since what passes as transformative learning is merely a difference of degree not of kind.[10] In place of the various components of transformative learning, he proffers nine aspects of what he calls simply "good learning" (the term he advocates).

Despite the criticism, the impact of Mezirow's theories can be seen in the plethora of scholarly literature engendered in the past twenty years in the broad area of transformative learning. Transformative education has gained currency in domains beyond adult education. Kalantzis defines education as incorporating institutions, curriculum, and pedagogy and she contrasts three models of education: didactic, authentic, and transformative. The major contribution of this research is the identification of seven dimensions of education: architectonic, discursive, intersubjective, socio-cultural, proprietary, pedagogical, and moral.[11] So, while initially confined to education faculties and applied to adult education, transformative learning theory has since the

---

10 Michael Newman, "Calling Transformative Learning into Question: Some Mutinous Thoughts," *Adult Education Quarterly* 62:1 (2012): 36-55.
11 M Kalantzis, "Elements of a Science of Education," *Australian Educational Researcher* 33:2 (2006): 15-42.

1990s extended to such diverse fields as general education (including secondary schooling), nursing and social work education, and business and leadership training programs. The general principles of adult learning – and the criticisms of Mezirow's concepts – have clear application to all areas of adult education. They have been especially warmly embraced in those areas which have emerged in recent times, such as business and social welfare. Yet in many more traditional disciplines, the application has been limited, even resisted, as the tenets of transformational learning present so many challenges to conventional pedagogic practice and, in some cases, to the traditional ideology underlying such pedagogy. Perhaps this is seen nowhere more clearly than in that most ancient and pedagogically conservative discipline of theological education.

Some Contemporary Statements
While the scholarly debates around transformative learning are of academic interest, it is in a number of emerging policy statements that some of the fundamental concepts of transformative ideals are finding expression, even if the convoluted terminology of the theory is avoided. Perhaps nowhere is this more pointed than in the transition in much recent educational literature and policy statements from content-centred to person-centred pedagogy, from a focus on teaching to a focus on learning. This has ramifications in areas such as curriculum aims and design as well as teaching/learning resources and methods of delivery and evaluation. Whereas not all such development calls for the Mezirow-style radical identity change, it does incorporate the underlying principle of the holistic development of the person as the heart of the educative process rather than a body of information to be transmitted and mastered. This transition is coming to typify a wide range of disciplines, most notably those associated with humanities and social engagement.

In a recent Report from the Grattan Institute, comparisons were made between Australian education attainment levels and those of several Asian countries, with Australia shown to be significantly lagging. While specifically referring to schools, the report highlighted shortcomings in tertiary teacher education and gave insights into the changing role of teachers in the more progressive countries. Put simply, these countries wanted students to develop learning skills rather than purely acquiring academic knowledge. Therefore they wanted teachers to move from directly transmitting knowledge to a constructivist approach: from the drilling of students to providing broad learning experiences. These included project and inquiry based learning to help students develop critical thinking, problem solving and communication skills. The approach involved integrated learning areas rather than compartmentalised subjects and moved beyond an exclusive focus on text books to adopt diversified learning and teaching resources to deliver curriculum. Formative assessments were emphasised, showing *how* students were learning, rather than simply *what* they learnt.[12] This emphasis on the development of the person as the basic goal of education has much in common with the ideals of transformative learning.

With reference to transformative curriculum, a 2011 UNESCO Curriculum Reform Manifesto also incorporated many of the ideals of transformative learning. In noting the radical structural transformations of such initiatives as the Bologna Process, the decline of public investment in American universities and the burgeoning of universities in developing Asian countries, the authors also noted the neglect of curriculum in tertiary dialogue. It thus promulgated a set of *Principles for Rethinking Undergraduate Curricula for the 21st Century*.[13] This document is a set of eleven overlapping principles designed to guide an experimental process of redesigning university undergraduate curricula worldwide. The principles have much to say regarding the personally transformative nature of what constitutes an undergraduate degree curriculum in the 21st century. They are set out below.

1. As a central guideline teach disciplines rigorously in introductory courses together with a set of parallel seminars devoted to complex real life problems that transcend disciplinary boundaries.
2. Teach knowledge in its social, cultural and political contexts. Teach not just the factual subject matter, but highlight the challenges, open questions and uncertainties of each discipline.
3. Create awareness of the great problems humanity is facing (hunger, poverty, public health, sustainability, climate change, water resources, security, etc.) and show that no single discipline can adequately address any of them.

---

12 Ben Jensen, "Catching up: learning from the best school systems in East Asia," Grattan Institute Report, February 2012, 14. http://www.grattan.edu.au/publications/129_report_learning_from_the_best_main.pdf.
13 UNESCO, "Curriculum Reform Manifesto: *Principles for Rethinking Undergraduate Curricula for the 21st Century*," 15 August 2011. http://curriculumreform.org/curriculum-reform-manifesto/.

4. Use these challenges to demonstrate and rigorously practice interdisciplinarity, avoiding the dangers of interdisciplinary dilettantism.
5. Treat knowledge historically and examine critically how it is generated, acquired, and used. Emphasize that different cultures have their own traditions and different ways of knowing. Do not treat knowledge as static and embedded in a fixed canon.
6. Provide all students with a fundamental understanding of the basics of the natural and the social sciences, as well as the humanities. Emphasize and illustrate the connections between these traditions of knowledge.
7. Engage with the world's complexity and messiness. This applies to the sciences as much as to the social, political and cultural dimensions of the world. Such an engagement will contribute to the education of concerned citizens.
8. Emphasize a broad and inclusive evolutionary mode of thinking in all areas of the curriculum.
9. Familiarize students with non-linear phenomena in all areas of knowledge.
10. Fuse theory and analytic rigor with practice and the application of knowledge to real-world problems.
11. Rethink the implications of modern communication and information technologies for education and the architecture of the university.

The transition from teaching to learning was stressed in a paper delivered by Royce Sadler, Director of Griffith University Institute for Higher Education, which focused on methods of engaging learners.[14] He contrasted the two pedagogical models of teaching as (a) what the teacher does and (b) bringing about learning (of the right kind). In the former model, the lecturer presents material to students as information "dissemination," "transmission," course "delivery." The student's role is to engage the material so transmitted: it is to be memorized, researched further, understood, interrelated, digested, applied or regurgitated in assignments and examinations. In the latter model, the argument is that no teaching has taken place unless learning has occurred. Going through the motions of teaching does not necessarily mean that any

---

14 D Royce Sadler, "What it means to teach." (Paper presented to Australian College of Theology Faculty Colloquium, Brisbane, 20 October 2008).

learning is taking place. There can be a serious disconnect. It is in what happens in and to the learner that authentic education consists. In noting the implications of these approaches, he included the following, which relate directly to the dynamics of transformative learning.

- Student backgrounds, entry (life and technical) skills, verbal facility and ages are often very diverse.
- In order to meet students where they are, we have to know them, and that involves knowing something about them.
- It means taking on board who they are, what they already know, and how they have structured that knowledge.
- It means ensuring that what we say, and what they read, can be interpreted in terms of appropriate concrete or abstract "referents." A springboard is needed.
- It involves helping learners build on their prior knowledge and experience so that there results an integrated, whole, and deep knowledge, skill, wisdom, discernment and compassion.

The emphasis in this presentation is on the need for effective teaching to take genuine cognizance of the learner's life experience and to see an educational program as an element in a life continuum rather than a "time out" from life. The centrality of the learner is clear.

A similar approach to grounding education in the dynamic real life experience of the learner is emerging in the increasingly significant field of online and distance learning. James Dalziel, Director of Macquarie University's E-learning Centre of Excellence, notes that e- learning has a well developed approach to the creation and sequencing of content-based, single learner, self-paced learning objects. However, a key dimension of education is learning which arises from interacting with teachers and peers (rather than simply interacting with content), and the lack of sequencing of multi-learner activities is a significant blind spot in e-learning today. Such "lesson planning" is largely absent from e- learning. He promotes the e-learning concept called the Learning Activity Management System (LAMS), a concept based on the need to go beyond mere content knowledge and mastery to facilitate the learners' engagement of context and the community of learners. It places emphasis on the creation of sequences of learning activities which involve groups of learners interacting within a structured set of collaborative environments, with particular reference to how teachers can make these sequences both authentic and easily re-usable.[15] Mark Nichols and Rosemary Dewerse, in an evaluation of a course on *Worship and Community* delivered as an online unit at Laidlaw College, NZ, highlight the importance of considering the student context, the effectiveness of core questions, course curricula, design challenges for facilitating perspective transformation, and the difficulties of assessing for transformation.[16] The creation of effectual personal communications (both teacher-learner and learner-learner) and the establishment of a community not dependent on geographical proximity are coming to be seen as more pressing than a coherent compilation and the attractive packaging of content. Again, the focus is shifting away from mere information transmission towards the holistic and potentially transformative development of the person within an authentic community.

2. What are They Saying about Transformative Education in Theology?

Developing Interest: Home and Abroad

While somewhat slower than in other disciplines, there has been a growing scholarly interest in transformative learning in theology. This has been particularly evident in North America where there is a far more widespread, diverse and progressive approach to theological education, in both universities and seminaries, than has been the case in Australia. The main areas of implementation have been in the ministry streams of seminaries, with a significant number of doctorates based on field research in education and ministry emerging on the topic. Many have simply taken Mezirow's work as a tool for application. Ted Dodd sought to articulate the factors and best practices of transformative theological education in a particular intensive module on ministry leadership.[17] Nella Roberts used Mezirow's theory as the basis of interviews of students to investigate the role of spirituality in

---

15 James Dalziel, "Implementing learning design: the learning activity management system (LAMS)" https://www.lamsfoundation.org/CD/html/resources/whitepapers/ASCILITE2003%20Dalzie%20Final.pdf
16 Mark Nichols and Rosemary Dewerse, "Evaluating Transformative Learning in Theological Education: a multi-faceted approach," *Journal of Adult Theological Education*, 7:1 (2010). http://www.equinoxjournals.com/index.php/JATE/article/view/9429.
17 Ted Dodd, "Sacred circle of learning: A Model of transformative theological education" (DMin dissertation; Vancouver School of Theology, 2008).

transformative learning.[18] Ellen Marmon used Mezirow's constructs as a lens to analyse the cross-cultural experiences of her seminary students.[19] Others have used Mezirow's theory as a means by which to evaluate the claims of teaching institutions to be in the business of providing transformative experiences. Marie-Claire Weinski conducted such an inquiry into the transformative learning of evangelical theological students in Germany and concluded that an informed theory for describing such a process was lacking.[20] Perhaps it is in her acknowledgement that theological education has yet to arrive at a clear articulation of transformative learning (and thus an operational understanding of transformative experiences) that a rich and urgent field of pedagogical endeavour – in theory and practice – is suggested.

While overseas theological educators have been willing to engage (if not yet master) the issue of theological transformative learning, there has been very little produced in Australia on the topic. An early study was conducted by Stephen Ball which analysed the Field Education program of a Queensland theological college in terms of Mezirow's theory. While he noted some obvious transformative development in the students being studied, he also noted some significant shortcomings of the application of the Mezirow model to account for all the transformative experiences of the students.[21] More recently, Stephen Haar presented a conference paper to a Lutheran Educational Consultation in Bangkok which constructively promoted the principles of transformative learning as a means by which theological schools may become more effectual agents of change and transformation in civil society.[22] While acknowledging some theological and ideological issues involved, he offered some practical ways in which transformative principles could well be married to theological ideals to enhance the learning experience and ultimate outcomes of the theological educational enterprise. Darren Cronshaw has expressed thoughts

---

18 Nella Ann Roberts, "The role of spirituality in transformative learning" (EdD dissertation; Florida International University, 2009).
19 Ellen L Marmon, "Cross-Cultural Field Education: A Transformative Learning Experience," *Christian Education Journal*. Series 3; 7:1 (2010), 70-84.
20 Marie-Claire Weinski, "An inquiry into the transformative learning of evangelical theological students in Germany" (PhD thesis; Trinity Evangelical Divinity School, 2006).
21 Stephen Ball, "The Usefulness of Transformation Theory in Understanding Student Learning in the Innovative Field Education Program of the Queensland Baptist College of Ministries: A Pilot Study" (MEd thesis; Queensland University of Technology, 1999).
22 Stephen Haar, "Enhancing the Capability of Theological Schools in Becoming Agents of Change and Transformation in Civil Society" (Consultation on Establishing a Regional Network of Lutheran Theological Institutions: Bangkok; 18 March 2010).

on his vision for transformative theological education and leadership formation by addressing three salient questions: how can we help our students be equipped and courageous to transform the world to be more in line with God's dream for it; how can we help our people to dream and work with God to transform the church in our different contexts; how can we work with God to reenvision and transform people's understanding of their self and their vocation?[23] His paper presents a case study of several approaches to missional, contemplative and integrative learning at Tabor, Forge and Whitley colleges in Victoria and their role in generating Spirit-attuned transformation.

As noted above, Charles Sherlock undertook a major scoping study in 2008 into Australian theological education on behalf of the Council of Deans of Theology – the first of its kind in this discipline in Australia. The research culminated in a publication which painted a broad canvas of the theological educational scene across all tertiary providers in Australia.[24] Sherlock noted the oft-cited claim by theological institutions that they were in the business of providing "transformative" experiences, a claim that was particularly prominent in the promotional publications of the various bodies. However, he could find no evidence of any clear definition of such transformative experience, of any indication that it was in fact intentionally or strategically incorporated into any set curriculum, or of any formal means of demonstrating or recognizing such experience. In this, his work echoed the findings of Weinski concerning the lack of an articulate understanding of transformative learning in theological education – clearly more work remains to be done.

Course Aims

A fundamental platform in the concept of transformative learning/education is the centrality of the learner in the whole process. If transformative learning is to be embraced, then it follows that statements of aims will have the learner as at least a significant focus.

Some challenging comments have been made recently in regard to the overarching transformative aim of theological education. Tolliver and Tisdell draw the connection between transformation and spirituality as a part of the theological process. "[If] transformative learning is partly about the trans-

---

[23] Darren Cronshaw, "Australian reenvisioning of theological education: In step with the Spirit?" *Australian eJournal of Theology* 18:3 (December 2011), 224.

[24] Charles Sherlock, *Uncovering Theology: The Depth, Reach and Utility of Australian Theological Education* (Adelaide: ATF Press, 2009).

formation of meaning schemes and spirituality is partly about meaning making, often transformation of meaning schemes naturally connects to the spiritual and can lead to transformation on either the individual or sociocultural level."[25] In a provocative address to Anglican theological educators in 2011, the Archbishop of Canterbury Rowan Williams presented what he termed a theological "position report," which in essence posited the major goal of theological education expressed in terms of answering three key questions under the general head of "where are you?" In expanding this question, he showed that the connecting dimension of theological understanding lay in the formative process within the learner.

> Where are you: in your understanding of God – yes; in your place in society – yes; but also in your understanding of yourself. Are you growing? Are you changing in your perspective of who you are before God? ... I'm not saying that that means theology is what feels right at this or that moment, but that into my full theological task comes this element of learning who I am as a person here and now.[26]

In a recent study of the education of clergy in America, Foster *et al* observed a number of pertinent elements of the pedagogical ethos of the institutions, which they termed "pedagogical intentions," as these directly impinge on curriculum aims. Foster's team identified four basic patterns of pedagogical intentions across the schools: (1) a pedagogy of *interpretation*, which is characterized by the interpretation of texts, situations and relationships; (2) a pedagogy of *formation*, which is characterized by the formation of spiritual and/or vocational identity; (3) a pedagogy of *contextualization*, which is characterized by the engagement of a specific context or agency; and (4) a pedagogy of *performance*, which is characterized by performing skills for ministry practice.[27] The notion of "apprenticeships" is used throughout the book as a means of analysing the pedagogies involved. The three apprenticeships evident in seminary education are identified as the *cognitive* or

---

25 Derise E Tolliver and Elizabeth J Tisdell, "Engaging Spirituality in the Transformative Higher Education Classroom," in Edward W Taylor ed, *Teaching for Change: Fostering Transformative Learning in the Classroom: New Directions for Adult and Continuing Education*, No 109 (San Francisco: Jossey-Bass, 2006), 39.

26 Rowan Williams, "Theological Education in the Anglican Communion" (TEAC Principals Address, London; 11 May 2011), 3.

27 Charles R Foster, Lisa E Dahill, Lawrence A Golemon, Barbara Wang Tolentino, *Educating Clergy: Teaching Practices and Pastoral Imagination* (San Francisco: Jossey-Bass, 2006).

intellectual apprenticeship; the *practical* or skill apprenticeship; and the *normative* or identity formation apprenticeship.[28] The cognitive domain (the "knowing what") is well known in all traditional curricula, including theological, but what needs to be in this area needs defining (and periodic re-defining). Many pedagogical methods have been effectively designed to develop the cognitive apprenticeship. The skills domain (the "knowing how") includes the ministerial skills that need to be mastered for vocational purposes. These will often require a different set of pedagogical strategies from those needed for the cognitive area. The normative apprenticeship (the "knowing who") was found to be often the most neglected part of the educational curriculum, being often treated as separate from any formal curriculum. In many cases, it was left to the "non-academy," with mentoring done outside of classes in separate formation classes or in a completely separate institution (eg local church). Often, such formation was assumed to happen after graduation and during "real experience." The analysis of an institution's pedagogical intention is perhaps the most significant intrinsic element in determining whether – or to what degree – it will commit to transformative curriculum aims. If it does commit, then the elements of the pedagogy of formation and the normative apprenticeship will find some explicit expression in the course aims.

In the Australian context, theological degrees are consistently very conservative in the statement of course aims, with the traditional emphasis on the engagement with the classical subject areas remaining dominant, and with a more recent addition of vocational skills emerging as an option.[29] In recent years, there has been a marked trend towards the formulation of sets of graduate outcomes and attributes, most of which are expressed in terms of the personal qualities of the graduate. As Sherlock noted, these graduate attributes are those qualities which an institution wishes to see in its graduates, the formation of which "pushes a college to ask what attributes its graduate should have, and how its courses should be formulated in the light of its overall graduate attributes." He also noted that these statements of attributes "are of little use if they are not fed back into the design of learning outcomes

---

28 Ibid, 25-26.
29 For example, an explicit focus on the development of personal attributes suited to a profession expressed in a contemporary nursing degree contrasts with the more traditional statement of cognitive knowledge of the theology degree at the same university, namely, Australian Catholic University (see ACU's Handbooks 2012). The focus on engaging the classical areas is common to all the major universities and consortia and most of the independent colleges.

for disciplines and units."[30] If transformative learning concepts are valued and are to be embraced within the curriculum, then the statement of course aims will need to be the starting point. The prevalent aim of a systematic and comprehensive study of received traditions stands at odds with Rowan Williams's three-fold "where are you" questions.

Curriculum

The broad parameters of the curriculum of any course will be largely determined by the overall curriculum of the whole institution, as reflected in its aims but also expressed in its conduct. Foster *et al* noted that every school has three curricula: (1) the *explicit* curriculum, which is visibly the main object of attention; (2) the *implicit* curriculum, that is, the values and practices of the institution which support or subvert the explicit curriculum; and (3) the *null* curriculum, which "exists" because it is absent, that is, the curriculum of non-attention, or what is omitted from the explicit and implicit curricula.[31] Griffith University's Stephen Billett has a variation on the different aspects of curriculum. He notes three sub-categories of curriculum, as follows. First, there is the intended curriculum, what is *intended* to occur by sponsors or developers in terms of educational goals (that is, what should be learnt) and learning outcomes as a result of the curriculum being implemented. Second, there is the enacted curriculum, what is enacted as shaped by the resources available, the experience and expertise of teachers and others, their interpretation of what was intended, their values and the range of situational factors that shape students' experiences. Third, there is the experienced curriculum, what students experience when they engage with what was intended through what was enacted, and how they learn through that experiencing, even that which is unintended by those who plan and enact the curriculum.[32] The curriculum is not simply an objective entity encompassing a set of classical subjects for study. Rather, the setting of a curriculum needs to take due cognizance of a complex set of elements, including the overall pedagogical ethos of the institution as well as the inter-connected issues of content, teaching delivery resources and learner experience.

30 Sherlock, *Uncovering Theology*, 85-86.
31 Foster et al, *Educating Clergy*, 49.
32 Stephen Billett, "Curriculum and Pedagogic Bases for Effectively Integrating Practice-based Experiences within Higher Education." http://altc.edu.au/resource-integrating-practice-based-experience-griffith-2011.

From the perspective of transformative learning, the question could be asked, "What comes first: the student or the survey?" David Clines recently related a watershed moment in his teaching career, which he described as the biggest upheaval in educational theory and practice that had happened in his lifetime. "It happened in a moment when I woke one morning vowing to stop teaching biblical studies and start teaching students."[33] This concept of putting the learner front and centre in the educative process is at the heart of transformative learning and it colours the very selection of what content to offer in the first and subsequent years of the program as well as the more obvious teaching methods.

In his discussion of theological curriculum, Clines notes and opposes the practice of determining curriculum on the basis of teacher expertise, interest and attitude to content rather than on the basis of student needs. Fundamental to the notion of transformative learning is the changed perspective of the role of the teacher. The teacher is not the focus of the learning process, the learner is. There is a significant role for the teacher, but it is as a facilitator of learning, not (merely) a transmitter of information. The teacher's role is that not of a dictator, but of a co-learner with the other learners in the class. Clines advocates a student-centred learning approach to curriculum which asks entirely different questions from the teacher's professional opinions, namely, "What do students want, what will benefit them, what outcomes are being sought by the curriculum?"[34] In the same manner, Haar summarises theological education in the 20th century as having devolved into a piecemeal transmission of knowledge and skills, with its traditional division of the curriculum into biblical, historical, systematic and practical theology. This has consequently provided a non-integrated, compartmentalised learning experience that has offered too little challenge for students to develop abilities as independent, lifelong learners, growing constantly, while engaged in the work of ministry in the church and the world.[35] If learners' perspectives are to be formed or transformed, then their existing perspectives need to be factored into the curriculum. Learners need to be allowed to be more responsible for their own learning and thus to take greater ownership of the content and processes of that learning. In short, the content of the curriculum needs to

---

33 David JA Clines, "Learning, Teaching, and Researching Biblical Studies, Today and Tomorrow," *Journal of Biblical Literature* 129:1 (Spring 2010), 7.
34 Ibid, 25.
35 Haar, "Enhancing the Capability of Theological Schools," 1.

start as much from the question "Where are you?" as it does from the statement "This is where you need to be."

In terms of the structure of curriculum, Clines also attacks the "myth of foundationalism," that is, the prevailing view that students must at the beginning of their education in biblical studies (and by extension other sub-disciplines) acquire sound foundations on which they can then build. There is, he claims, no particular starting place, no agreed body of facts that students must begin by learning. "There is no right place to start, except the place where each student is, ramshackle and half-baked though their ideas may be."[36] His preferred subject matter for an introductory course in biblical studies is one small book from which could be educed as many principles for biblical study as possible, drawn from the situation of the learners themselves as they engage the book. Haar has noted that many students entering theological education have already had some significant transformative experience, some challenge to their view of self or God, which led them to enrol. Consequently, the very entering into the world of theological education is a step in their transformative journey. However, they are generally presented with the traditional first year offering of factual knowledge which provides an overview and/or a common knowledge base for further studies. This, says Haar, is counter-productive to transformative development, as it completely misses the learning needs of students at their particular stage of growth. Rather, to promote transformative learning, students need opportunities to grapple with and critically examine theological issues.[37]

From such considerations emerge questions of what content to include in a curriculum and what content to place at the beginning of the course, both related directly to the more fundamental question of what is the overall purpose of the institution and the program. If the student need is to be central, then some appreciation of the student's prior experience, knowledge and perspectives is needed. However, in most institutionalised situations, especially in large institutions, the notion of an individualized curriculum seems fanciful at best. As well, given the historical and creedal base of Christian theology, there is a real agenda of traditional transmission, preservation and promotion. As Haar has noted, the challenge for any theological school that promotes transformative learning is to avoid theological chaos and to remain faithful to its confession of

---

36 Clines, "Learning, Teaching, and Researching Biblical Studies," 27.
37 Haar, "Enhancing the Capability of Theological Schools," 4-5.

faith. So there is a general corpus of content to which the student needs to be introduced. However, it is questionable that an emphasis on comprehensively "covering" all the content of Christian traditions, beliefs and praxis is the best or even an appropriate way of doing so – even if such a coverage were possible to achieve within a three or four year course of study. Coverage of content in itself is no guarantee of students' retention of that content and neither does it guarantee students' ability to analyse it and use it in their professional and personal lives. The value of the course content is reduced if there is a lack of guidance and practice in what to do with that content.[38] Yet still there is the common plaint from theological teachers that there is too little time to cover the vast amount of necessary content to allow much time for the apparently secondary matters of process. "Once I set a foundation for what we're doing, I only have time in a quarter (term) to spend about ten minutes on each chapter of the Gospels. If I start stealing time from that to deal with all these 'process things,' the students will leave here under-prepared."[39] It has long been acknowledged in educational circles that learners learn by assimilation (of new knowledge into their existing frameworks) or accommodation (by way of revising existing frameworks in light of new knowledge), rather than by the memorization of discrete and unrelated facts. Thus any new knowledge needs both time and opportunity to be related effectively to existing frameworks of knowledge and understanding. An information overload of vast amounts of survey units in the first year can present a formidable roadblock at a pivotal juncture in this process. So too an accumulation of disconnected and unintegrated advanced units in later years can produce a fragmented outcome of much learning but limited holistic formation.

In summary, two overriding considerations have emerged that colour the discussion of curriculum design which promotes transformative learning. The first year needs to take deliberate steps to ascertain just what are the existing theological and experiential frameworks of commencing students and to structure content so that students are enabled to *review critically those existing frameworks* in light of new theological knowledge encountered. This will entail the creation of a learning environment in which such reflective practice is facilitated, with limited content and an emphasis on critical

---

38 Mary-Ann Winkelmes, "The Classroom as a Place of Formation: Purposefully Creating a Transformative Environment for Today's Diverse Seminary Population," *Teaching Theology and Religion* 7:4 (2004), 218.
39 Ibid, 217.

thinking practices relevant to the various disciplines (if indeed the traditional sub-disciplines need to be retained). Second, advanced units of study need to be a continuation not a cessation of this process, but with strategic opportunities provided for a holistic *integration of units* taught. This may well require a revision of the traditionally discrete fields of study ("majors"), or at least a deliberate and effectual means of integrating the world views that are being formed across the curriculum. In short, transformative learning ideals promote the concepts of a student being taught to think critically and reflectively and to form a clear set of perspectives of God, self and the world that are coherently integrated and cogently articulated.

Methods

In addressing the aspect of educational methods suited to the attainment of transformative learning, there are some important preliminary issues that affect the methods employed, especially the issues of *where* and *how* transformative learning takes place. Despite the common reliance on experiential and transformative development beyond the classroom, Winkelmes has pointed out that, in the current climate of non-residential and scattered seminary and theological communities, the only place and time where teachers can ensure a gathered formative learning community is in the classroom during their scheduled class time. Hence, the classroom is "the most feasible locus for the kind of gradual, intellectual, and spiritual formation that seems to have happened within the supportive, residential seminary communities of generations past."[40] Even when the unit involves a field placement, Billett has stressed the important role of teacher-facilitated classroom contributions to field placements in preparation for and critical reflection on the field experiences.[41] Even when the classroom is the virtual space of online learning, instructional strategies need to be designed to enhance personal and spiritual formation by focusing on the affective domain, especially encouraging relational interaction and promoting a sense of community, and incorporating the important arenas of interactive learning: student-to-student, student-to-teacher, and student-to-content.[42]

As for the issue of how does transformative learning take place, if effectual

---

40 Winkelmes, "The Classroom as a Place of Formation," 213.
41 Billett, "Curriculum and Pedagogic Bases."
42 Roger White, "Promoting spiritual formation in distance education," *Christian Education Journal* 3:2 (2006), 311.

learning is to happen, then recognition and utilisation of various individual learning styles must be a part of the educative process. A focus on learning styles will shape the discussion of educational methods – specifically, should we be discussing teaching methods or learning methods, since this distinction will effectively govern all that actually happens in the classroom. There is a growing recognition of the need for holistic learning to involve not just the cognitive aspects of learning but styles such as affective and kinaesthetic as well. When students are required to respond to an assumed learning method which is counter to their nature, an alienation from the learning process can result, with a resistance and even resentment towards those very methods.[43] A commitment to transformative learning involves a re-consideration of the role of the teacher as well as a consideration of the diversity of the learners.

The role adopted by the teacher is vital in any educational situation. The term "lecturer" evokes an image of a thoroughly knowledgeable sage who stands and delivers new and important information to a group of relatively passive listeners. The lecture remains the most widely practised method of imparting vast amounts of such content in limited contact time, which is its legitimate and efficient use. However, as Long has pointed out, the lecture is largely the primary method of theological education, which runs counter to the need for holistic learning.[44] Unless the lecture is punctuated by moments of reflective processing on the part of the students, the opportunities for genuinely transformative experience will be very limited. For transformative learning to occur, the teacher's role needs to be seen less as a "lecturer" and more as a "learning facilitator." Transformative learning as applied to theology requires a holistic view of education that incorporates the whole person including mind, emotions, body and spirituality.[45] While there are innumerable ways of being an effective learning facilitator, there are several general and inter-connected principles which seem to apply universally, namely, the principles of transparency, collegiality and peer learning.

Transparency involves a willingness on the part of the learning facilitator to discuss openly and consistently the aims and strategies of the learning-teaching programs and processes. This includes the aims, procedures and assessment elements of any unit. This transparency generates in students a

---

43 Winkelmes, "The Classroom as a Place of Formation," 216.
44 Jude Long. "Teaching Adults: Insights from Educational Philosophy," *Journal of Christian Education* 53:1 (May 2010), 50-51.
45 Ibid, 52.

greater awareness of their learning practices and encourages them to take a more responsible role in their own education.[46] It also forms part of that corporate discourse which promotes critical reflection in community that is fundamental to transformative development.[47] Collegiality involves such communal discourse, but it goes further. The learning facilitator not only facilitates the learning of others, but is a participant as a co-learner in the developmental process. This involves both humility before the students and an attitude of vulnerable risk-taking as, in serving as a co-learner, the facilitator reflects these Christian values of humility and authenticity.[48] Peer learning takes this stance a step further, as it respects the capacity of all students to be contributors to the learning of others. This does not mean an abdication of the role of the teacher; indeed, education literature emphasizes the significant role of the reflection facilitator in transformative learning.[49] The teacher as reflection facilitator acts as *provocateur* to instigate critical reflection and discourse; orchestrates a safe and challenging space in which the discourse takes place; and ensures a clear understanding by all participants of the purpose, procedure and product of the peer learning agenda.[50] These principles do not in any way devalue the role of the teacher, but they do suggest significant ways of re-defining that role.[51]

A major challenge for all teachers is the identification of individual learning styles, especially in large classes and most significantly in introductory classes. Once again, while much research has been done in this area of learning styles, it is rare to find a tertiary teacher who proactively seeks to discover the preferred learning styles of students before teaching them. There are programs available for such an identification exercise.[52] While most people have multi-modal learning styles, yet some 40% are estimated as being significantly hindered if they are not free to learn in their own dominant style.[53] If this

---

46 Winkelmes, "The Classroom as a Place of Formation," 220.
47 Marmon, "Cross-Cultural Field Education," 74.
48 Ibid, 76.
49 Ibid, 75.
50 Ibid, 75-76; Winkelmes, "The Classroom as a Place of Formation," 220.
51 A useful chart contrasting the characteristics of what he terms "Traditional Teacher" and "Facilitator" is provided by Clines. See Clines, "Learning, Teaching, and Researching Biblical Studies," 16.
52 One such program is that constructed by Neil Fleming, based on his VARK model, which identifies the four predominant learning styles as Visual, Aural, Read/Write and Kinesthetic. Fleming has developed a quick online questionnaire which could well be taken as a pre-teaching orientation activity. See his website at www.vark-learn.com.
53 Clines, "Learning, Teaching, and Researching Biblical Studies," 11.

issue is to be taken seriously, then opportunities must be orchestrated that will allow the teacher to reinforce any pre-teaching insights by an ongoing analysis in the early stages of the program. Opportunities in various reflective critical method units which connect with the individual student's actual experience and background could well replace the content-driven survey units in introductory programs.

When it comes to specific suggestions for delivery methods which promote transformative learning, two chief observations emerge. The first of these is the need for integrative teaching. Transformative learning requires a high amount of energy and time, so the issue of work load is important. For the majority of students, a high work load is a hindering factor for transformative learning, which may contribute to burnout rather than integrative learning.[54] Another consideration is the setting of a text. Course texts can help facilitate the way students "read their worlds" and contribute to transforming perspectives.[55] Once in the classroom, the onus is on the teacher to introduce and progress the material in such a way as to facilitate an integrative appropriation of the topic. This will be enhanced by a process of contextual framing: an explicit introductory comment by the teacher about the purpose of the lesson, its main goals and issues, its place in the overall course design, and its relation to previous topics or readings, and a matching explicit comment at the end of the class to summarize these connections and pre-emptively link with the next topic.[56] A topic may be introduced by an initial dilemma or problem that requires the forthcoming class material for its solution. Integration of the material is more likely if the class engages work related or real-life issues and questions that they are currently experiencing or are likely to confront in their foreseeable future roles.[57] The inclusion of real world problems that address inequalities can also be a powerfully transformative encounter.[58] Towards the end of a lesson, some simple student exercise such as a one minute paper to summarize the key idea the student is taking from the class and what questions still remain can be an effective means of helping the teacher to maintain an integrative focus in the ongoing teaching.[59]

The second main observation on transformative learning methods is the

---

54 Haar, "Enhancing the Capability of Theological Schools," 6.
55 Marmon, "Cross-Cultural Field Education," 78.
56 Winkelmes, "The Classroom as a Place of Formation," 218.
57 Clines, "Learning, Teaching, and Researching Biblical Studies," 25.
58 Haar, "Enhancing the Capability of Theological Schools," 8.
59 Winkelmes, "The Classroom as a Place of Formation," 219.

transition from teacher-focused delivery to student-centred learning. An effective promotion of transformative learning requires, among other things, a respect for the learner as a responsible adult. This includes allowing students a role in the *instructional design* of their program by choosing and deciding the direction of their learning.[60] Such an approach will lead more naturally into an inductive process of discovery rather than allowing the questions of the scholarly (and often arcane) tradition to set the agenda in the classroom.[61] The use of regular *peer processing* of encountered material will enhance both the individual learner's immediate critical reflection and the communal element of social learning. Some simple ways of doing this are the provision within each class period of several two minute group processing opportunities, where students are required to apply the new concept to a new situation proposed by the teacher, or engagement in specific case-study discussions in seminar settings.[62] Collaborative research projects, problem-based instruction and discussion, and brief role plays are other common and simple strategies that promote student participation and engagement.[63] In field education units, preparatory sessions can draw on students' existing experiences, while challenges to personal confidence and competence encountered in the field experience can be redressed by effective group processes, including sharing of and reflection on that experience.[64]

As well as such general techniques, consideration is warranted of the fundamental philosophical approach to learning and teaching. The traditional model of *didactic delivery* of what has been predetermined to be the necessary and important content removes the learner from the active process and assumes a more or less passive receptivity on the part of the student. A popular method of generating relevance and application of such content has been to adopt a *problem-solving* approach, particularly in practical ministry units. Such an approach assumes that there is a problem (in the organization, the practice, the system, etc) and that an effective analysis of contributing factors and contextual conditions will lead to a solution. However, this clearly useful approach has limitations, as it tends to see the learner as an external analyst rather than an active and positive participant. It naturally focuses on

---

60 Haar, "Enhancing the Capability of Theological Schools," 5.
61 Clines, "Learning, Teaching, and Researching Biblical Studies," 22.
62 Winkelmes, "The Classroom as a Place of Formation," 219.
63 Haar, "Enhancing the Capability of Theological Schools," 8.
64 Billett, "Curriculum and Pedagogic Bases."

what is wrong, rather than on how a learner's personal situation and experience may be taken as the base of a continuing journey. If the transformation of the learner is to be the focus, then something more than didactic information transmittal and problem-solving analysis will be needed.

One model suited to transformative learning is *inquiry-based learning*. Here, the teacher proffers an issue, a realm of study that the learner will personally investigate with the support of the teacher. The learning task becomes a heuristic process, where the learner draws upon previous personal experience and prior knowledge in order to continue a journey of discovery. Such inquiry is best (and more likely to be transformative) if it is open-ended, that is, the discoveries or solutions are not pre-determined. While clearly more "risky," such an approach generates intrinsic motivation for learning as against the more extrinsic motivation of attaining good grades or being affirmed as having reached the "right" conclusion.[65] However, such inquiry learning need not be unstructured. In fact, it needs to be structured so as to ensure the learners do not feel abandoned or out of their depth. Clear direction needs to be established for the purpose and parameters of inquiry and resources need to be available to facilitate the inquiry, but the journey of discovery is an individual story to be inductively unfolded. Possibly the most formative (and potentially transformative) version of inquiry-based learning is that of *appreciative inquiry*. In appreciative inquiry, instead of framing a problem to be solved, the learner is asked to reflect on past successes which can then be built on to shape future triumphs. "Rather than focusing on problems that need solving, appreciative inquiry focuses on the examples of the system at its best, its highest values and aspirations, its noblest actions."[66] The principles of appreciative inquiry can be readily applied to individual learning in all theological studies. While such inquiry-based learning is often criticised as being a time-consuming "re-invention of the wheel," none the less the process of having students learn for themselves just how wheels are made can be a powerful element in their personal development.[67] Inquiry-based learning may be used as a segment of a unit and at any stage of the course, not just the later stages of individual research units. Such inquiry is likely to flow naturally into action-oriented outcomes, in both the individual's life and

---

65 Clines, "Learning, Teaching, and Researching Biblical Studies," 20.
66 GR Bushe and AF Kassam, "When is Appreciative Inquiry Transformational? A Meta-Case Analysis," *The Journal of Applied Behavioural Science*, 41:2 (2005), 166.
67 Clines, "Learning, Teaching, and Researching Biblical Studies," 27.

in a social context. Such action-outcome is a marker of transformative learning.[68] The intrinsically powerful motivation of facilitating the students' development of their own understanding and perspectives through their own self-directed inquiry is a strong contributor to active transformative learning.

The issue of assessment methods always looms large in educational delivery. Charles de Jongh has analysed the difference between *deep* and *surface* learning and its implications for constructing assessment instruments that foster deep learning. He suggests ways of encouraging deep learning such as teaching and assessment tasks that encourage a deep approach, rather than a breadth of coverage; meaningfully building on learners' previous experiences and prior knowledge; an emphasis on principles and structure, rather than examples and facts; affording the learner the opportunity to choose aspects of the content and method of learning; and the rewarding of more than the recall of facts or information.[69] He warns against the danger of the "backwash effect," where learners simply learn what they think they will be tested on, when assessment determines what and how students learn more than the curriculum does.[70] He proceeds to outline seven principles for deep learning assessment, all of which have clear reference to the facilitation of transformative learning.

1. Assessment is integral to course design and should be centred on the learner's envisaged achievement.
2. Assessment requirements focus on the significant principles and structures of the course material.
3. Assessment is based on clear and stated objectives and outcomes, which are directly associated with the aims and purpose of the course.
4. Assessment for deep learning makes use of a wide variety of methods and types.
5. Assessment requirements and criteria are clearly and explicitly stated.
6. Assessment for deep learning is supported by good preparatory guidance, material and personal support, and appropriate resourcing.
7. Assessment gives early and comprehensive feedback, with the intention of addressing weaknesses and improving learning.[71]

---

68 Haar, "Enhancing the Capability of Theological Schools," 9.
69 Charles De Jongh, "Theories of Multiple Intelligences and Learning Assessment for Deep Learning in Higher Education" (EdD thesis; University of Johannesburg, 2010).
70 Ibid, 51.
71 Ibid, 53–57.

Outcomes

Whereas the discussion of course aims focused on what is intended to happen during the delivery of the course, course outcomes are more to do with what sort of product results from the overall program of theological education. Since that "product" is essentially a theological graduate, the question really reduces itself to what sort of person is the intended outcome as a theological graduate who has experienced a process of transformative learning.

Haar has noted that it is only in the modern era that earlier concepts of transformative learning were superseded by a notion of education as the transmission of a body of knowledge, taught and explained by teachers, learnt by students and periodically tested by examinations, with little or no understanding of the role played by the background, beliefs, emotions and interests of individual learners.[72] However, over the past decade or so, various educators have sought to develop alternative models for theological education which re- engage with the real life and social context of the learner, in such things as the missional model of Robert Banks and the programs of the Forge Mission Training Network.[73] The desired outcome of such transformative models is a graduate equipped to think, pray, live and lead from a Christian perspective in all areas of society.[74] Clines expresses course outcomes in terms of what students will be able *to do* on successful completion of the course, rather than what they *will know*, that is, the skills that they will be able to deploy, not just the knowledge they will have absorbed.[75] Such an approach finds common recent expression in many course accreditation documents. These statements echo Foster *et al's* categories of cognitive (intellectual) and practical (skills) apprenticeships, but they stop short of including the normative apprenticeship of identity formation, of what a graduate actually *becomes* as a person.

Winkelmes has observed that, more than professors in most other disciplines and contexts, teachers in seminaries belong to a culture in which the overall educational and developmental experience of students warrants serious consideration. She adds a comment that the goal of such consideration is to help diverse learners to understand the relationships between what they learn in the classroom, how they navigate the larger institutional community, and how they

---

72   Haar, "Enhancing the Capability of Theological Schools," 1.
73   Cronshaw, "Australian reenvisioning of theological education," 226-232.
74   Haar, "Enhancing the Capability of Theological Schools," 2.
75   Clines, "Learning, Teaching, and Researching Biblical Studies," 12-14.

function in the world.⁷⁶ Consequently, the practices within the classroom – the transparently explicit aims of any unit, the selection and ordering of content, the methods of students' engaging and processing that content – need to be aligned with such transformative perspective development and consolidation. The outcome of any unit needs to be seen not in terms (only) of a grade but (also) as a demonstrated development of person. Clines bemoans the "fixation on grades, which represent the commodification of learning," a fixation which often accompanies a massive misunderstanding of what education can be. In noting the "superfluity of data the Internet provides," he longs to see the replacement of the unhealthy practice of the deliberate memorization of unrelated facts with the realization that all that really matters is not the data but what we do with the data.⁷⁷ While this description may contain an element of caricature, it does prompt the thought that, in terms of transformative learning, we might well extend the statement to, "and what the processing of the data can do to us."

Transformative learning involves a symbiosis of teaching and learning that offers even more than a place for formative learning. It allows the teacher to model the kind of formative facilitator the students will ideally become after graduation: one who enables learners to educate themselves.⁷⁸ It includes what Rowan Williams refers to as "an adult self- awareness," wherein a minister (or other theologically educated person) will naturally talk in an adult awareness of themselves, their limits, their struggles, their strengths.⁷⁹ This is what marks a healthy and creative theological community, be it church or college. Williams describes the desired outcome of a theological education in terms of the person in ministry:

> So the ordained, ministering, teaching theologian is there in order to make a *learning church*, because they themselves are learners, growing in understanding; they will look for the kind of context in the parish or college or wherever in which a learning conversation is being taken forward at every level.⁸⁰

It is not inappropriate to substitute the words "seminary" or "college" or "theology faculty" for "church" in the above statement.

---

76 Winkelmes, "The Classroom as a Place of Formation," 215-217.
77 Clines, "Learning, Teaching, and Researching Biblical Studies," 19-20.
78 Winkelmes, "The Classroom as a Place of Formation," 220.
79 Williams, "Theological Education in the Anglican Communion", 5.
80 Ibid, 6.

3. Conclusions

This review reinforces the historical and creedal bases of traditional theological teaching and the value of the important development of practical skills as a legitimate component of contemporary theological education, particularly in those institutions which have been established to service the needs of churches. At the same time, it serves to inform further thinking (and perhaps to provoke further action) in the area of theological curriculum design and delivery. Clearly, no theological curriculum can be designed or delivered in isolation from its traditional and socio-political context, which legitimately involves a complex set of competing agenda, shaped by the demands of theological and ecclesiological distinctives, vocational needs and institutional ethos and resources. Yet within all of these parameters, there is the desire for (and arguably the duty of) theological institutions to take seriously their role in the formation of people and the transformation of both individuals and society. Nor is this really a new idea, despite the terminology and recent popularizing of the concepts. Indeed, it is essentially a return to some ancient views of education (at least as old as the time of Jesus) as the transformation of lives and society. It comes by way of reaction against the dissatisfaction with the limitations of the knowledge transmission philosophy of modernism and it seeks to re-locate the person as a legitimate focus in the educative process. This placing of the learner at the centre of learning – in course aims, curriculum design, delivery methods and desired outcomes – is fundamental to the philosophy of transformative learning.

However, while such theory has been around for some time now, its practical implementation has lagged significantly, and perhaps nowhere is this lagging more pronounced than in the educationally conservative field of theological education. Malcolm Knowles, a leading thinker in adult education, wrote as follows:

> [T]here is an urgent need for all programmes of higher education ... to be geared to developing the skills of autonomous learning.... To reorient higher education ... in this direction is a tremendous challenge. It is a concept that is foreign to most educators. It has not been part of their training It requires a redefinition of their role away from that of transmitter and controller of instruction to

that of facilitator and resource person to self- directed learners. It is frightening. They do not know how to do it.[81]

Perhaps what is even more "frightening" is that Knowles wrote this thirty years ago, yet curriculum designers in particular seem still not to know how to do it. The constraints of tradition and context notwithstanding, the framers and deliverers of theological curricula have an opportunity to engage and drive the process of transformative learning with all its potential for individual and social transformation. The opportunity involves humility, risk and creativity, but these are the elements of any progressive venture. There seems no reason why theological educators should not take positive steps to developing a more intentional and strategic approach to transformative educational curriculum development.

4. Postscript: A Personal Reflection

What then is the ultimate outcome desired for a genuinely transformative theological education? The thinking that has emerged from the current research has caused me to reflect critically on my own teaching career of some forty years. It has made me wonder, "What contribution has my teaching made to the transformation of the lives of my students?" While the current project is not geared to reviewing the post-graduate experiences of students, none the less some graduates have been included in interviews and there have been numerous intentional discussions on this matter with other of my own past students, some from fifteen-twenty years ago. A couple of conversations in particular stand out. I had taught these students at different times a number of undergraduate courses in Church History, including what I had considered some lucid expositions of the historical and theological contributions of the Church Fathers and the Reformers. Both students reported enjoying my classes, both successfully graduated more than ten years ago, both are actively involved in church ministry, and both are currently near completing a PhD in a leading university. Neither of them could recall any of the details of my explanation of Origen's complex theology, neither had a clear picture of the geography of Wycliffe or Huss. However, both independently reported very

---

81 Malcolm S Knowles, "Preface," in *Developing Student Autonomy in Learning* (ed David Boud; London: Kogan Page, 1981), 8.

emphatically that some of the most crucial things they had learned about themselves, their church, their approach to ministry and the shaping of their world view came as a direct result of my teaching them how to think historically and critically. This had become a natural part of the way in which they thought about virtually everything, from study techniques now being used in their doctorates to church constitutions, from biblical and theological interpretation to personal letters received from family overseas. In other words, the only real thing of permanent value my teaching had contributed (apart from some good grades in Church History) was what they had appropriated as a part of their own personhood. I readily acknowledge the research weakness of such anecdotal stories, but I offer this account as a sample of what I have come to believe is at the heart of transformative learning. The screeds of lecture notes taken during classes but never revisited after examination are not the essential outcome of a healthy education. What the person does with the content encountered and, ultimately, what the content does to and for the person are surely the things of lasting value.

3 | CURRICULUM DESIGN AND DEVELOPMENTS

LEARNING FROM HISTORY

A comprehensive analysis of curriculum documents from major providers – both universities and theological colleges – was conducted. This analysis examined the historical curriculum documents over the period 1973-2010, which covers the delivery of Australian bachelor degrees in Theology. The focus of the analysis was on the design of curriculum, with particular reference to the role of learner experience and the structural incorporation of transformative learning opportunities. The review showed that there have been very few and limited "watershed" developments in curriculum design, with the traditional bases of theological degrees being commonly retained as a strong platform of biblical studies and systematic theology. There is a high degree of uniformity in course design and content, despite the varying philosophical and institutional bases of the teaching bodies.[1]

1. A Brief Historical Review

The evolution of theological curriculum has been closely linked to the institutional evolution of the bodies providing the programs and the changing

---

[1] The review included historical curriculum documents from Adelaide College of Divinity, Australian Catholic University, Australian College of Theology, Brisbane College of Theology, Charles Sturt University, Christian Heritage College, Flinders University, Malyon College, Melbourne College of Divinity, Moore Theological College, Murdoch University, Sydney College of Divinity, Tabor Adelaide, The University of Newcastle.

social context in which they have operated. Most denominations had very early in-house training of some sort: Catholic seminaries; the Anglican Colleges of Moore and Ridley, with the Australian College of Theology's (ACTh) establishment in 1891 "to foster and direct the systematic study of Divinity, especially among the clergy;" Presbyterian and Baptist Theological Halls and Colleges in Melbourne, Sydney and Brisbane. All were well established by the early 20th century, with the narrowly defined purpose of providing the classical theological study required for denominationally ordained ministry within a largely Christianised cultural context. In 1910, the Melbourne College of Divinity (MCD) was established as a consortium of Church of England, Baptist, Congregational, Presbyterian and Methodist colleges, with an Oxford style collegiate system of independent colleges under a Bachelor of Divinity awarding institution. Various independent trans-denominational evangelical Bible Colleges, with an emphasis on lay and missions training, emerged in the first half of the 20th century. The general picture of these colleges was one of small independent institutions with limited student numbers and focused non-accredited programs geared to the provision of clergy, with some inter-denominational commitment to foreign missions.

The Martin Report of 1965 allowed non-universities to offer degrees, which led to a rapid expansion of accredited theological institutions and awards. Among others, ACTh expanded its programs, offering the Bachelor of Theology from 1975. A number of theological consortia soon commenced: Adelaide College of Divinity (1979), Sydney College of Divinity (1983), Brisbane College of Theology (1983). Pentecostal churches also entered the field in a significant way: Tabor SA (1979); Harvest Bible College (1985), Christian Heritage College (1986). The general picture in the 1970s-1990s was a move towards more colleges and greater recognition of degree programs. However, within this rush to open local colleges, very little attention was given to curriculum development, with the standard offerings of a conventionally solid suite of Bible, languages, theology and church history being the staple of all courses, with little or no interaction between providers in matters of pedagogical development.

The "New Age" of theological education really commenced in the 1990s. The dominant motif became "Accreditation." For the first time, Australia saw direct governmental engagement of private tertiary education delivery, prompted largely by the explosion in overseas marketing. This entailed government accreditation, with various forms of associated financial support, of private institutions and their academic courses, with a subsequent proliferation of independent Non Self-Accrediting Institutions and government registered Higher Education Providers. This development has brought all major theological providers within the ambit of government policy, protocols and operational guidelines. Recently, some colleges have found the regulatory impost too heavy a burden and have forgone their independence to affiliate with a larger consortium or one of the six Australian universities offering a theology program. Perhaps the most notable trend in the last few years has been the more aggressive (re-)entry of universities into theological education, with the establishment of the University of Newcastle Theology School in 2006 (absorbing Broken Bay Institute in 2010); the creation of the Australian Catholic University's Faculty of Theology in 2009 (absorbing the theology degree offerings of two private theological colleges in 2010-2011); Charles Sturt University's absorption of a number of colleges since 2009; the Theology Schools of Murdoch and Flinders Universities and the University of Notre Dame Australia with campuses in several States. While government accrediting bodies and university regulations do not mandate curriculum content or design, the impact of such a regulatory regime has been, *inter alia*, to encourage a high degree of uniformity in matters of course rationales, aims, structures, contents and conditions of delivery, all required in the name of quality control and cross-institutional benchmarking. There has consequently been a very conservative approach to theological curriculum development over the past twenty years.

2. The General Picture

Course Aims

If students' life experience and transformative perspective development are important components of theological education, they could be expected to find a place in the statement of course aims. For example, in formulating guidelines for integrating practice-based experiences within higher education, particularly in professional vocationally oriented fields, Stephen Billett lists seven key learning outcomes, one of which is "transformation of students' personal perspectives."[2] However, a review of the statements of course aims of

---

[2] Stephen Billett, "Curriculum and Pedagogic Bases for Effectively Integrating Practice-based Experiences within Higher Education." http://altc.edu.au/resource-integrating-practice-based-experience-griffith-2011.

the theological degrees offered within Australia shows that such personal transformation does not feature in the stated aims of universities or theological colleges' offerings. Rather, the stated aims are almost universally expressed in terms of the systematic acquisition of the traditional content areas of theological studies – scripture, theology, church history, philosophy – "a thorough and comprehensive grounding in the principal areas of theological studies."[3] The universities at times offer an additional option of more liberal arts units, but these are also listed as content areas. Typically, the universities add a statement about the interaction between theological traditions and society, couched in terms of the various theories and arguments that have occurred in the history of theology and the intellectual basis of core faith teachings. The major theological consortia, which include a host of smaller teaching institutions under their respective umbrellas, generally (though not universally) add a ministry vocational application to their aims, with a systematic body of traditional theological disciplines undergirding practical ministry skills. The following statement of the largest consortium is a good synopsis of the stated aims of the major private providers, with its focus on the traditional academic content of theology, with an optional extension into vocational skills acquisition. "The aim of the (Bachelor of Theology) is to guide students in a systematic manner to the acquisition of the body of coherent knowledge that is the classical discipline of theology as a means of preparing men and women for the responsibility of communicating Christian knowledge as leaders in the church, and if students so choose, to the acquisition of skills appropriate to ministry in one or more areas of pastoral practice."[4] The independent stand-alone providers also typically focus on systematic engagement with academic traditions as a means of preparation for ministry: "(the degree) is designed for men and women who desire a biblical and theological foundation for full-time Christian ministry."[5] Occasionally, there is a reference to the development of "godly attitudes and values,"[6] but in general, the emphasis remains on the development of "academic skills designed to equip students with the practical skills to function effectively in a professional ministry context."[7]

So then, while the language of transformation occurs frequently in promotional literature and slogans, it has not historically translated into formal

---

[3] University of Notre Dame Australia, Bachelor of Theology, *Handbook 2011*.
[4] Australian College of Theology, Bachelor of Theology, Aims and Rationale, *Handbook 2011*.
[5] Moore Theological College, Bachelor of Divinity, *Handbook 2011*.
[6] Perth Bible College, Bachelor of Ministry, *Handbook 2011*.
[7] Christian Heritage College, Bachelor of Ministry, *Handbook 2011*.

course aims. Such a disjunction may result from a combination of intrinsic and extrinsic factors. The intrinsic factors are those which arise from the very nature of the teaching institution itself: its institutional purpose, its regulatory policies, the received and dominant traditions in which it is located. Such factors are within the control of the institution and its constituency, even though any radical changes may involve considerable and possibly traumatic challenges. The extrinsic factors are those which are imposed by external agencies: particularly accrediting and funding agencies. While these factors are not so readily within the control of the teaching institution, none the less they need to be managed constructively (and at times creatively) in order to avoid institutional stagnation.

Theological teaching institutions in Australia, whether in universities or theological colleges, have historically been initiated by churches or other religious orders or individuals. Consequently, they have always tended to reflect the religious tradition and need of the establishing agency. Thus, the institution's theological *raison d'être* has been a major determinant of the curriculum aims. Even the theology schools of the six universities which deliver theological degrees in Australia, while generally adopting a public stance of avoiding any particular faith position, have been set up to serve the needs of churches and in large measure depend on church support for their existence.[8] This historical and ecclesial background needs to be kept in mind in any discussion of pedagogical matters in theological provision.

In the Australian context, a major extrinsic factor is the influence exerted by the accreditation charters governing the official recognition of courses. Universities are required to uphold the academic disciplines and to show socio-cultural relevance of their courses. However, while skills development in such areas as social work is well established in universities, there has been a general reluctance to engage "non-academic" ministry skills or the "spiritual" areas of personal religious formation. Private institutions which require government accreditation (and, generally, the support of churches) need to

---

8   Australian Catholic University consistently uses terms such as "within the Catholic tradition, ... within this Catholic perspective" in its course literature; University of Notre Dame Australia also stands explicitly within the Catholic tradition; the Theology faculty of Newcastle University was endowed by a gift of the Anglican Church; the Theology schools of Charles Sturt, Flinders and Murdoch Universities consist essentially of a consortium of denominational theological schools joined under the banner of the university. While none is directly charged with serving the individual churches involved, there remains a close nexus between the university's theology school and the supporting churches. The recent absorption of several Catholic, Anglican and Uniting Church theological colleges into Australian Catholic University, Charles Sturt University and Newcastle University reinforces this connection.

demonstrate both academic rigour and the vocational utility of their courses, which constrains them in the statement of aims. However, despite such external pragmatic factors, other disciplines such as nursing seem to be less conservative in expressing aims in terms of personal development rather than in terms of content areas. For example, in Australian Catholic University, where a Bachelor of Theology has the stated aim of pursuing "an in-depth study in scripture, theology and philosophy," the Bachelor of Nursing has the following aims:

> The Bachelor of Nursing course aims to develop a caring professional nurse, who is proactive and adaptable, a competent safe and ethical clinician, a creative and critical thinker, an informed consumer of practice evidence, and an independent lifelong learner. The course uses learner-centred approaches including inquiry and situation-based learning to enhance students' experiences during the course as well as their readiness for the workplace.

Course Structures

There has been very little radical surgery performed on the body of theological curricula in Australia. The essential skeleton of course structures remained in 2010 very much what it had been for thirty years or more. The main structural change has been in the general semesterisation of delivery in place of the historical year-long subjects, but this has had no real effect on course content and structure other than to spread a year-long subject over two semester units.[9] A comparative analysis of the Fields of Study, the Major foci of the awards and the Core Requirements reveals a common approach to the structure of undergraduate degrees across the wide spectrum of providers for most of the history of the awards. Structurally, the degrees have been crafted around three main Fields of Study, namely, Biblical Studies, Christian Thought (comprising Systematic Theology, Church History, Philosophy and Ethics) and Christian Practice (by various names such as Ministry in Practice, Mission and Ministry, Practical Theology). Occasionally, some have added a Liberal Arts Field, which has allowed some broadening of academic horizons and is often used to

---

9   Semesterisation has had other impacts, especially in combination with the associated internalising of assessment. Most particularly, content has less time for processing, as assessment instruments are far more numerous and dominant throughout all semesters. There are other issues involved in the difference between semesterisation and year-long subjects, but with reference to course structure, little difference occurs in terms of content and sequencing.

encompass a limited number of units which are tangential to the discipline of theology or do not comfortably fit into the other specialised Fields (eg biblical and other ancient languages or general studies of religion). The Liberal Arts Field has not generally contributed greatly to the overall degrees in Theology. Concentrations within the awards have been typically designated as "Majors," comprising a selection of 25-33% of the total degree drawn from units within a certain Field or sub-field (eg New Testament Studies). A degree would typically require one or two Majors to be taken, thus ensuring a solid base within the specialised field. As well as the Majors, courses commonly included a small number of Core Units, generally introductions to biblical, theological and historical studies and key doctrinal units such as Christology. This general pattern has historically dominated the theological degree structures.

The earliest providers of Australian bachelor's degrees in theology were Melbourne College of Divinity (MCD) and Australian College of Theology (ACTh), both being consortia catering to a diverse range of affiliated institutions. The evolution of the structures of ACTh (the largest consortium) serves to illustrate the general development. From 1975 to 1991, ACTh had just one accredited undergraduate degree, the Bachelor of Theology, with the three Fields of Biblical Studies, Theology and Church History, and Christian Studies. This degree consisted of twelve year-long subjects with the dominant assessment item being a uniform external examination at the end of the year in each unit. Until 1981, the prescribed units were Greek I, OTI, OTII, NTI, NTII, OT/NTIII, CHI, THI, THII, THII/IV or CHII/III/IV with two Electives drawn from a limited suite of units in Bible, Liturgiology, Philosophy of Religion, Christian Ethics, Christian Education, Study of Religions and Christian Missions. There was no practical component in any unit. In 1981, a couple of minor amendments were made to allow the final Core CH/TH unit to become an Elective, two units were expanded to two subjects each, and Pastoral Ministry was added to the Electives. With a couple of very minor adjustments to the Electives in Christian Studies, this remained the pattern until 2001.

In 1992, ACTh made a major addition to its bachelor's awards, largely resulting from pressure from its increasingly diverse constituents, namely, the Bachelor of Ministries. This degree was framed around the three Fields of Bible and Language, Christian Thought, and Ministry and Practice. This was a semesterised degree with internal assessment and external moderation. While there were no Majors, there were prescribed minimum requirements for the degree in the various Fields, which ensured its distinction from the traditional Bachelor of Theology and allowed for an extensive expansion into the field of applied practical ministry, with a suite of eighteen units in Ministry and Practice incorporating a practical component, typically weighted at 20%. It also included a unit of Supervised Experience Based Learning, which was flexibly designed to assist a student's personal spiritual growth across the duration of the course.

In 2002, ACTh implemented a sweeping change to its bachelor degree offerings, by rationalising the structures of the two discrete degrees in Theology and Ministries. Both degrees were semesterised and incorporated the same Fields, units and overall structures as had been developed within the Bachelor of Ministries (then changed to Bachelor of Ministry). The respective regulations concerning minimum requirements in the fields ensured the Bachelor of Theology retained its emphasis on language, biblical and theological study. For the first time, provision was made for some limited inclusion of a practical Elective in the Bachelor of Theology. Core Foundational Units were mandated, but there was a high degree of choice available in the combination of other units to meet the regulatory requirements. In some ways, the more flexible structures of Electives within the two awards tended to blur the distinction in practice, but they did allow individual colleges within the consortium a large degree of autonomy in structuring the degree that best suited their purposes.

As one of the largest theological providers over the past two decades, ACTh has been arguably the benchmark for course structures and the developments detailed above reflect the general story of course development in that period. Other consortia and independent colleges have followed more or less along similar lines, with similar approaches to Fields, Majors and Core requirements. Melbourne College of Divinity's awards featured four Fields and required two Majors each containing 25% of the overall degree and one sub-Major of 16% of the degree. Two of these foci had to be in Bible and Systematic Theology. The MCD Humanities Field incorporated a small number of units in languages, philosophy, history and religious studies, while the Mission and Ministry Field was mainly theoretical with very little by way of practical components in the church ministry units. Sydney College of Divinity (SCD), a relatively late starter in the sector (commencing in 1983), sought to cater for a very wide range of constituent members and ecclesial traditions with a more overtly liberal approach to education. Its approach was a federal system, whereby it did not have a central syllabus but invited member institutions to submit their own proposal for a course which satisfied the general parameters of SCD and was then approved as the SCD Bachelor degree. Consequently, the Bachelor of Theology degree contained up to eleven Fields, although many of these were in effect amplifications of what others included within Christian Thought (eg Theology, Church History, Ethics, Philosophy) and Christian Practice (eg Pastoral Theology, Counselling, Liturgy, Missiology, Spirituality). The Major and sub-Major requirements were the same as for MCD. The vast array of individual units listed within the Fields, while an attractive option for the member institutions, was none the less an expression of the individual and un-coordinated courses offered at member colleges and included considerable duplication in content, despite slight variations in unit titles. While this was eventually to cause significant issues for government re-accreditation, it theoretically allowed member colleges much freedom in structuring their individual courses. However, in practice, the individual structures were remarkably similar, with the conventional selection of and concentration on biblical and theological units with some (though limited) variety within the practical and other Electives. Similar structures to those of the major consortia were historically adopted by the other groups such as Adelaide College of Divinity and Brisbane College of Theology up to around 2010.

Government accreditation requirements tended to assess the degrees of private providers according to a benchmarking criterion: essentially, all Bachelor of Theology degrees should look alike. Therefore, it is perhaps not surprising that even the independent colleges which emerged in the last thirty years shaped their degrees in strikingly similar ways. However, while basic structures of Fields and Majors remained the norm, these colleges all seemed to be concerned with how they developed skills of ministry as a part of the overall training enterprise and, as independent bodies, they incorporated their distinctive philosophical approach to doing this. Tabor College in Adelaide (and later in other States) placed great emphasis on performance skills, thus reducing the emphasis on the conventional "academic" biblical and theological units and focusing more on the "applied" Christian Practice Field with significantly more practical components in these units. Christian Heritage College in Brisbane, while retaining the conventional three Fields and two Majors in Bible and Christian Thought, intentionally incorporated key units such as Spiritual Formation, Christian Worldview, and a series of Experiential Units (Practicums) within the degree. Thus, the Pentecostal colleges were able to infuse the conventional structures of the degree with their own tradition's distinctive ethos of training. Malyon Baptist College in Brisbane based its Bachelor of Ministry on a central Supervised Field Education ethos, whereby up to 30% of the degree could be taken in partnership with approved field placements, supervised by college trained and accredited practitioners under the overall leadership of a full-time faculty director. Standing in a different theological tradition, Moore Theological College in Sydney also developed its own philosophically based training structure. From 1992 to 2009, Moore offered its four year Bachelor of Divinity as year-long subjects, with a total focus on Bible, Theology and Philosophy.[10] To accommodate the practical ministry skills, up to 2005, students heading for ministry were required to complete an additional twenty-one relatively small units of practical ministry which were spread across the course but not included in the degree. In 2006, this system was replaced with the inclusion of four Ministry and Mission units (one per year) within the degree itself. So, while adhering to the general benchmarking structural norms, these independent colleges were able to take greater initiative in incorporating their distinctive requirements for training within or alongside their accredited programs.

Australian universities have been relatively recent entrants into the provision of theology degrees. Indeed, there has been a sensitivity on their part as to the place of Theology (and even more so Ministry) in a university. Consequently, there has been a studied insistence on avoiding reference to such traditionally non-academic issues as faith, spiritual or ministry development in their curriculum documentation. However, as previously noted, the six university theology providers are primarily associated with supporting and/or participating churches and the curriculum contents and structures are shaped very much by the ordination requirements of those churches, albeit while sitting within the overall regulatory framework of the university. Since it is the agencies of the Roman Catholic, Anglican and Uniting Churches which are associated with the university schools, the respective requirements of those participating church agencies dominate the curriculum contents and structures of the university awards. At Australian Catholic University, until 2003, all Bachelor of Theology units were chosen from designated minor and major sequences within the schools of Theology and Philosophy, but in 2004, the three Fields of Biblical Studies, Christian Thought and Christian Practice were

---

10 Partial semesterisation was introduced in 2010, in year 1 and year 4 units and some year 2-3 units.

adopted. Reflecting the Catholic tradition of the university, there were eight Core Units (seven Theology, one Philosophy) and two Majors, including at least one in Theology. To cater for the vocational teaching needs of some students, in 2004 a Liberal Arts requirement was added to the Bachelor of Theology, with a Liberal Arts Major optional from 2004. However, at the same time, the previous twenty-one advanced Philosophy Units were transferred from Theology to Liberal Arts, which allowed a degree of flexibility while still accommodating the retention of the Catholic tradition's emphasis on Philosophy within the Bachelor of Theology. The Christian Practice Field contained predominantly theoretical units such as Ethics, with one option of a unit in Christian Community Experience. The 2008 review provided some more flexibility by expanding the fields to five (by adding Philosophy and Studies of Religion) and allowing Philosophy to be included as either a sub-major in the Bachelor of Theology or a major as a liberal arts sequence. The affiliation of Trinity (Uniting Church) Theological College with the university in 2010 saw the addition of a number of practical units pertinent to the ordination requirements of the Uniting Church. The academic formation of the churches' ministry candidates underlies the structure of the overall degree, with the ministerial formation being generally left to other agencies (such as the seminary or the church).

A similar situation pertains at other universities. In the Bachelor of Theology current to 2012 in Charles Sturt University (incorporating Anglican and Uniting Church colleges as its Theology School), conventional Majors, optional Liberal Arts Minor and minimum Core Units in Bible and Christian Thought operate, but in the limited Mission and Pastoral Studies Field, there are no Supervised Field Education or other experiential units.[11] Murdoch University is a little different. It offers a three year BA(Theology) within the Humanities and Social Sciences Faculty, whereby 50% of the degree needs to be taken from Theology units as a Theology Major. There are no separate Fields within Theology, but the spread of units covers the conventional fields of biblical, theological and historical units required by the churches for their ministry candidates, along with the optional provision of a pastoral practicum. The Bachelor of Theology requires an additional year of Theology Units

---

11 The revised Charles Sturt Bachelor of Theology, operative from 2013, has removed the majors and established in place two compulsory foundational subjects in each of the four sub-disciplines of Biblical Studies, Church History, Practical Theology and Systematic Theology. As well, there are further compulsory subjects in Biblical Studies and Systematic Theology at 200 and 300 levels.

(including further optional pastoral practicums) as a supplement to the three year award. Such an approach to structure allows for a less concentrated focus on specific fields of theological study, since Theology is taken as a whole rather than having its traditional sub-divisions. This is in keeping with the overall university ethos, but it has the potential for more fragmented theological study. In general, the structures of the university Theology degrees have mirrored, and are consequently barely distinguishable from, those of the theological colleges which essentially shape the university schools. The overlay of university regulation has more to do with general operations and quality management than with specific details of curriculum.

While allowing for variations in some details and terminology, the following Table A is generally indicative of the typical traditional structure of most Bachelor degrees in Theology. It shows a strong emphasis on a first year devoted to introductory units in various sub-disciplines and a heavy concentration of biblical and theological studies throughout the course, with a relatively lesser emphasis on practical units and even less on personal development units.

Table A: Typical Traditional Course Structure

Year	Biblical Studies	Christian Thought	Christian Practice	Electives
1	Intro to Biblical Languages Intro to OT Intro to NT Hermeneutics	Foundational Theology Early Church History (or Church History Survey)	Intro to Ministry Intro to (Missions, Youth, Christian Education)	Christian Worldview Spiritual Formation Field Placement
2	Advanced Greek/ Hebrew OT Exegesis NT Exegesis	Systematic Theology Ethics Philosophy Reformation or Aust Church Hist	Core Pastoral Unit Supervised Field Education	Bible, Theology, Pastoral Units
3	OT Exegesis NT Exegesis	Systematic Theology Philosophy	Core Pastoral Unit Supervised Field Education	Bible, Theology, Pastoral Units Independent Studies
(4)	OT/NT Exegesis	Theology	Internship	Research Project

Summarising the General Picture

Whether university, large consortium or smaller independent college, the traditional emphasis in Bachelor degrees has been on a heavy concentration of biblical studies (with a progressive decline in biblical languages over the past twenty years apart from the Reformed tradition) and systematic theology accompanied by some compulsory but relatively limited church history (particularly that of the early church and the 16-18th centuries). The Catholic tradition has incorporated a large component of philosophy as well as biblical, systematic and historical studies. The last twenty years have seen some general (although not universal) development in the inclusion of ministry skills, especially in the Bachelor of Ministry type degrees. This has been more evident in the Bible colleges than in the more traditional denominational systems (especially Catholic, Anglican and Uniting Church) which have tended to retain "ministry skills" in formation programs outside the degree itself, while reserving the degree for the academic "theology" component. Most awards featuring such ministry skills components, however, include them mainly as class-room based teaching, with an occasional minor element of field placement or practical project work. The main exception to this is in the growing inclusion of Supervised Field Education units, which still feature generally as a relatively minor elective in most awards and only occasionally have pedagogical conditions clearly spelt out. While there is a growth in the number of awards that (claim to) seek to integrate theoretical learning with practical experience, there was no clearly discernible evidence of curriculum which intentionally or strategically connects with a student's prior life experience. Similarly, while there is a clear indication recently of the growing importance of ministry skills development, there was no clear evidence discovered of intentional transformative learning in the historical curriculum documents.

3. Lessons (to be) Learnt from History

Issues of Concern

In the survey of literature in the field (chapter 2), a number of concerns were highlighted, which can now be applied to this historical review of theological curriculum, since they have significance for the overall consideration of the strategic incorporation of transformative learning opportunities. The two elements that warrant particular attention are the issues of what Haar referred to as the "piecemeal compartmentalisation" of theological learning and what Clines referred to as the "myth of foundationalism." These two aspects carry with them the attendant consideration of student work load.

Stephen Haar has lamented the devolution of theological education into the fragmented impartation of knowledge and skills, resulting in a non-integrated, compartmentalised learning experience.[12] This is not dissimilar to the issue of lack of appropriate sequencing, which is required if material is not to be presented in a way that appears to be disconnected or irrelevant.[13] The historical review of curriculum documents suggests that such observations are accurate. The review shows that curricula have been almost universally delivered as "compartments" of knowledge, with little if any structural integration of the discrete fields of Old Testament, New Testament, Systematic Theology, Church History and Ministry Skills. There was virtually no evidence of any continuous or exit level study which brought all these compartments into harmony with one another, by way of either thematic synthesis or inter-disciplinary skills congruence. Each field of study (and even the various sub-fields) seemed to be domains in their own right. The separation of "theological formation" from "ministerial formation" so common in many traditions and institutions tended to reinforce this imperial segregation. There was a general lack of connection between fields of study; far less was there any sense of connection between the fields of study and the actual lives of students, who were uniformly exposed to a common corpus of content within the framework of the conventional but discrete theological compartments.

David Clines strongly opposed the "myth of foundationalism" which dominated theological education.[14] Again, the historical review supports his observation. Virtually all courses took their starting point as the various Introductions to the Compartments: a standard survey of the world and literature of the Bible, a compendium of major theological doctrines, a chronology of the main events in the history of the church, a review of dominant issues in church or missionary matters. Often, these Introductions addressed some discipline specific study skills, but the emphasis on delivering vast quantities

---

12 Stephen Haar, "Enhancing the Capability of Theological Schools in Becoming Agents of Change and Transformation in Civil Society" (Consultation on Establishing a Regional Network of Lutheran Theological Institutions: Bangkok; 18 March 2010), 1.
13 Jude Long, "Teaching Adults: Insights from Educational Philosophy," *Journal of Christian Education* 53:1 (May 2010), 53-54.
14 David JA Clines, "Learning, Teaching, and Researching Biblical Studies, Today and Tomorrow," *Journal of Biblical Literature* 129:1 (Spring 2010), 27.

of content in a very limited time militated against mastery of such skills. The operational assumption seems to have been that all students need to start and finish at the same place, regardless of personal background, experience and knowledge or individual needs and aspirations. There was no evidence that introductory units were structured in order to locate the student in the learning program or in such a way as to provide a coherently integrated approach to theological study. Nor was there any evidence that, despite idealistic claims made, advanced units within the compartments actually did build on these foundational units in any structured way. As Clines pointed out, there is no consensus on what these Introductions should look like, nor what their real purpose is, yet there seems to be an historical consensus that they are needed as a starting platform.

The attendant issue of student work load and its significance for personal transformation also emerged. With such a concentration of heavy content delivery at all points of the course, the reception and retention of that content becomes a major burden. The fact that commencing students in particular are confronted with a barrage of new and often discomforting knowledge ideally requires significant time for due internal processing. This is particularly important when issues of intensely deep theological moment are involved. The recent trend towards semesterisation with progressive assessment has added to the rush and pressure of content processing. Given that many schools also place heavy extra-curricular demands on students by way of parallel ministerial formation programs or community life, the overall load on undergraduate theological students has historically been extremely high. When all these elements – the internal wrestling with theological issues and the external pressure of the waves of assessment and extra-curricular demands – combine, the time and resources available for a student to practise skills and to grow personally are inevitably reduced. The historical insistence on covering a voluminous amount of content – at all levels of the course – has been an obstacle to the provision of opportunities for personal transformation.

Who Determines the Curriculum?

The review of theological curriculum documents has shown theological education to be a rather unusual beast in terms of how it is shaped and delivered. Unlike most other tertiary programs, it is very closely connected to various ecclesiastical organizations as well as secular regulatory bodies (universities and government agencies). Then there is the overlay of the dominant consortial bodies, which tend to operate often even within university schools. While various other professional courses have external influences from professional associations (such as medical boards and teacher registration bodies), it is rare (perhaps even unknown) for other agencies beyond the actual teaching organ to constitute such a complex of determinative forces in curriculum as happens in theology.

So, a tangential issue that arose from this documentary review is that of who actually determines the theological curriculum. It became clear that this is as much an issue of ecclesiology as it is of pedagogy, with the dominant influence in curriculum design being the ordination requirements of the supporting church's tradition (with its typically conservative constraints), and a secondary influence being the pragmatically necessary aspect of consortial cooperation (with its typically implicit compromises). Since both of these factors involve inhibitors to local innovation, they present a significant issue for curriculum development. In general, the ecclesiastical tradition seems to represent a more significantly conservative element than the consortial arrangements, since most consortia have reasonably flexible structures which allow member institutions to implement their own emphases. However, within the ecclesiastical traditions, there is a variety of expressions and a range of opportunities for local curriculum innovation. In all tertiary programs, there are regulatory limitations on innovative freedoms, but in theology, the degree to which local teaching institutions have the freedom to develop and implement curriculum has these additional layers of restriction, which vary according to the tradition in which they stand. Hence it is important that the recognition of this factor be a part of any projected curriculum development. In general, the more hierarchical the ecclesiastical control, the less the potential for local innovation; the more local that control, the greater the potential for local innovation. As an indicative guide, Table B gives an idea of the level of external control associated with various institutions, the realistic implications of which need to be appreciated by members operating within the various systems.

Table B: Influences on Theological Curriculum

Dominant Influence	Typical Institutions	Impact on Curriculum Content and Delivery
Global Ecclesiastical Regulation	Nazarene Orthodox Roman Catholic Salvation Army	Global ordination rules set limited parameters of courses. Strong priority in content and delivery given to needs of seminary/ordination candidates.
National/State Hierarchical Ecclesiastical Systems	Anglican Presbyterian Uniting Church	Ordination requirements for candidates dominate curriculum content. Strong distinction in delivery between candidates and general (non-ordination) students.
Congregationally Autonomous Ecclesiastical Traditions	Baptist Churches of Christ (typically within teaching consortia because of small size)	Ordination requirements are accommodated but not exclusive. No discrimination between ordination and general students in delivery. Greater local college flexibility in curriculum decision-making.
Locally Independent Colleges	Bible Colleges Pentecostal Colleges	Not limited by external requirements. No discrimination between ordination and general students. More freedom to develop and innovate at college level.
University Regulation	Private Universities (UNDA) Public Universities (ACU, CSU, Flinders, Murdoch, Newcastle)	Legally separate from church control (and explicitly not faith-based in the public universities), yet strongly influenced by requirements of participating churches (specifically Roman Catholic, Anglican, Uniting Church). Curriculum is subject to university regulation, commonly demanding rationalisation of offerings and paring down of (typically) small classes. Innovation prompted by churches is slow and limited.

4. What are Others Doing?

While the exclusive province of this study is theological education, it has been useful to look at developments in other disciplines. Somewhat surprisingly, the curriculum structures of many universities have been remarkably conservative, with reforms in matters of governance, marketing and operational rationalisation having far outweighed considerations of curriculum reforms. While content has been continuously updated and delivery methods are being regularly reviewed, the core business of curriculum design has been largely neglected (as noted by the recent UNESCO Curriculum Reform Manifesto). However, two disciplines which seem to have much in common with theology are the human service areas of education and nursing. While in no way meant to be exhaustive, a brief look at some developments in local universities in these two areas is informative, with particular reference to the two key issues of compartmentalisation and foundationalism.[15]

The Bachelor of Education degrees of several major Australian universities were examined in detail. In all cases, there is a strong emphasis on developing the theory of human development and the pedagogical methods pertinent to specific school subject areas such as English, Mathematics, Science and so on. All include extensive mandatory placements in practical teaching situations in each year of the program, with an increase of these placements in the final years. Thus they combine theoretical knowledge delivered in the classroom and relevant professional skills development in classroom-based theory and practice in real situations. However, in all cases, the structures reveal a similar "compartmentalisation," with no evidence of integration or coordination of the school subject areas where teaching methods are being taught. There is also no suggestion of any connection with a student's life experience either prior to the course or in any aspect beyond the university or school classroom. The focus is very heavily on the development of vocational skills – with an occasional and brief foray into the realm of teachers' professional responsibilities – but this development does not involve a coherent approach across the whole degree, nor does it make specific reference to the formation of the person of the teacher beyond the vocational skills.

---

15 The undergraduate programs in education and nursing of Australian Catholic University, Griffith University, Queensland University of Technology, The University of Queensland, University of New South Wales, University of Sydney, Deakin University, Monash University, University of Tasmania, Flinders University, University of South Australia, Curtin University and Murdoch University were reviewed for this exercise. The three specific programs discussed in each field of Education and Nursing are generally representative examples of the types of degree programs offered across the board.

The other strongly noticeable feature is the general adherence to the doctrine of foundationalism. All courses begin from a set suite of introductory units and progress through the discrete suites of compartmentalised units. The University of Queensland's program begins with the four set units *Introduction to Education, Child and Adolescent Development for Educators, Numeracy in Primary and Middle Years of Schooling Contexts*, and *Education and Creativity: Pedagogical Content Knowledge*. The Core Unit *Introduction to Education* is offered as a starting point to provide students "with a framework on which to build an understanding of education as a discipline during their undergraduate years." Similarly, Queensland University of Technology's course begins with *Introduction To Education, Teaching and Learning Studies 1: Teaching in New Times, Learning Networks*, and *Foundation: Scientific and Quantitative Literacy*. The Core Unit *Introduction To Education* is placed early in the course "to introduce foundational theories and practices in the design of curriculum, pedagogy and assessment that you will then build on throughout the remainder of your course." The objectives of the unit are all in terms of knowledge and understanding of content and skills, with no reference to personal development of the student beyond these two dimensions. However, in contrast to this unit, the companion unit Teaching in New Times has all of its outcomes expressed in terms of problem-solving and inquiry-based learning, critical reflection and integrated strategies for teaching. This degree is distinctive in its inclusion of a final year teaching internship which is taken after the completion of all other course requirements, an initiative designed to ground the vocational skills in a real-world context. The University of Sydney's degree is perhaps the most clearly compartmentalised of all three with a very early and consistently maintained segmentation of the school-based subjects. However, in its introductory units, there is a motif of integration of knowledge and personal development of the student. Its introductory unit *Education, Teachers and Teaching* sets out to provide a general introduction to education and teaching, by integrating knowledge, culture and the curriculum; teaching as a process and way of life; and teachers as life-long learners and researchers. Within this unit, students are also mentored by more experienced students during their first semester transition to the university so that, by the conclusion of the unit, they will have developed and demonstrated an understanding of the complex character of teachers' work. While the tenets of foundationalism are prominent in all courses, there are signs emerging that the universities are placing a growing emphasis on professional skills development within the formal structures of the degrees and, while still to a lesser degree, on the personal integration of the various facets of learning and the personal journey involved in progressing through this process. The variability in the units suggests that this process is still in its embryonic stage and has yet to be more strategically systematised within the institutions.

The Bachelor of Nursing degrees of the universities provided more pertinent insights. The University of Queensland course structure is perhaps the most conservative, in terms of both its compartmentalisation and its foundationalism, although several other established programs are quite comparable. Its first semester incorporates three introductory units covering the range of human development from embryo to old age, based largely on anatomy and physiology, along with a placement in Clinical Practice, which comprises one quarter of the semester's load. This pattern continues through the first two years of the three year program. The third year moves to a heavy emphasis on Clinical Practice, with just one class-room unit in first semester. That is, the third year is virtually a field experience unit of Clinical Practice. There is throughout a pronounced emphasis on the acquisition of anatomical and physiological knowledge grounded in the experiential context of clinical practice. Thus it is centred on health issues in potential clients, with no obvious reference in content or objectives to the development of the nurse as a person.

In 2012, the University of Sydney Nursing School introduced a new three-year Bachelor of Nursing (Advanced Studies) degree, designed to give a strong foundation for professional nursing practice. The structural reforms incorporated into this degree see a greater emphasis on integration of nursing issues and care, with teaching and research across all the health disciplines of medicine, nursing, pharmacy, dentistry, public health and the health sciences. This is designed to generate an interdisciplinary practice by having students learn from a range of clinical experts and academics. Rather than the compartmentalised knowledge based on anatomy and physiology, the focus is on leadership, evidence-based practice and international health, with practical hands-on experience catered for in the 900 hours of clinical practice provided across the range of nursing contexts. A similar approach is being taken by a small number of recently developed courses in other universities. The aim of the Sydney course is explicitly stated as preparing students "to respond to and thrive in health care environments that are evolving and changing (and therefore) we are moving from a reliance on hospital-based care to an integrated system which focuses on the person as the patient and the support they need in managing their health and health care." The twin foci of this award are the integration of learning and practice and the personal development of the nurse practitioner. This general philosophy is reflected in the statements in the first semester's individual introductory units, with their emphasis on critical reflection on public health data and the establishment of evidence-based analyses. The introductory unit *Nursing Knowledge, Practice and Policy* aims "to cultivate knowing and mindful action in nursing practice by introducing students to the Framework for Practice Thinking and person- centred nursing." The explicit and strategic integration of person (both nurse and client), context and learning marks this award.

The Australian Catholic University claims to be the largest provider of graduate nurses in Australia. Its Bachelor of Nursing degree makes a strong commitment to person-centred nursing education. From the outset, it states its aim of developing "a caring professional nurse, who is proactive and adaptable, a competent, safe and ethical clinician, a creative and critical thinker, an informed consumer of practice evidence, and an independent lifelong learner." This aim is reinforced by a commitment to learner-centred methods of inquiry and situation-based learning. While generally adhering to the concepts of foundationalism, with introductory units such as *Human Biological Science 1 and 2* and *Beginning Professional Practice*, it has some interesting additions. The course includes two Core Curriculum units, the introductory level *Community and Vulnerability: Action and Advocacy* and the final year *Understanding Self and Society: Contemporary Perspectives*. These book-end units provide a world view dimension to the overall program not commonly associated with such professional courses. The program lays stress on the person as the centre of the nursing enterprise, in both study and professional performance. This is established early in the course right in the foundational units, as typified in the description of the unit *The Person, Health and Wellbeing*:

> This inter-professional unit focuses on the person as the centre of the health care experience. Emotional, cognitive, motivational and behavioural factors that influence health, illness and the health care experience will be explored. There will be a major emphasis on psychological resilience and coping across the lifespan. This foundational knowledge in human behaviour and development will enable the health professional to understand how individuals

respond to the challenge of health maintenance, illness and hospitalisation in the contemporary health care environment.

This focus on "the person as the centre of the health care experience" contrasts starkly with the more traditional content-based segmentation of anatomy and physiology.

In summary, the current undergraduate degrees in education and nursing show a growing trend towards placing the person and the person's experience at the centre of the learning enterprise and professional practice. First, there is the now universal emphasis on situating the theoretical classroom learning in a real-life practical context by way of school classroom or clinical practice as a structured and integrated component of the degree, rather than depending on extra- or post-curricular experience to provide such grounding. But even beyond this aspect, there is a development which is embryonic and piecemeal in education but more progressively consistent in nursing, namely, the re-orientation of the course structures, aims and methods around the situation of the learner rather than the acquisition of specialised knowledge. It is not that this knowledge is abandoned; rather, it is being shaped in its delivery around the situation of the learner and ultimately the "client" to be served in subsequent professional practice. The ramifications for theological degrees are obvious, with consideration warranted of the strategic integration (as distinct from incidental inclusion) of supervised field education within the degree, the role and nature of student-centred learning methods in the classroom and beyond, and the strategic design of curriculum to promote the development of the integrated person within the theological enterprise.

4 | A CONTINUING JOURNEY

LIFE EXPERIENCE AND LEARNING

1. Life Experience and Transformative Learning

A fundamental premise of transformative learning is that adult education is a stage in a lifelong journey, not a detached "time out" in isolation from the reality of a student's life. The formal educative stage starts from the recognition of pre-existent life experience and critically reviews the frames of reference already established by that prior experience. It proceeds by way of assimilation (of new knowledge into the existing frameworks) or accommodation (by revising existing frameworks in light of new knowledge encountered), rather than by the memorization of discrete and unrelated facts. It continues to bring new knowledge into dynamic connection with ongoing life experience, not simply as a learning method but as a holistic development of a critically reviewed and shaped world view which is more inclusive of others' philosophies and life styles, and which serves as a platform for future experience. Hence, any attempt to structure a curriculum with a transformative goal must take seriously the intentional connection between the program of study and the students' pre-existent experience-derived frames of reference. Further, it will need to develop a strategy for the meaningful connection between new learning and concurrent experience to provide a ground for holistic integration. This recognition of the connection between transformative learning and students' life experience is the starting point for any such curriculum development.

The review of historical curriculum documents produced virtually no evidence of curriculum which intentionally or strategically connected with a student's prior life experience. It did reveal a recent trend towards incorporating some experiential learning in field placements or other practical learning exercises, but this was more to do with the development of ministry skills than a critical review and re-shaping of an overall and potentially transformed world view. Connection with a student's concurrent life experience was generally not strategically structured within a curriculum. Given this evident omission from documented materials, the research undertook an extensive field study of this aspect to discover and to analyse both what are the actual practices of teaching institutions and what are the aspirations that typify the sector in this regard. This field research comprised extensive surveys, focus groups and interviews of students, graduates, faculty, church leaders and other stakeholders.

2. The Student Profile

The profile of students who undertake theological undergraduate degree study gives an insight into some significant dimensions of the life experience, the frames of reference and the expectations that are brought to the study programs by the students. While not individually detailed, the following profile has been built up from responses to surveys received from 583 current students and 646 recent graduates across all Australian States, all institutional types and numerous denominational traditions.[1]

(a) Age at Enrolment of Current Students - 2011 (%)

	1st Year (n= 236)	Final Year (n = 141)	Overall (n = 565)
Under 20	6.4	5.7	6.9
20-30	58.5	51.8	58.2
31-40	16.9	21.3	17.7
41-50	14.4	13.5	12.0
51-60	2.5	5.0	3.4
Over 60	0.4	2.8	1.6

The dominant age group is 20-30 (58%) with a significant group in the 30-50 range (30%). There are very few school leavers entering directly into theological studies.

---

1   While overall figures are presented in this chapter's profile, a breakdown of noted variations across denominations is provided in Appendix B.

(b) Sex of Current Students - 2011

In all groups, the ratio of males to females was consistent at approximately 2:1 (First year: 66:34; Final Year: 63:37; Overall: 67:33)

(c) Highest Level of Prior Education of Current Students - 2011 (%)

	1st Year (n= 234)	Final Year (n = 141)	Overall (n = 565)
Primary School	0.4	2.1	0.7
Secondary School	25.2	24.1	24.2
Post-secondary Certificate/Diploma	23.1	21.3	20.7
Bachelor Degree	36.3	40.4	41.5
Post-graduate award	15.0	12.1	12.9

The great majority (75%) have completed post-secondary qualifications prior to entering theological studies. More than half have at least a bachelor's degree and a significant number have post-graduate qualifications. The combination of age and prior qualifications indicates a more mature and educationally advanced cohort than in most other undergraduate programs.

(d) Nationality or cultural background of Current Students - 2011 (%)

	1st Year (n= 230)	Final Year (n = 141)	Overall (n = 548)
Australian	72	72	72.6
Asian (incl Australian born Chinese)	11	14	11.5
British	6	2	3.6
New Zealand/Pacific Islands	3	3	3.8
European	3	3	3.5
African	2	3	2.2
Americas	1	1	1.3
Other	2	2	1.5

The great majority of students identify as simply Australian (including one Australian Aboriginal). However, a significant number of students (16%) are of Asian (especially Chinese and Korean), Polynesian and African background. While an Australian cultural background and a Western educational system can be generally assumed, the significant minority for whom this is not true needs to be noted and accommodated.

(e) Enrolment Status of Current Students - 2011

In all groups, the ratio of full-time to part-time was 75:25. This figure was influenced by the large returns from two colleges where full-time enrolment is encouraged. In other institutions, the ratio was consistently around 65:35.

(f) Attendance Mode of Current Students - 2011 (%)

	1st Year (n= 237)	Final Year (n = 141)	Overall (n = 548)
Day classes	86.5	83.7	88.6
Evening classes	8.0	3.5	4.8
Distance/online	5.5	12.8	6.2

By far the great majority of courses are taken in day classes, with evening classes being a major mode for only a small number of students, especially beyond the first year. There is an increase in online enrolments in the final year, but it remains a major mode of delivery for a relatively small number of students. However, it should be noted that, while this survey invited online students to participate, it was largely conducted with on-campus students, and most of these were in day classes.

(g) Vocational Outcomes

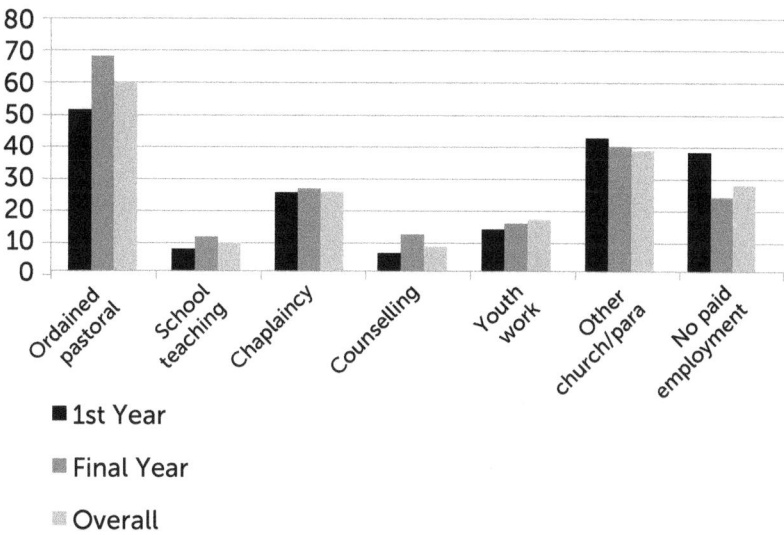

Current students were asked to indicate their expectations of vocational outcomes resulting from their theological studies. Respondents were allowed to indicate more than one possibility, which was particularly evident in the matching of ordained pastoral ministry, chaplaincy and para-church work.

Ordained pastoral ministry is the main vocational expectation of theological education, with half of commencing students and an even higher number of final year students having that goal. Specific professional careers with a Christian world view and para-church ministry (cross-cultural missions and social work in particular) are the other major areas of vocational outcomes. One third of incoming students have no expectations of paid employment and, while this figure is lower by the final year, it remains significant, with an overall 27% of responses falling in this category.

From this item, it seems that the traditional emphasis on preparing students for vocational pastoral ministry is justified. However, very significant numbers of students are now not preparing for such ministry and are seeking to develop their professions within a Christian world view. For these students, the emphasis on priestly performance is not significant, yet it remains necessary for the pastoral candidates. As well, the need to deliver theological education in ways that are relevant to this wider range of careers is emerging strongly. The third dimension of this item that warrants attention is the large number of students studying with no employment in view, but who are seeking personal growth in knowledge and spirituality.

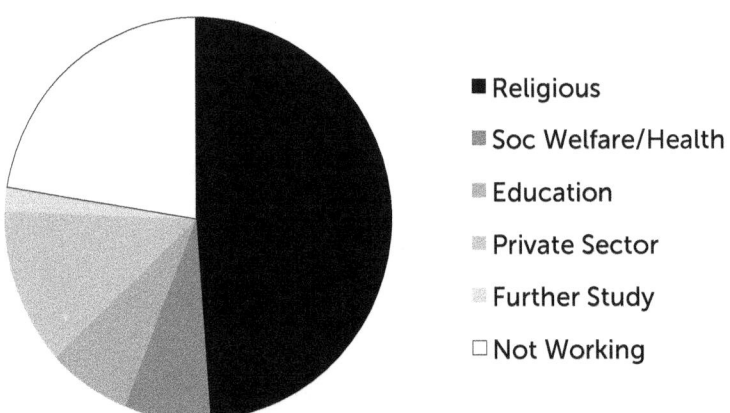

A similar picture emerged from the Graduate Destinations Surveys from the period 2005- 2009, as indicated in the chart above. While ordination requirements of churches dominate curriculum construction and delivery, only half the graduates enter religious occupations, including non-ordained positions. Therefore, while such religious occupations remain the major destination of theology graduates, there is an equally numerous proportion of the student body who do not enter such vocations. This has a three-fold ramification.

- Given that religious service (including ordained ministry) remains the main vocational destination, there is a case for the greater and more deliberate integration of theological principles and ministry practices within the degree itself.
- Given that a significant number enter (or remain in) human service occupations such as health, social welfare and education, there is a case for an intentional integration of vocational profession and theology.
- Similarly, since another significant number do not enter paid employment, there is a case for the intentional integration of theology and general world view within the degree itself.

A major challenge is to construct a curriculum that incorporates flexible opportunities for students to have exposure to and develop mastery in ministry skills within a personally articulated theological world view, while at the same time not limiting the scope for personal and other vocational developmental opportunities by imposing the narrowness of ordained requirements on students who are not heading that way.

3. Making Connections: Actual Practice

(a) Connecting with Prior Life Experience

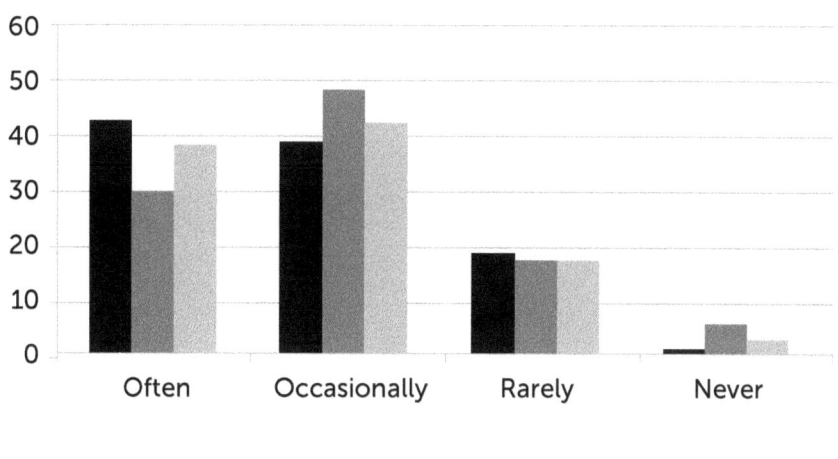

In the early student survey and focus groups, there was very limited connection expressed between the theological study and prior life experience. What was mentioned was stated as incidental only, with some empathy with and expansion of prior experience (especially noted by mature-aged part-time students), but there was no report of structured or intentional engagement with prior experience, even in Field Education units.

In the more extensive follow-up student surveys, which included first year students, final year students and a group of continuing students followed over a twelve months' period, a more detailed picture emerged. In these surveys, students were asked if, during the course of their theological studies, there had been explicit links made with their prior life experience. While fewer than half the responses indicated that such a connection was often made, yet most reported at least occasional such connection. Very few (2.6%) reported that there had never been such a connection.

Students were given the option of making comments on the connections made, but only 26% of respondents did so. The vast majority of these comments related to links made between studies (especially Bible studies) and previous ministry experiences or understanding of church-related issues. A considerably smaller number related connections to specific personal issues in their life which had helped to explain and/or evaluate these issues. A few isolated responses made reference to re-evaluation of interpersonal relationships, social experiences beyond the church, or a connection with a prior world view. While comments were largely positive, it was noticeable that, in the final year student responses, there was a significant number (12%) of negative comments, typically citing the over-intellectual approach to theology and its lack of practical connection to life or ministry, with virtually no connection with the secular world which is a large part of the context of lived Christianity.

The series of intensive one-to-one interviews with various stakeholders also probed the issue of making connection with students' prior life experience, particularly with senior faculty and recent graduates. The overwhelmingly dominant response by faculty was that, while acknowledging and valuing the diversity of incoming students, there is no policy or strategy for linking the teaching program with that experience. Some skipped this element of the question, but of the responses offered, 70% indicated that there was no connection drawn with a student's prior life experience. Of the remainder, 10% reported that such prior experience was shared meaningfully at the "behind the scenes" level, where teachers and students came to know each other more closely than they thought would commonly be associated with larger public universities. Another 10% said that such linkages were occasionally made in class, on an informal *ad hoc* basis, but these linkages were not part of any specific strategy. The remaining 10% reported that such experiential connectedness was featured in the extra-curricular ministry formation program, although not in the classroom.

The workshop of some seventy senior teaching faculty held in 2012 generally supported the faculty views expressed in the interviews. The workshop groups addressed two basic questions: why is it pertinent to connect with a student's prior experience/ future life; what has the institution done to link successfully theological studies and prior life experience? In discussing the first item, there was general agreement that diversity of cultures and backgrounds of students is far different from classrooms thirty years ago, that there is a diversity of religious experience, denominational affiliation and spirituality within any one classroom, and that since these cultures and stories are in the room and are having an effect, it makes sense to incorporate these stories as an explicit part of the educational process. That is, there is the need for the explication of the life experience that brought the student to theology: the motivation of the students to be in the classroom needs to be honoured. It was also noted that, while many other areas of human service education (such as nursing and social sciences) make extensive use of the life experience of students, there remains a question as to whether theological curriculum has changed over the years in line with the changes in students and society, or whether it remains something of a faculty creation based on some notion of an "ideal" student, but not related to the actual reality of current students. Consequently, while many faculty teach using illustrations and applications related to life experience, there is the challenging question (also prominent in student focus groups and graduate interviews) as to whether faculty are connecting in the classroom with their own prior life and ministry experience or with the students' life experience. Hence there is a need to make such connections intentional and systemic, with the aim of teaching students how to use experience and do theology from that experience.

In addressing the second issue of what has been successfully done in the area of life connections, the workshop groups provided some worthwhile insights. One report detailed the way in which teaching is seen as an open invitation, with a "syllabus by questions" approach to the subject as a series of questions to be explored. Another approach included a discussion with students in first year of the institution's graduate attributes and their place in shaping their learning, revisiting them again when the students are in their final year to see whether these are the attributes that they have attained, and then asking graduates five years out of college about the relevance of the attributes (though institutional size and organizational logistics were problematic, especially in the last stage). As well as the usual role of applied assignments, practical components within units and the formal recognition of prior learning, there was an encouragement to develop an organizational culture that is open to a central role for student experience with an expanded "imagination" of the college, to promote a movement away from seeing the college as central, but seeing it from the student perspective as just one of many parts that make up a student's life: that is, seeing the student as central, not the institution.

The responses from recent graduates in the series of interviews generally indicated that there was no (or at most very limited) direct or structured connection drawn between studies and prior life experience. A common comment was as stated by one respondent: "There was no connection with my prior life experience. The college did not address any such connection." One response put it more starkly (and disapprovingly): "There was no attempt to link with anyone's prior experience or knowledge. It was a case of, 'You are all on the same page, that page is zero, let's start from here'." Many responses indicated frequent connections arising in informal and *ad hoc* class discussions as the main means of any such connection. A significant variant in this was the age of entry of students, with the young acknowledging their limited prior life and especially ministry experience, and the older students noting their natural and more prevalent reflection on their prior experience. It was also noted that the more introverted students did not experience the same degree of involvement in such conversations.

While such linkages were limited in scope, there were some examples given of how the consideration of prior experience has been constructively incorporated. Some faculty noted the application of assignment topics to prior life situations, while a couple told of using some theological concept mapping and action reflection to review critically some previously held views and practices. Two faculty members reported the use of entry interviews to determine past experience and future goals, with a tailoring of the course to suit these situations (although in one case this was limited to ordination candidates only). There was a small number of specific examples of where the actual unit design and content was amended to suit the prior experience of incoming students. These included changing study topics in the unit, amending the *Introduction to Ministry Formation* unit to accommodate a changing demographic now based on inexperienced young students instead of the previously more mature intakes, encouraging

Non-English Speaking Background students to use the Bible in their own language for exegesis and to draw classroom comparisons with English versions, and the employment of a scaffolding approach to teaching methods to ensure an appropriate developmental progression in learning activities.

The recent graduates reported more limited meaningful connections with prior experience, and where these were detailed, they fell into two categories: ministry and secular career. Most connection was made with prior experience in church-based ministry, especially where college study had been immediately preceded by a church-based ministry internship or traineeship. In some other cases, where the previous ministry (especially youth ministry) was ongoing during college study, the connection was also noted positively. In all these cases, the ability to reflect critically on and evaluate prior ministry praxis was appreciated. However, where students had no significant prior ministry experience, the connections were very limited. In terms of engaging critically with a prior secular profession, connections were rare. An interesting post-interview conversation occurred with one respondent and his previous ethics lecturer. The lecturer related how he had taught a unit in the ethics of war to a class including this student who, unbeknown to the lecturer, had just returned from active duty as an armed serviceman in Iraq. "I had the theory; you had the experience – how much more you could have taught me," lamented the lecturer. One respondent cited the encouragement to use the creative talent of a previous role as a creative artist in learning tasks and assessments. Another professional musician was encouraged to integrate theology and music in a ministry outcome. However, another media graduate expressed disappointment at the lack of opportunity to link theology with media in today's world.

Over all, there were some (though few) examples of intentional connection between theological studies and prior life experience. Only one respondent indicated an institutional approach to tailoring individual study programs to connect with prior and ongoing life experience and goals, accompanied by strategic field placement and support, recognition of different learning types and encouragement of creativity in learning and assessment tasks. This response correlated with input from other stakeholders associated with this college. In a few other cases, significant connection with prior secular and professional experience was facilitated in response to the student's individual initiative. Apart from these few cases, however, the only real connection with prior life experience was in unstructured class discussions which mainly came from pastoral perspectives, not secular engagement. This promoted reflection on and evaluation of prior ministry experience, albeit limited in scope. Yet, as acknowledged pointedly in the case of the returned serviceman, how much more sense could the theory have made of the student's experience had he been able to focus on the connection as the topic arose in class.

(b) Connecting with Current Life Experience

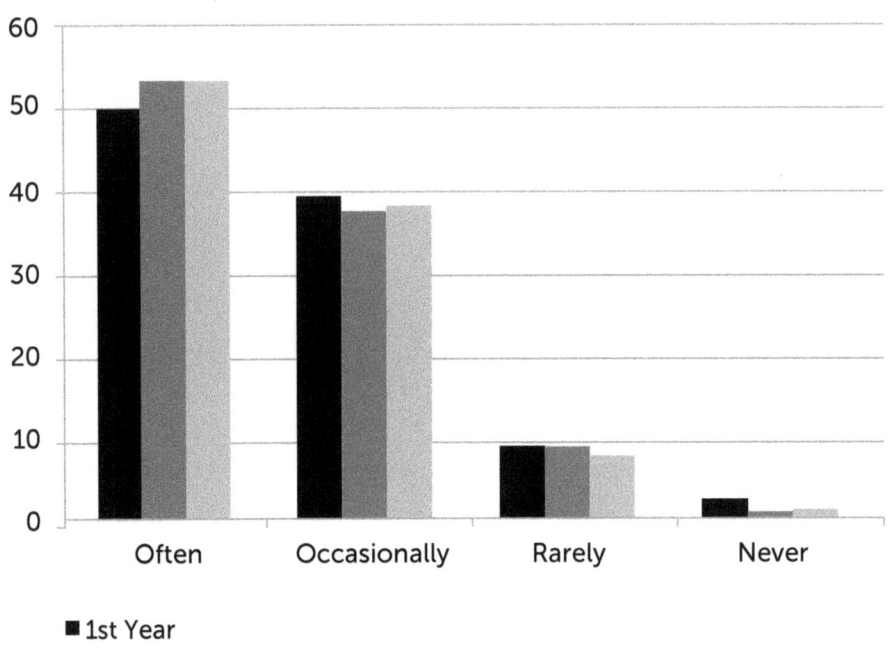

With regard to current life experiences, especially ministry situations, the early student survey and focus groups reported that such intersection occurred more clearly and intentionally. The integration of theology and liturgy with life issues was commonly noted.

Some reported changes in jobs and family conflict management as a direct result of their theological progression while others noted the impact of theological studies on their personal and public ethics, where previously held moral absolutes were commonly replaced with a more pluralistic perspective. The integration of study and ministry was particularly noted within Field Education placements in those colleges where such units form part of the actual degree.

Once again, the later student surveys asked students if, during the course of their theological studies, there had been explicit links made with their current life experience. These surveys provided more detailed responses. All groups reported that explicit connections to current life experience were made far more often than those to prior life experience. This was particularly noticeable with the final years, with more than half the group reporting frequentsuch connections with current life experience. The overall number of "Rarely" or "Never" responses was noticeably lower.

Over 50% of respondents made comments on the connections made, with the highest proportion of such comments coming from the final year group. Comments were quite evenly split between connections to current church ministry (especially sermon preparation and Bible study leading) and issues of personal spirituality and Christian conduct or understanding of and relationship with God. There was very little reference to anything beyond personal piety or church-based ministry, with a total of three responses listing evangelistic outreach and three listing social justice and world view challenges (from an overall total of 539 responses).

In the student surveys, a closer connection between class work and current life experience was noted, especially with regard to ministry placements. However, somewhat surprisingly, this was not reflected in the faculty workshop groups and interviews. The workshop groups noted that many of the colleges have small classes for three hours at a time, which effectively means that there has already been a movement from "lectures" to "teaching," especially small group teaching, which facilitates individual applications, albeit in an unstructured way. The workshop groups also cited the (variable) use of assessment tasks that have a section that applies the research specifically to a life experience or placement, which is seen to be an ongoing effective integration of life and learning some years later. However, most individual faculty interview responses indicated no such connection at all or, at most, an occasional and incidental applicative discussion. About 30% of responses referred to the church placement as the arena where such practical applications of class work are made, a practice which is commonly restricted to ordination candidates. Two universities reported the development of a university-wide innovation that is still a work in progress, namely, the incorporation of a *Work Integrated Learning* or *Community Engagement and Transformation* unit. Details of how such connections are made were sketchy, with only a few responses offering any indication, and these were generally limited to critical reflection and individual student reports on their experience, some occasional assignment focus and unstructured applicative discussions. One response stated the aim of practical theology units to integrate life and theology, but provided no details of how this was done.

The recent graduates' responses indicated that connections with current life experience were a little more frequent, but still generally limited and narrow, essentially reflecting the pastoral perspective of an individual lecturer or denominationally-oriented minister (often the same person). Commonly, such connections were dependent on student initiative rather than a result of an intentional strategy, and again consisted largely of unstructured *ad hoc* class discussion and occasional applications. "While there was perhaps no direct connection made with my life experience, there was a general tendency for my study to be informed by my life experience." There was no specific reference anywhere to connections drawn in biblical or historical subjects and very little in theology units; however, a few respondents referred to the possibility of the optional inclusion of their own experience in assignments. There were more examples of connections between practical units and field ministry placements, especially where mentored reflection was an integral part of Supervised Field Education, and in special electives such as Youth Ministry and Church Planting.

Within this generally limited kind of connectedness, there were several positive examples detailed by the graduates. One noted involvement in a church plant during second and third years, which involved a good link between church and college. The associated Partners in Training Scheme was regarded as very helpful in this arrangement. The creative artist mentioned earlier was very enthusiastic about the connections and encouragement by the college at a systemic level, manifest in a recognition of different learning styles, encouragement of experimentation and creativity in ministry and in strategic placement and support in a field placement. Two respondents articulated very clearly a strong integration of theology and continuing life and profession. One described how the third year integrative project had allowed him to establish an integration of the sacred and the secular in regard to his prior and ongoing profession, the real purpose in his coming to college, which had eventuated in his particular ministry beyond college. The other particularly noted the nexus of theology and his secular specialist teaching profession, which provided a framework to interact with his students with equality and dignity. "It allowed me to proceed from theology first and then to pastoral theology second .... This understanding gave me a consistent platform for my interaction with the people I work with."

While there was a higher degree of connection with current life experience than with prior life experience, this was again largely restricted to ministry placements in Supervised Field Education and some practical units. Occasional reference was made to Systematic and Moral Theology, but none at all to biblical and historical units, despite their dominance in all curricula. Another noteworthy absence from all graduates' responses was the college community, which was held in very high esteem by faculty as a major element in students' experiential development. In fact, the only such graduates' references were negative in this regard, tending to see the college community as "a bit contrived" and as a barrier from real life: "In some ways, I pulled out of life to be a student, to become involved in 'the College Community' but separated from any other 'real' community. What I have found since graduation is that the implication of this approach is that re-entry into the 'real world' requires a steep learning curve."

In drawing together the input regarding both prior and current life experience, some conclusions can be drawn concerning the issue of explicit and strategic connections made between classroom lessons and a student's life experience beyond the classroom. These connections were more common with current experience than with prior experience and, in both categories, were most commonly related to church-based experience, particularly formal ministry praxis. Other connections focused on personal spirituality and individual Christian living. Rarely were there connections made with life beyond the individual Christian or church ministry. Given that other survey items revealed that half the students are not involved in or heading to formal pastoral ministry, the lack of connection to the world beyond the church seems to indicate an experiential gap. While connections made were generally appreciated by students, there seemed to be no great concern with any perceived lack in this area. However, it is worth noting the significant minority of comments by final year students critical of the gap between intellectualized theological theory and practical life and ministry. The significant exceptions to this general picture were the two graduates who are working either beyond or on the fringe of a church context, who both affirmed a strong integration of theology and career, based on firm theological principles issuing in a coherent professional praxis.

(c)Experiential Learning

While not exactly the same as connecting with life experience beyond college, the issue of experiential learning (that is, experience-based practice as a method of learning) was addressed in the interviews with faculty and academic chairs and so warrants recording. While there was quite clear understanding in various other questions concerning who was responsible for curriculum development and the various institutions' main foci and strengths, there was far less clear articulation of this experiential dimension of delivery.

The issue of intentional incorporation of experiential learning into the curriculum was generally very low key among the faculty. Only one response clearly stated that such learning was intentional and strategic, and formed part of the official written policy of the institution by being incorporated into the rationale for the Bachelor of Ministry stream. This rationale, however, did not flow into the Bachelor of Theology in the same institution, where any such learning was reported as minimal, informal and incidental only. The most common response was that there was no evidence of significant experiential learning within the undergraduate programs. The other almost equally common response was the reference to Supervised Field Education (SFE) units, which generally were limited to one or two units within the degree and were not generally taken by students other than ordination candidates, and occasionally a Guided Spiritual Formation unit, which ran throughout the duration of the course. There was some more limited reference to a small number of practical electives which include practical assignments or projects, but most indicated that experiential learning does not feature significantly in the majority of so-called academic units. Most emphasis seemed to be on the informal community life of the college, such as chapel and college missions, and extra-curricular ministry formation programs which stand alongside the degree program and do not include non-ordination students, including extra-curricular internships or other church placements. There was little suggestion that such extra-curricular activity is integrated with the academic program of the degree, although in at least two cases the degree teaching faculty were increasingly involved in the ministry formation programs and were strategically attempting a higher level of such integration. One comment which perhaps sums up the general approach to experiential learning was, "We tend to be more academic. We are very content driven."

As with the faculty, the majority of academic chairs' responses listed extra-curricular campus activities such as ordination formation programs, community activities, college mission or ministry week, and student groups and chapel times as the main expressions of experiential learning. Other responses cited SFE and a small number of elective practical ministry and liturgical units as including some practical components. There were some, though few, dynamic expressions within these units, such as the structured engaging within ethnic communities in designated suburbs, interaction with members of other religions as a part of the program and *in situ* church planting experiences. There was little reference to the teacher's role in managing such experiential activity, as most of it happened beyond the classroom and not in association with the unit teacher. The main reference to teachers' roles listed the teacher's style of classroom dialogue and informal communication with the students as the main encouragement to link student experience with theological study, while a small number mentioned the value of well organised field trips as an integral part of certain church history units.

In the rather small incidence of experiential learning cited, the main method is the use of group activities, generally in the classroom. The concept of collaborative learning is being actively developed in one institution. In the SFE units, supervised critical reflection and reports are common, although the level of college-based supervision or observation of practical work in the external placement is minimal. The relatively few units in missiology often incorporate field trips to sites of other religions with associated reflective exercises. One college noted its door-knocking activity as a part of its evangelism unit. Two very specific examples of curriculum design which intentionally and strategically incorporate experiential learning were reported. One university now includes a Core Unit *Community Engagement and Transformation* as a part of its Bachelor of Theology (and also as a university-wide requirement), in which all students undertake a community placement as a part of the degree program. Another college, which has defined a specific Social Engagement Stream within its ministry degree, mandates community engagement in its units, such as working with the homeless in *Theology of Global Poverty*, a four day trip to Canberra to lobby politicians as a part of *Theology of Political Engagement*, and explaining the theology of the trinity to a Muslim as a part of *Theology of the Trinity*.

In light of the low incidence of experiential learning, it is not surprising that little comment was offered on the results of such learning. One response listed the development of some usable tools for ministry and one college, which sought to utilise more such learning, reported an increased attraction of younger students. However, there was virtually no specific comment offered on the overall effectiveness of experiential learning. Indeed, when asked to comment on the results of any experiential learning in their institutions, most respondents had very little to offer, with only four responses presenting any observations, and only one of them being specific. There was virtually no assessment of experiential learning offered. One response noted that, in classroom dialogue, mature aged students were more likely to draw on their personal experience, while two acknowledged the shortcomings of SFE units, in terms of their limitation (generally to ordination students) and their inconsistency of quality (with the faculty not having involvement in or control over the implementation of these units). The one active outcome reported was from the college with the Social Engagement Stream, which related a significant increase in enrolments of younger students who tended to be more actively involved in ministry and who were "more engaged on the street than in abstract classes in Theology." However, even here, there was no mention of the attainment of any specific outcomes of the experiences.

4. Making Connections: Aspirational Expressions

There were various expressions of how people would like to see more enhanced connections with students' prior life experiences, especially from students and recent graduates, and occasionally from academic chairs. Current students in particular offered numerous suggestions for incorporating students' life experiences strategically into the curriculum. Most were positive and proactive suggestions for consideration; some were negative and reactive ways of highlighting perceived shortcomings of current practice.

Positive suggestions mainly centred on the intentional inclusion of opportunities in various units for life application, by way of structured tutorial/seminar or other group discussion and by set assignments, either essay or project based. The sharing of personal stories with critique of variant world views was seen as a positive thing, provided it was facilitated in a non-judgemental way. Such personal experiences, while being respected in themselves, should also be filtered through the lens of the Bible rather than be automatically received as authoritative.

The more reactive commentary centred on the need for more consideration of and support for contemporary theological students and the elimination of presuppositions concerning who such students are and what their needs and motivations are. Issues highlighted include the danger of assuming common prior experience and motivation of all students and the need to recognise the shift in the composition of the student body from the former tradition of full-time males gearing for vocational ministry to the current preponderance of part-time female students not heading for ordination. This has ramifications in areas of delivery such as what load is a realistic "full-time" load; what hours of access are available (for classes, libraries and lecturer consultation); mode of delivery (day class attendance, evening classes, timetabling, weekends, vacation periods, online etc). There was also significant concern at the lack of support services typically available (or not available in most non-university colleges). While much praise was expressed concerning lecturers' general helpfulness, the lack of formal student centres, academic development support, chaplains and other personal support personnel and resources was seen to be in stark contrast with the provisions of most universities. Consequently, suggestions for catering for individual students' life experiences and situations included the provision of chaplains; the implementation of introductory programs in theological language and thinking as an orientation element; the development and implementation of student support and learning management systems; flexibility of delivery times and modes and access to lecturers; and a commitment to the valuing of all students' experience (including that of youth in a generally older cohort and of part-time women in a male-oriented institution) rather than merely the "traditional" or lecturer's personal experience.

One other observation made in the context of this topic is worth noting. It was noted by a number of students that, commonly, ordination students have a parallel formation program for practical ministry development and, while this is generally integrated with academic studies when the formation program is intentionally linked to the degree (by virtue of curriculum design or by common lecturers), when the formation program is quite separate from and independent of the delivery of the degree, such integration, even compatibility, is not always evident. The desire for more intentional and strategically structured integration of theological studies and such formation programs was a strongly voiced aspiration from students within the formation programs.

There were limited suggestions from the recent graduates with regard to ways in which such life experiences could be enhanced. Essentially, these suggestions involved seeing prior life experience (both ministerial and secular) as a beneficial resource to be enhanced not limited. This was seen to have two-way benefit, for both those with the experience and the peer group involved in its processing. One suggestion was that all students should do some Supervised Field Education, provided that such programs involve the setting of clear and appropriate individual goals, are well structured and mentored, and manage to escape the bondage of excessive paper work. It was considered worthwhile to develop a blend of theology and whole-of-life rather than seeing theological study as an interruption to life. It would also allow (and require) more individually tailored course pathways and learning experiences (as happens in one college as a matter of policy), which would in turn lead to more varied and enriched outcomes. To follow up on a previous metaphor, one respondent put it: "I think there should be specific curriculum for needs, tailored to meet such specific individual needs and to produce specific outcomes, not just 'page zero becomes page five'."

Suggestions for enhancing experiential learning were even more limited than the previous elements, with only three responses offered by academic chairs. One person quite strongly declared the need to expand the perspectives of *Worship* classes by involving a wider range of practitioners as teachers and the need to incorporate a practical component in the *Youth Ministry* unit, but that was the limit of any specific suggestion. The two remaining responses noted the need to ground experiential learning in appropriate theory and scholarship, so the student's experiential learning is well informed and facilitated by the lecturer, rather than simply being a case of asking, "What is your experience?" In general, the responses indicated a sense of "We should do more, but "

5. Summary

There is very little formal incorporation of structured connections with students' life experience (prior or current) with associated learning opportunities within the curriculum, with such learning being very limited in extent and narrow in scope. There is a similarly limited employment of structured experiential learning methods across the breadth of the curriculum, particularly in the biblical and theological areas which dominate the programs. Any life-based connectedness within the curriculum is typically *ad hoc* and intuitive rather than intentional or strategic. The classroom is seen as the place to transmit information rather than to engage students in learning activity. Occasionally, some pastoral ministry units have a small practical project component and, even less frequently, some history and missions units incorporate experiential field trips. Supervised Field Education is the one significant area which features experiential learning, but this is commonly (though not universally) limited to a small component of the course, commonly taken by the minority ordination candidates only, and commonly conducted in external church placements and not under the direct supervision of teaching faculty, thus reducing the integrating connections that may be made between "academic" and "field" work. There are but few examples of intentional and strategic curriculum planning that incorporates significant and well planned experiential learning by way of community engagement, involving both unit design and creative learning and assessment tasks. Apart from these curriculum elements, most experiential development is associated with extra-curricular activities, especially the separate Formation programs and the highly valued (though limited and at times seen as contrived) campus community life. While many endorse the value of experiential learning, there is little evidence of any expertise in designing or implementing specific programs for its attainment. This suggests an area in need of significant attention and development, if experiential learning is to be seen as an authentic element in theological education.

While there is a common recognition of the value of the variety of students' life experiences and backgrounds, both before and during the study program, there is an equally common exclusion of those experiences and backgrounds from the teaching/learning enterprise. Field placements are rarely integrated with classroom curriculum and it is only by way of informal class discussion that connections are made. Any such connections (with a few notable exceptions) are incidental and at the student's initiative. This is an area where faculty generally seem to have a lack of either capacity to initiate or confidence to implement, despite the good results noted in those few cases where connectedness occurs. There are very few examples of an institutional approach to tailoring individual study programs to connect with prior and ongoing life experience and goals, accompanied by strategic field placement and support, recognition of different learning types and encouragement of creativity in learning and assessment tasks. Generally, there is no formal connection with a student's life beyond the course, with college seen as a discrete time out to study rather than a part of an ongoing organic life process. There are a couple of interesting innovations in universities, who are increasingly seeing their mission within the context of community engagement and integrated experiential learning rather than in social isolation.

The general disconnection between theological studies and life experience is seen as a limiting feature of the programs, and one which has significant room for enrichment.

5 | A CHALLENGING JOURNEY

TRANSFORMATION THROUGH LEARNING

1. Transformation as the Heart of the Project

The central focus of this project is the concept of transformation of a student's life as an integral element within undergraduate theological degrees. To discover the extent to which this concept is currently incorporated in such degree programs, and some ways in which the concept may be enhanced in future developments of curriculum, an extensive inquiry was undertaken to learn precisely what is actually being experienced and what is actually desired by all interested parties. In keeping with the ideals of transformative learning, the centrality of the student was taken as the starting point. Hence, the first voice sought in the investigation was that of current students as the key beneficiaries of current programs, by means of an initial survey of current students and a series of student focus groups, which served to set the parameters of further investigation among a wider range of students, faculty and other stakeholders. Given the vital significance of this topic, it was gratifying to receive such clear, comprehensive and candid input concerning just what current students are experiencing in this regard, what recent graduates report as their experience, and how these reports correlate with what faculty claim is happening and what key stakeholders such as church leaders and other employers of theological graduates are saying they see in theological graduates. As a result of this input, we are able to articulate what it is that all parties want and to collate a number of proposals for promoting the furtherance of the transformative cause in theological degree programs.

2. What the Students Say

The Initial Student Survey explored student experiences of personal transformation. While nearly all students reported an expansion of intellectual horizons and critical thinking and a broadening of tolerance towards other theological and ecclesial positions, there was little suggestion of radical changes in world view. A significant number related challenges in coping with the critical study of sacred texts and revered doctrines with an associated sense of isolation (and common lack of personal support) experienced in that process. However, this struggle typically resulted in an affirmation of faith and an expansion of theological parameters rather than a paradigmatic change of any sort. A few exceptions to this were noted in responses from students from a non-Western or non-Christian background, who at times expressed the development of an entirely different understanding of the world and their place in it as a result of their theological study. A strong note to emerge was the acknowledgement of the influence of role modelling of lecturers in theological colleges in shaping their attitudes to the subject of their studies. A summary of the responses to main items follows.

Responses generally indicated a significant degree of personal growth in self-confidence and self-esteem. This was a product of perceived growth in both the capacity for critical thinking and personal spirituality. There was a noticeable affective element in the responses, which reported a sense of personal enjoyment of study in a different field, noted by graduates from other disciplines as greater than in previous studies. Expanded intellectual horizons were accompanied by enhanced inter-personal dialogue, especially theological dialogue, and an increased understanding of and tolerance towards different views of theology, culture and ecclesiology. The social environment of learning was held to be significant, but some environmental restraints were also noted in relation to residentiality.

Most reported an affirmation of personal faith, with an increased trust in, reliance on and intimacy with God during the course of their study, despite the challenges. This had found concrete expression in a more consistent and informed connection of gospel principles and values with the whole of life (though this was not consistently reported). As well as these affirmations, the study had caused some disruptions to, or even negations of, previously held views or perspectives. These included some previously held "foundational" doctrines and understanding of scripture, particularly a simplistic reliance on scripture, and the importance of denominational distinctives, which progressively became viewed as less binding or relevant in the modern world.

Several important challenges were reported. The most profound was that of being confronted with the need to question academically their held belief systems. The critical study of scripture was particularly unnerving, especially early in the course. Often, this was associated with a sense of loneliness or isolation, manifest in several ways: a "theological loneliness" in coping with challenges to held beliefs; a "social loneliness" in a felt pressure to "keep a happy face" despite personal struggles within a theological college context; and noticeably the felt isolation of young single women in a cultural context generally shaped by older married or established males. The need for colleges to manage these spiritual, psychological and emotional challenges to facilitate an enjoyable experience emerged clearly.

There was little if any change noted in regard to the students' regular life role. While there was some report of greater job satisfaction (especially among Catholic teachers), there was no change in professions reported. There was an increased awareness of ministry opportunities that accompanied the study. However, the general picture was that of an affirmation of previous attitudes and goals, with increased commitment and more intentional activity. Only occasionally was there any reference to the rejection or reshaping of previous ministry or professional goals. Similarly, students' world view was generally described as expanded rather than radically changed. This particularly related to a new awareness of the environment and the relation and centrality of Jesus in their world view. A noticeable exception to this was in those from a non-Western/non-Christian background (eg Asia, Africa), who commonly reported a radical re-orientation of values and a re- defining of their role in the world.

The Student Focus Groups also probed the extent to which the students saw their theological studies as being instrumental in personal transformation. In general, prior expectations of students entering theological studies centred on the acquisition of deeper biblical and theological knowledge, the development of enhanced thinking processes and the attainment of practical ministry skills. There was little if any expectation of personal change, although personal challenges and some sense of deepening one's relationship with God were vaguely anticipated. However, the most commonly reported and profound development experienced during the course of study was in a vastly expanded (rather than radically different) world view which necessitated at times significant personal changes. Growth in theological knowledge and understanding led to a greater degree of simultaneous humility and confidence as one's identity in Christ became more fully understood and appropriated. At the same time, concepts of God and his creation were enlarged, leading to a far more defined recognition of and more inclusive respect for the diversity of creation (including people, cultures and churches) and an accompanying diminution of judgementalism towards others' thoughts and praxis. Personal development was seen more in terms of growing into the person one is capable of being – not necessarily a different person but possibly a hitherto unknown person. The main pertinent responses are summarised as follows.

All respondents reported a significant growth in terms of an expanded world view occasioned by their theological studies, with concomitant recognition of the need to grow or change in order to respond to that enlarged perspective. This led to a growth in personal understanding of self, God and the world, which in turn led to a widespread rejection of dichotomous and judgemental absolutes regarding God and the world. The main element of personal growth was expressed in terms of a greater sense of God's being in control rather than oneself. One person put it as, "The language of 'me' has disappeared from my vocabulary;" another expressed it as, "Previously, I was telling God what to do in me; now, it is God telling me what he is doing in me." This growing sense of God-dependency in place of self-sufficiency resulted in a vastly expanded understanding of the nature and various expressions of God, in terms of both individual mystical contemplation and a pluralistic community.

While not widespread, some limiting factors on such personal growth were noted. The pressure and academic orientation of units at times limited or truncated the opportunity for development. Some lecturers' attitudes (requiring conformity) and personal engagement (especially by way of negative off-handed comments) at times hampered growth. (However, generally, lecturers were praised for their openness and helpfulness in creating a "safe" environment for personal inquiry.)

All respondents reported a greatly expanded view of the nature, variety and value of variant cultures and people. This resulted in greater tolerance towards and genuine respect for others' views and cultures and an increased openness to dialogue. The world was now seen not as a dichotomous "opposite" to the church, but as the locus of God's overarching creativity. Hence it is essentially good, although damaged and in need of restoration to God's image. Similarly, the view of creation had become more holistic, going beyond mere humanity and the church and embracing the totality of God's creation(s). Within this perspective, there was noted a greater sense of the lostness of people combined with love and respect for them. In light of the greater sense of confidence in God, his world and his justice, there was a greater willingness to take a counter-cultural stand.

The dominant response concerning the students' developing sense of self was that of a growing sense of one's personal identity in Christ. This had the double effect of a growth in both humility and confidence, as they became less self-focused and more God-dependent. The increased awareness of personal weaknesses was accompanied by an increased confidence in God: "my frailty; God's 'bigness'." Increased understanding of doctrines of grace, justification and sanctification led to greater acceptance of oneself as identified with Christ, with more courage to enter new fields and "to run with a vision."

The other outcome of this personal growth was expressed in terms of a less judgemental attitude to others. There was a removal of the previous sense of superiority towards non-church people, now seeing all God's creatures as equals. There was now an understanding of their role as being to reflect Christ positively in the world rather than to judge the world, with a desire to care deeply about people and to relate to them at a deep level, with a view to improving the world.

In summaries of the most important thing about their theological education, two main responses dominated. First was the need for the application of theological knowledge to real life rather than the mere development of a set of propositional truths. Second was the importance of the educational process and community in which the education occurred. These two elements came together in the willingness and openness to learn (even when this is discomforting) with a resultant respect for diversity and acceptance (of the people studied with, of churchly expressions, of the world at large), with an attitudinal development growing from exclusion to inclusion.

These initial student investigations were followed up by a more comprehensive series of student surveys among a wide range of current students. First year students were typically asked to relate their expectations and aspirations in commencing theological study and their initial experiences, while final year students were asked to review their actual experiences and to note significant changes that had occurred during that study. Significant responses collated across the range of surveys are provided in the following section.

Students were asked to indicate the elements they had expected (first years) and found (final years) to be most important to them personally. The element rated as most important by both groups was their increased biblical and theological knowledge. There was a high correlation in both groups between such increased knowledge and personal spiritual growth, which was consistent across all ecclesial traditions as well as the universities. The element of skills acquisition leading to vocational or paid employment rated very low. Relatively few attributed great importance to changed perspectives on interpersonal relations, with only a few more attaching great importance to growth in social awareness or understanding of social and cultural issues. In general, such socio-cultural development tended to be important to younger students and those in Pentecostal colleges. Hence, the main motivation and benefit for students in studying theology is the acquisition of biblical and theological knowledge. Personal spiritual growth is also sought and achieved, particularly in terms of its connection with the increased understanding of scripture and theology. However, it seems to be more internal and individual, with not a lot of connection with development in interpersonal or broader social and cultural awareness.

First year students were asked to indicate if they had expected their theological study to cause significant changes in certain areas and final year students were asked to indicate if they had experienced a great deal of significant or unexpected change in the same areas. The longitudinal survey asked respondents to note changes actually experienced. This is one area where there was a noticeable variation between the expectations of incoming students and the experiences of second year and final year students. Responses in the two surveys involving advanced year students produced very similar results in every category, with a slightly lower incidence of significant changes reported by second year students as compared with final year students.

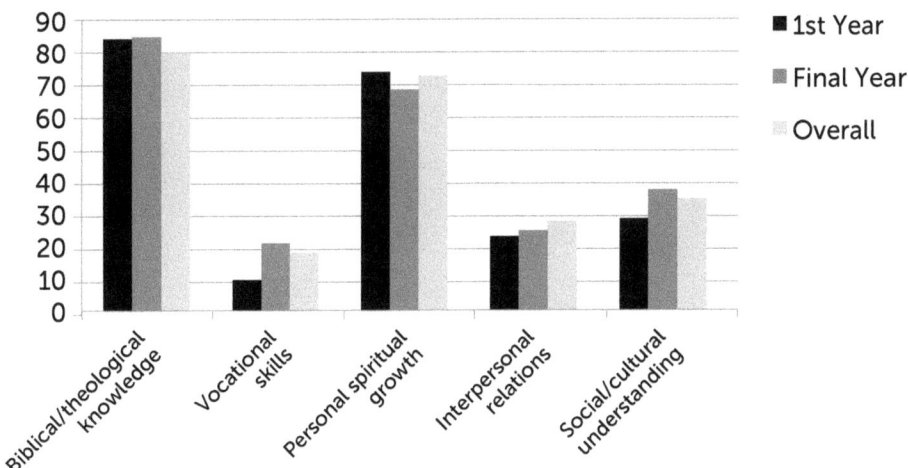

While most responses in the longitudinal survey reported some changes in most areas in the period between the two stages of the survey, those who reported "a great deal" of change in any area were few (with a maximum of 44% in any area), with a far greater number (up to 68%) reporting "very little" change in most areas. In an associated item in the final stage of the longitudinal survey, whereas most rated the attainment of their original expectations as "significantly achieved," only 12.5% rated it as "completely achieved," while an equal number rated it as "slightly achieved" or "not at all achieved." A large majority of incoming students expected significant changes in their understanding of God and the Bible, which aligns with their motivation for enrolling. While half of the advanced year students reported significant changes in these areas, this proportion was markedly lower than the parallel expectation of first years. Again, while similar numbers of first years indicated an expectation of significant change in all other areas, the actual degree of significant change reported by advanced year students was markedly lower in all the social and cultural attitudes and church practices. The areas where most change was reported were theological and scriptural understanding, while the areas where least change was reported were relations to non-Christians and the world in general beyond the church and in areas of personal and spiritual development. Growth (rather than change) in biblical and theological knowledge was valued and effective, but it seems to have been associated with internal personal understanding rather than having a significant impact on how the students relate to the world around them.

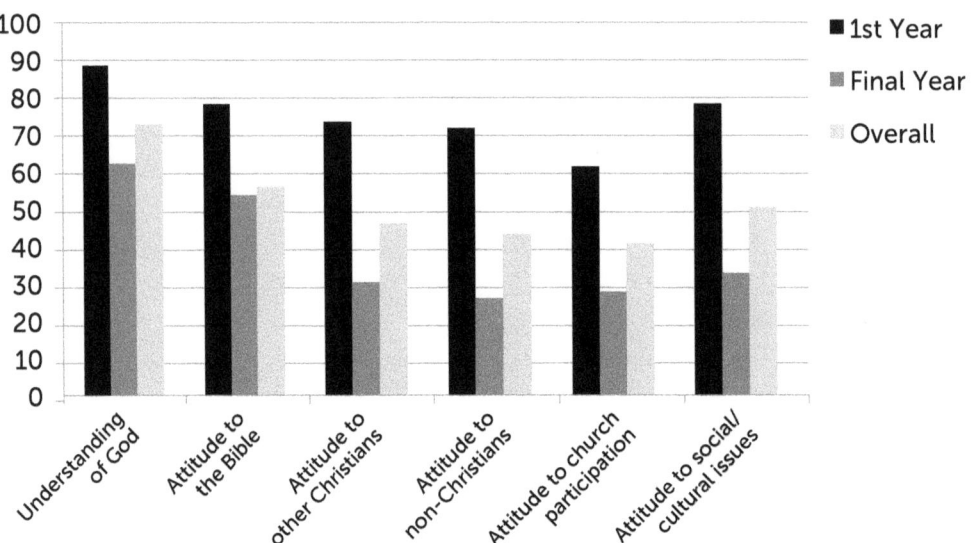

Students were asked whether, in the course of their theological studies, they had encountered new ideas or practices that had brought them to face significant and unexpected challenges. More than three-quarters of all responses indicated that they had encountered such new ideas or challenges occasionally or often, while only 4% reported no such encounter.

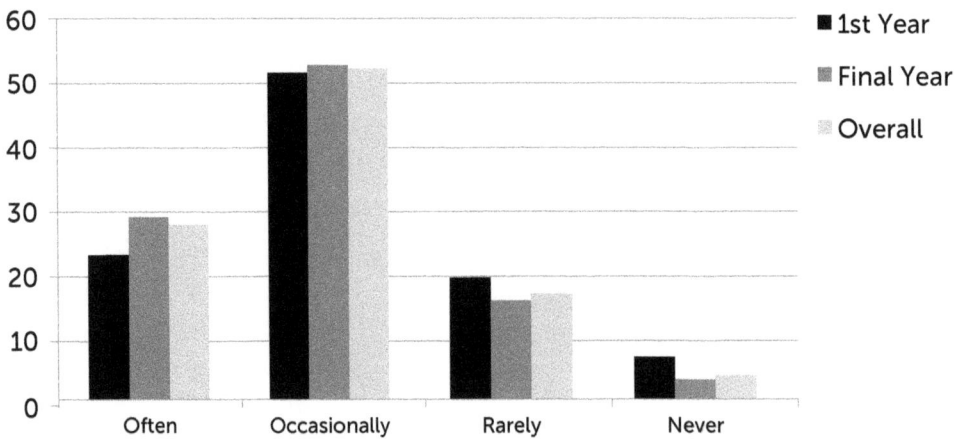

Students were asked to provide a brief description of such experiences, and 42% of the students did so. The two major areas of challenge were in the intellectual challenges presented by the academic study of theology and the critical study of scripture. Issues of biblicity were particularly challenging for first years, while theological dilemmas which challenged previously held views troubled the final years more. These two areas accounted for more than 60% of the total number of challenges reported. The next most prominent area was in the acquisition and application of new skills of ministry or the challenges to held views on doing church and related church issues, particularly prominent in the first year responses. Some 10% of the first year responses noted the challenge of coping with formal study, in terms of both formal academic requirements and personal self-discipline. The other main area, especially for first years, was the challenges to their Christian spirituality or Christian living. Fewer than 2% recorded significant challenges in areas of social justice or evangelism.

In the main, new ideas and challenges were experienced in the intellectual domain of theological thinking and critical biblical study. These challenges were expressed largely in terms of the conflict generated by a limited set of views held before starting the course and the need to confront a plethora of other accepted ways of thinking theologically or approaching the Bible. The active dimension of challenge was largely in terms of individual piety and Christian living, often expressed as the challenge to be more Christ-like in religious faith and life. While there were a few references to trying some new approaches to ministry (eg storytelling as preaching), these were minimal. Apart from these, there was virtually no reference to new practices and there were only a couple of vague references to new engagements with the wider society.

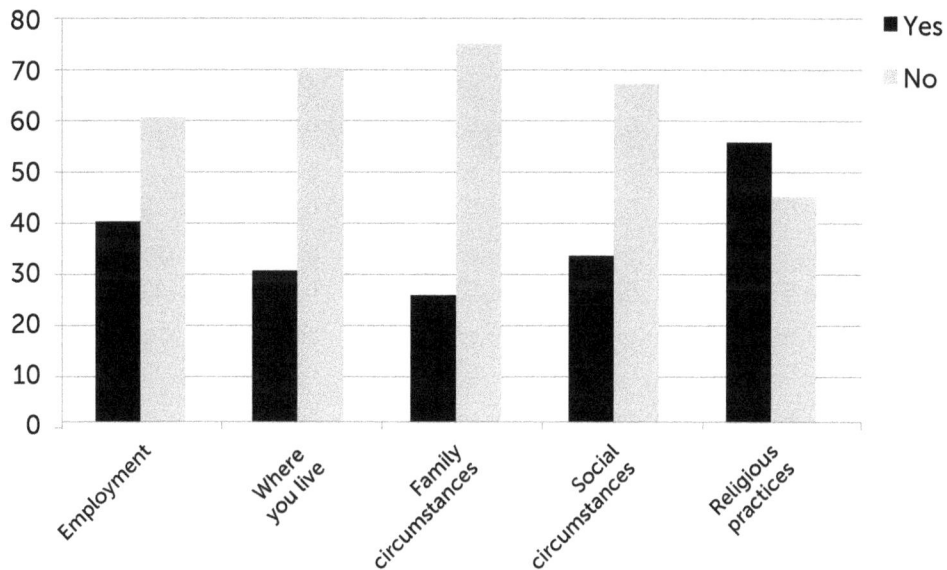

The final year students were asked to indicate if any of the challenges cited in the previous item had resulted in significant personal changes in a number of areas. Most responses indicated a relatively low degree of significant life changes, apart from the area of their religious practices, where 55% reported significant change. This was commonly associated with a change in employment, especially among candidates for ordination. However, it is questionable whether this change resulted from the course or from a decision made prior to enrolment. That distinction was not investigated. A small number of responses made it clear that the change of employment was directly a result of the theological study. There was relatively little significant change noted in the areas of interpersonal relationships such as residence, family and social circumstances.

Students were also asked to indicate their attitude to any personal changes that had occurred. There was an overwhelmingly positive response indicated, with 75.8% recording "Very Positive" and 20.3% reporting "Slightly Positive," with almost none (1 response in total) reporting "Very Negative." This suggests a high degree of satisfaction among final year students with regard to their personal development.

3. What the Graduates Say

Recent graduate surveys and course experience questionnaires, while not specifically addressing transformative learning *per se*, do give some pertinent insights into the experiences of recent graduates. Not surprisingly, the most commonly endorsed strengths of all institutions were two-fold: the quality of the faculty and the development of enhanced written communication skills. There was a widespread esteem for the personal quality of lecturers, with their commitment to their lesson and resource preparation; the quality, suitability and currency of the resources they made available; the quality of feedback provided; and their genuine concern for individual students. In terms of the attainment of generic skills, most responses listed written communication skills as the dominant attainment, following by the development of analytic skills and critical thinking. While the standardised forms did not facilitate comments on the content of the units, the open-ended instrument included many responses which listed the acquisition of biblical knowledge as an appreciated strength of their program. A less frequent but still significant response was the value placed on the community interaction with other students.

However, despite these almost universal affirmations, there were several areas consistently noted for desired improvement, both from institution to institution (which suggests a systemic situation) and from year to year (which suggests a static situation). There were two areas most commonly rated relatively poorly. One was the provision of health, welfare and counselling services, which generally earned at best a 50% approval rating, compared with common ratings of 75-90% in most other areas. Given that most theological institutions are quite small and community-oriented, this perceived lack of welfare provision seems odd; however, while the informal individual care of students by faculty members is impressive, it seems that the formal institutional provision of student services is not effective. Even lower than welfare provision in its overall rating was that of developing the student's ability to work as a team member, which rarely rated as high as a 50% approval. This is an obvious issue of concern, especially in light of the common vocational objective of congregational ministry. Other main areas expressed as concerns needing improvement were those of work load, including the load and lack of coordination of assessment, and the poor use of and/or access to technology, both by lecturers in the classroom and in the overall institutional environment. Of lesser but still significant concern were the lack of attainment of pertinent skills in problem-solving and practical ministry and the poor teaching too commonly in evidence. While faculty were consistently rated as high in their commitment, resourcing and care, there were frequent references to poor teaching delivery and classroom methods – often with a plea for more effectual teacher training of faculty. While the personal quality of the lecturing faculty is strongly endorsed, in terms of the transformative quality of the educative experience, this range of noted shortcomings is worthy of significant attention.

The graduate interviews focused on exploring the extent to which the institutional emphasis was on vocational equipping or personal development, the main area of individual development identified by the graduate, and an overall assessment of the experience. In terms of the school's emphasis, the dominant response was clearly the focus on training for ministry. A small number of responses indicated that shaping the person of the student was important, but this was done so in terms of shaping the person in preparation for ministry, that is, developing a ministry persona. In all of these responses, attention to personal growth, if at all present, was secondary to ministry training. In only one case, in a non-denominationally aligned college, was the primary emphasis reported clearly as shaping the student as a person: "I was constantly encouraged to ask good questions and to think theologically, beyond absolutes." In terms of programs, the main avenues for personal growth, again typically associated with developing ministry preparedness, were in the extracurricular formation and other community programs, with their typical emphasis on ministry topics, personnel and activities. The aspect of informal campus interaction with other students was mentioned by some respondents, but not as having any profound impact on growth or ministry formation apart from exposure to a range of personalities and perspectives, worthwhile and enjoyable but not greatly significant.

In the one case where the shaping of the person was detailed, there were some interesting comments offered. Although these comments came from just one respondent, they are of sufficient interest to report here since, while others reported the openness and integrity of lecturers and their encouragement of independent thinking, this response actually described it. The predominant motif of this response was the individually liberating force of the educational program and the lecturers who provided it.

> In missiological units, evangelism and social action were presented as two arms of the church's mission. I had come from a background where evangelism was the sole focus, so this challenged my previous thinking. We were presented with no absolutes but were encouraged to think of holding the two in a tension and arrive at our own conclusions. While this did not result in any active changes for me, it helped me to clarify my thinking, and reduced my fundamentalist angst. It generated within me an intellectual liberation where I could find authenticity for myself, to find what is real for me. It freed me from the need to accept what I could not believe.

The concept of challenging previously held views and freeing an individual to think differently and arrive at independent conclusions was reported as a very transformative experience, which allowed for what the student perceived as an authentic expression of self.

In reporting the main area of individual development experienced during their course of study, most respondents strongly affirmed what has been reported elsewhere by current students, namely, growth in biblical and theological knowledge. It was commonly noted as the main reason for entering college and its value was variously stated as having influenced hermeneutical understanding with a consequent impact on ministry and relationships. The acquisition of practical ministry skills was, interestingly, not stated by any respondent as a main outcome, despite their common vocational interests and ultimate occupations. Of the few who listed personal growth as the main area of development, most were very young (school leavers) when they entered theological education and expressed their growth in terms of a marked increase in personal confidence in relating to other people and in the intense development of a passion for theological learning. The one other respondent described it as a "breakthrough moment (which) came near the end of the course when it all came together in my sense of identity as a minister. This was a moment of personal identity integration. It included all the huge biblical and theological knowledge I had gained, but it all came together in what I can only describe as an *integrated identity*."

While most respondents expressed a high degree of satisfaction with the outcomes of their theological education, several made the observation that they would have appreciated more time to consolidate the issues that arose in the content of the course. Some suggestions for enhancement included spending more time on pragmatic issues and less time on the academic side of the Christian faith, and the incorporation of practical skills early in the course (as distinct from the current practice of generally later placement) to help put biblical knowledge into action. One strongly expressed thought was the need to incorporate apologetics, contemporary issues and cultural engagement, along with methods for doing so. Only a few respondents suggested more development in the area of personal growth, typically expressed in terms of a plea for more attention to the spiritual and personal formation of students, especially lay students who are not incorporated in the many formation programs available to ordination candidates. One respondent made a more expansive comment aimed at expanding the personal growth of students, by enunciating the danger of allowing intense scrutiny of sacred texts to become an unintended means of producing a personal and spiritual aridity:

> As a minister (or for anyone else), biblical knowledge only goes so far. We could have benefited from having some non-Christian teaching texts. I would like the college to facilitate more growth in passion for Christ and a zeal to serve. We spend so much time thinking that it becomes a dry exercise. We need to foster a personal life in Christ.

While growth in biblical and theological knowledge clearly topped the list of positive outcomes, the concern for concurrent personal growth ran as an undercurrent throughout the interviews. The area of personal growth throughout the course was largely seen as an aside or a corollary to knowledge mastery, with the young students being more likely to be more profoundly shaped by their course. As one respondent put it, "Personal growth tended to come along for the ride." Yet running alongside the legitimate quest for biblical and theological advancement is the less tangible but earnest desire for authentic personal spiritual growth. In all the graduate interviews, it was apparent that the graduates have a high regard for the development they had undergone during their theological studies: "We gained more than we had hoped for in coming to college." But as with all good products, there was an undertone of, "Yet it could be better." In the challenging words of one particularly articulate graduate: "It would be wonderful if all knowledge was transformative."

The graduates' evaluation of the various colleges' strengths and areas for improvement understandably echoed the findings of the course experience questionnaires and graduate surveys. Once again, of outstanding note is the emphatic description of the centrality of the lecturer in the effective educative process, not only because of subject expertise (which is acknowledged but generally assumed as a normal prerequisite), but more because of the personhood of the lecturer in terms of accessibility and openness, respectfulness and inclusiveness, and exemplary Christian character and values. The widespread attribution by graduates of such qualities stands as a strong commendation of the theological faculty in all colleges. Also valued is the consistent focus on biblical orthodoxy and principles and the breadth and depth of biblical and theological scholarship fostered in the colleges, another point consistently endorsed by all categories of stakeholders. While these aspects are more to do with what the college presents, there is also value ascribed to the personal outcomes in the students themselves, with most focus on the development of independent thinking in biblical and theological areas, again a reflection of the content focus of the courses. However, there is revealed only a limited focus on the development of an individual identity or the facilitation of an individual vocational outcome.

It is mainly in the area of integration that possible improvements are suggested. Such integration involves intentional and strategic *curriculum co-ordination* to replace the currently fragmented approach of separate disciplines; cohesive and accountable systems of integrating *church and college* in the formal curriculum, to establish a more effective connection of theology, practice and personhood of the students, including those students who are not specifically ordination candidates; and intentional strategies to inspire and energise the student, to promote the development of *character and values* as well as knowledge. Thus it is hoped to facilitate the holistic graduate outcome that is often expressed as the desirable end of theological education.

In the workshop session on graduate experience, it was noted that there are few avenues for direct input by graduates into curriculum development. Only a small number of colleges include graduates in course reviews and even fewer have graduates represented on institutional committees. The main input by graduates is in the course experience questionnaires, but there is an acknowledged shortcoming as regards implementing remediation of noted deficiencies. Some recognition of graduates' concerns have resulted in some curriculum changes (such as the incorporation of some practical ministry skills components and some field placements throughout the degree) and, in one case, the requirement for newly appointed academic staff to undertake a graduate certificate in Tertiary Learning and Teaching. However, in general, there was very little impact on curriculum provided by graduates' input.

4. What the Faculty Say

The areas investigated with students and recent graduates were also the focus of the interviews conducted with senior faculty and academic committee chairs. This was done in order to compare the responses from the recipients of the education with the responses from the deliverers of it. The faculty perspective on the most valued and most effective emphasis of the institutions correlated strongly with the perspectives of the student and graduate groups, namely, the rigorous teaching of biblical and theological knowledge. Indeed, the emphasis in all responses was on the overarching priority of biblical/theological knowledge as the major, if not sole, priority in the courses. All responses included this element as basic even if other elements may have been the objective. No response listed personal growth as a major focus. There were, however, some nuances within the overall response. Some responses stressed the positive nexus between their success in biblical teaching and the personal growth of students that accompanied it, while others similarly noted the causative link between biblical knowledge and ministry skills development, that is, the learning of biblical knowledge with relevant application to ministry. However, there were just as many responses which quite noticeably described their achievements in the area of personal growth as weak and their results in the development of ministry skills as weak. Most of these responses accorded with the responses of the student and graduate groups.

However, in assessing the factors which contribute to such successful outcomes, the faculty response varied somewhat from that of the other groups. While acknowledging the significance of the teachers (as the student groups had so strongly reported), the faculty laid far more emphasis on a coherent educational philosophy and consequent curriculum design and delivery than the student groups had noted. Many stressed the philosophical ethos of the curriculum that stems from a consistent and coherent hermeneutical, ecclesiastical and overarching world view held and promoted by the faculty. In one case, this was managed by the staff selection policy, with all teaching appointments coming from their own graduates, thus ensuring a continuity of the institutional philosophy. In another, *Christian World View* was placed as a core introductory unit which laid the basis of later philosophical teaching, while in another, the introductory unit in hermeneutics concentrated on the distinctive hermeneutic of the institution and was thereafter the touchstone of all biblical, theological and applied teaching. In others, an explicit commitment to an evangelical tradition and the priority of the Bible as transformative pervaded all teaching and community life in the college. In one university, there was the strategic development of a new introductory unit in theology, taught by several faculty, which taught the skills of theological thinking as a base for all later units in Bible, theology and church history. In general, there was a strong indication that the consistent, coherent and explicit philosophical approach to teaching, learning and curriculum design and delivery was an important element in achieving success. Yet this strong focus by faculty on philosophical and curriculum coherence seemed at odds with the common observation by students and graduates of a disjointed and compartmentalised curriculum, lacking in overarching integration. This variance in perception is a matter of concern and warrants further attention.

Far more detailed investigation was undertaken with faculty with regard to the opportunities and strategies for transformative learning that are exemplified in their institution's delivery. The first thing to emerge most noticeably was a concern for a clear understanding of the language of "transformative learning." This preliminary concern was echoed in the workshop groups, which began with the thought that we need to understand what transformative learning actually is, and asked, since transformative learning seems to mean different things for different providers, whether we can have a set of descriptions of transformative learning that will allow academics to choose one description that best fits their current context that they will be able to use intentionally. The workshop groups generally agreed that transformative learning is an on-going, lifelong process that commenced *before* students began to study theology and *will continue* throughout their lives. The faculty interviews also revealed a generally workable idea of the concept. While it was not always certain that all faculty had a common understanding of transformation, one respondent summarised the general concept succinctly: "Transformational education is not the same as formational education. Formation has an end in mind; transformation is more open-ended." His colleague added, "Transformational education means the integration of praxis into the being of a person." On the other hand, there was one strand of thought that maintained a strong distinction between the role of the academy (to provide intellectual development) and the role of the seminary (to develop the formation of a priestly persona and the transformation of personal qualities). The latter position was most pronounced in the Catholic tradition, although others who have a clear and separate formation program for ordination candidates tended to work along similar lines. However, notwithstanding this nuanced tension of terminology, there was a reasonable consensus in the meaning of the term, if not in the idea of whose responsibility it is.

This point affected the degree to which transformational opportunities were seen as intentional in a particular institution. Half the responses indicated that the provision of transformational opportunities was not strategic but hopeful and/or incidental, with most of these referring such provision to the seminary or an equivalent ministry formation program. Even beyond this half of the responses, for the most part transformational opportunities were described in terms of a prevailing institutional atmosphere or a general teaching style rather than as strategic facilitation. As one person put it, "Transformation, I would say, is encouraged and allowed, but it is not really deliberate or facilitated." With a couple of exceptions (including one response which strongly declared the intentionality and expressed strategicality of such provision), most accounts of transformational opportunities within the curriculum were in very general terms.

One quite commonly presented statement was that studying theology (or scripture or hermeneutics) is inherently transformative and so the whole undertaking is potentially transformative. "Doing theology is profoundly transformational. It frequently leads to the 'Aha!' moments." Other responses cited the Supervised Field Education and a small number of pastoral or practical units as the area where such opportunities naturally arise, as students are confronted with the need to process their own understandings of themselves and their practices. But the most common place where transformational opportunities were seen to be presented was in the rich community life of the theological colleges. Such activities as structured campus community events, regular chapel times, chaplaincy groups, ministry or missions awareness sessions, annual ministry weeks, and spiritual and meditative retreats were common and highly valued in many colleges. Although inevitably absent from the universities, some of these activities were a part of the co-curricular program of most colleges working within the universities. However, in all such extra-curricular activities, the focus was on full-time students attending campus, and in some cases limited to ordination candidates, with only minimal participation by other part-time, distance or non-ordination candidates.

Within the degree curriculum itself, transformational opportunities were seen to be generated by course design and teaching approaches. Some noted the intentional inclusion of transformative outcomes in Unit Learning Outcomes and the general direction to faculty to promote such outcomes. Others made reference to the development and strategic placement within the curriculum of Core Units designed to facilitate personal transformation. One institution has developed a Core First Year unit *Thinking Theologically*, which is designed to de-construct students' assumptions and to develop an openness to theological processes in five fields (biblical, systematic, etc), not just one theological model. Another college has developed a Core First Year Theology unit which intentionally provides a common base of theological understanding to balance prior experience, wherein the focus is on what are the specific ways in which each topic transforms the student's theology and relationship to God. Elsewhere, a Core Unit *Theology and Spiritual Formation* is taken about mid-way through the course and is designed strategically to help students to process their own theology and spirituality and personality.

The matter of teaching style was seen as significant more commonly than was course design. The encouraging and engaging style of the teacher was noted in numerous responses, with an important observation of the need to cultivate a suitable atmosphere wherein transformation may occur within the classroom. As one person described this deliberately cultivated atmosphere in their institution, "There is an institutional ethos of respect and safe challenges, including open and free classroom questions and dialogue, in a safe environment... it employs the cycle of Affirm-Stretch-Re-affirm, which is done in a consistent and deliberately non-judgemental way." Other elements in this area were various attempts to teach units *in situ*, such as teaching New Testament in an Aboriginal setting in the field and provocative field trips to cross-cultural or cross-religious settings.

Faculty were asked to relate examples of observed results of such transformative opportunities. There was a very limited response to this request and details offered were generally sketchy. The large majority made no comment on this point, while a smaller number stated that they had anecdotal evidence only, based on some generally favourable feedback from students by way of informal conversations or course evaluations, but did not give specific details. The few responses which did describe observable outcomes centred on three areas: the development of a greater openness to and critical thinking in doctrinal matters; an expanded world view with a concomitant increased awareness of issues in society, ministry and, especially, missions, which resulted in changed practices or engagements; and a marked discernible growth in personal confidence, manifest in personal bearing, social interaction and ministry performance.

There was one further interesting observation made by a number of academic committee chairs. Those colleges (including church-dependent university schools) whose declared primary interest was in ordination or ministry preparation were more intent on ministerial leadership development, while those institutions which had a less direct connection with specific churches or traditions and serviced a wide range of students or a younger profile of students tended towards individual development and personal transformation as a focus. It was noted that in these latter institutions, the dominantly lay students were more likely to be interested in personal development than in vocational training for leadership roles. While most responses saw no intrinsic difference between forming leaders and transforming individual lives, many noted some limiting factors. As one put it, "There is probably not (a difference), but it affects an institution's motivation for training." In addressing the question, "Why are we here?" a college will establish its primary purpose and orient its teaching accordingly.

There are several conclusions that can be drawn from the faculty input on this element. The issue of transformational learning is clearly important to faculty, but equally clearly it is elusive in description let alone attainment. It strongly emerged as an aspirational goal, even though there was no real consensus on just whose role it is to achieve it (the academy or the seminary or the church). Consequently, it is not so clearly in focus in curriculum considerations, notwithstanding its presence in some Learning Outcomes statements. Indeed, in terms of curriculum design and development, there seems to be a reluctance to grasp the nettle of transformative ideals in a structured and deliberate way – "this is not strategic, just hopeful." Consequently, there are few deliberately structured transformative elements within the formal degree program beyond Supervised Field Education units (which largely consist in external practical placements with limited class input) and a few practical elective units (whose main emphasis remains on the development of practical skills). In many cases, these two practical areas focus on attending ordination candidates rather than lay or distance students.

By far the most commonly cited area of transformative development is that of the informal extra-curricular agenda of colleges – its campus community life, regular chapel participation, chaplaincy or growth groups involving students and faculty, college ministry/mission weeks. Even in the universities, where the Theology school effectively involves or is closely associated with theological colleges, such extra-curricular activity is seen as highly significant for transformative development, although it may not be included in official degree considerations. A noteworthy limitation here is the emphasis on ordination candidates in most such transformative discussions, a point of concern since many theology students are thereby often effectively excluded from such opportunities. However, given that there is virtually no theological college that does not value such activity so highly, the question arises as to what really is a curriculum. As the workshop groups stated, any moves toward a curriculum based on transformative learning must carefully consider both the overt and the hidden curricula. Is "curriculum" necessarily restricted to the academic content of core disciplines, or is there a case to be made for including what is commonly termed "extra-curriculum" as a part of the "curriculum" in some way?

There are some recent developments in actual curriculum design that attempt to incorporate transformative learning strategically in the degree. The design and placement of specifically transformative units within the degree curriculum are clear and tangible strategies for the facilitation of transformative opportunities within the curriculum. While these are currently few and often limited to introductory units as a sort of institutional ethos marker, there is considerable scope for the expansion of such thinking throughout the degree, and in particular, more focus could be given to this aspect in the later stages of the degree, when students are more likely to have confronted more theological concepts and challenges demanding more intense personal integration. The role of the teacher in achieving transformative growth is clear, both in personal style and in the facilitation of an open and safe yet challenging atmosphere in which growth may occur. The whole notion of integrated learning necessitates an integrated faculty in its attainment and any attempt to achieve such integration will need to involve collegiate development across all departments. (No response mentioned the idea of capstone units as a means of integration in the later stages of the course, but it seems an obvious consideration and one that would involve multiple faculty in its execution.)

A particular difficulty emerged in the interviews, namely, noting and reporting the results of transformative learning, be it in formal SFE or in informal group life. This was manifest in the relatively vague and generally intuitive terms used in responses. While no clear answer to this problem was presented, it was clear that, if transformative learning is to become a key part of what institutions are offering, then some means of demonstrating transformation need to be established.

In all of this, there emerged an underlying sense that theological lecturers are keen on seeing their students graduate as persons with a holistic integration of theology and life not just as those who are theologically informed or ministerially skilled. Yet there remains an elusiveness in the whole venture and a sense that if transformation is really happening, it is more by chance than by design. The desire is there; the intention is developing; some strategies are being developed; more is possible. A succinct summary of the general scene was provided by an experienced faculty member about his own school's historical approach to transformative learning:

> It is extra-curricular and has mixed results. There is anecdotal evidence only of challenge and change about how to do ministry, which seems to be limited. Over all, this probably reflects a lack of intentionality in the conduct of the program, and unclear strategy. We began eight years ago with "hopeful," then became "aspirational," now probably "intentional," but still need to become more clearly "strategic."

5. What the Stakeholders Say

The interviews with church leaders and other employers provided a different sort of perspective from the viewpoints of those at the delivery point of the educational programs. The leaders included officials such as bishops and superintendents, denominational training and placement officers, missions directors and senior clergy in parish positions. They offered a somewhat more critically detached perspective, while having an intense personal and professional interest in the quality of the graduates produced by the programs. While all reported a high level of satisfaction with their associated teaching institutions, most offered some qualifications and concerns for areas clearly needing improvement.

In the eyes of the leaders, the major focus of virtually all theological educational institutions is seen as the biblical and theological content of the Christian faith. This emphasis is held by the church leadership to be of primary importance and is endorsed as a strength of the institutions. Even where there is the additional or growing emphasis on ministry skills development, the primacy of biblical and theological knowledge is upheld. While many institutions subscribe to the significance of ministry applications of that knowledge base, only a few have gone to the extent of formally re-structuring their curriculum to facilitate this dimension, while many acknowledge a significant shortcoming in the area. The dimension of personal growth and spiritual formation, while also acknowledged as supremely important, especially for ministry preparation, is recognised as largely neglected in formal programs.

While most leaders support the focus of their associated institutions, some qualifications have been expressed about the lack of a suitably wide world view and the inability of graduates to integrate their learning and their life/ministry. The most serious concern is the inadequacy of personal preparation of graduates for "real-world" ministry. The insularity often generated by theological colleges is seen as a feature to be recognised and a challenge to be overcome. Most agree that such issues are not the sole responsibility of the training colleges, but there is a sense in which this is a part of the challenge for colleges to confront. While theological expertise is seen to be in good shape, various suggestions have been made to enhance both the practical ministry skills and the personal growth aspects of the students' learning experience. What all these suggestions have in common is their aim to produce more integrated persons who can think, relate and live theologically and skilfully in a contemporary world context, rather than simply to produce informed and articulate theologians.

While the leaders' evaluation of their schools was almost universally positive and their negative observations were relatively few, those observations are worth taking seriously, since they were virtually all in the area of transformative outcomes for the graduates. Many of the qualifications expressed centred on the issues of a too narrow focus and a lack of integrated learning. "The biblical focus is good, but the singularity of that focus is not. Personal growth is also important and needs further development While I agree that the high academic standards are to be maintained, this should not be at the expense of the lack of holistic integration of growth and skills." One officer responsible for ministerial accreditation, while speaking highly of his denominational college, made the following comment: "Personal transformation is the most neglected, yet it is the most important element in (ministerial) accreditation." Another noted some good ministry skills, but also added the qualification: "There is a relatively (but to a limited degree only) limited capacity to interact biblically with missiological issues. When confronted by a problem issue, they tend to go straight to pragmatics first, rather than to start from a biblical basis to find a solution."

A minority of responses (about 10%) indicated a significant degree of dissatisfaction with graduate outcomes. The sole issue for this dissatisfaction was the personal quality of the graduates and their personal unsuitability for ministry, despite their generally commendable theological knowledge. One attributed this partly to the relatively poor prior theological and personal formation of incoming students from the churches, which caused the colleges to adopt a remedial role. However, a far more harsh assessment was given by a senior denominational accreditation officer:

> Personal growth is the area of most concern from the perspective of the (ministerial accreditation) panel. At the interviews of potential ordinands we see a shortfall in the area of personal growth. The main concern at this point is their lack of personal awareness of the effect they have on other people, a lack of empathy and understanding on life matters, and a general lack of consultancy. They present as having a sense of positional pride. (None of our colleges) is addressing these issues well, although I add that it is not necessarily the task of the colleges solely.

While most starkly articulated in this response, the matter of an inadequately formed personhood in graduates arose at various points in the interviews. One placement officer (also a faculty member) attributed this to the pragmatic self-interest of typical students and the negative impact of assessment requirements:

> We are really rigorous in our academic programs, but this means that assessment is a high priority in students' minds. Therefore, we have a way to go to get past this content-obsession and self-centredness. We want to keep the rigour but add values. I would like to see students come to the college to continue in ministry and to be better equipped, not just to have a "time out" to learn how to do ministry. I would like to leverage case studies and prior experience, to use that experience effectively as grounds for reflection and improvement.

However they were expressed, all these observations focused on the desire to form coherent and effectual persons in ministry and life.

As well as these general observations, the church leaders were asked to comment on the specific perceived strengths of their graduates and any areas which they would like to see significantly improved. By far the most dominant strength reported was the graduates' almost universally acknowledged rigorous grounding in theology and Bible associated at times with confessional and/or liturgical purity. However, while acknowledging this strength, one denominational leader also expressed a negative aspect of such purity: "This is accompanied by a liturgical purity, but it is a quite narrow liturgy. It is dated, not culturally relevant, with the emphasis still on the pastor as being the one in charge of worship. The main strength seems to be in maintaining the *status quo* of the church. They tend to present as a summary of others." However, it should be noted that this concern for a too narrow theological and liturgical knowledge was at most an undercurrent of other conversations rather than a strongly expressed concern.

A secondary area of noted strengths was that of practical ministry skills. Half the responses identified a variety of ministry skills, with a small number noting that graduates are "competent in ministry, ready to be employed, ready to go." A very small number cited preaching skills, the capacity to integrate theology and pastoral issues, and a demonstrated capacity to engage effectively with their church and wider community contexts: "Their ability to read a missional context and confidence to lead in that context. Their leadership development is based on their having internalized the basic principles of leadership." These practical skills, though not as pronounced as the knowledge component and generally more recent in development, were seen as significant qualities of graduates.

The third area of strength, though far less common than the previous two, was that of personal qualities in the graduates. A few responses (about 15%) noted a commendable passion for ministry, for God and for godliness, associated with a clear and consistent sense of vocation. A similar number referred to such qualities as an ability to cope with pressure, the development of a broader world view, critical and adaptable thinking in matters of theology and attitudes of tolerance and respect in personal engagement. While less emphasised in general than biblical and theological knowledge or practical ministry skills, these personal attributes were seen as significant parts of the make-up of an effective graduate.

In response to the question of areas in need of improvement, it was not surprising that no one listed any knowledge component, apart from one comment that more of the core faith content should be committed to memory. The three areas widely suggested for improvement were leadership, contemporary engagement and personal integration. In the area of leadership, some called for more effective experience in a wider range of ministerial duties (doing and reflecting upon them, not just being informed about them), more effective large church and team leadership, and a variety of specialised learning pathways to facilitate the development of expertise in such roles. Others noted the need to master not only time and program management but also people management, in particular, the need to learn to listen better to lay leaders and to enfold the congregation into their ministry more effectively and "to talk the language of people not the academy."

The area of contemporary engagement focused on both the church and the wider community beyond academic halls. Some responses called for more effective relationships, partnerships and overall communication with relevant churches, at both denominational and local levels, "to overcome the chasm between the college and the churches" and to help the colleges to develop "the concept and practice of collegiality as a member of a wider theological cohort." There were also some calls for a more experimental and creative approach to liturgy to facilitate a more contemporary expression of church worship. Beyond the church, there was a desire to expand the world view and the capacity for effectual dialogue with the broader society, something which is seen as largely missing from the narrow biblical and theological agenda of many schools. Several leaders expressed the desire for "better grappling with contemporary culture; more creativity in cultural engagement, to see the gospel, the church and culture in dialogue ... the need to expand the horizons of our graduates, to enable them to engage in public dialogue, in universities and so on." The contemporary integration of theological world view and contemporary social action was mentioned: "I would like to see a deeper understanding of their world view, how their theology links with politics, ethics etc at a social level, in engagement with global issues."

Finally, the issue of personal integration of knowledge, skills and personhood in a graduate was expressed as an area needing improvement. Essentially, this was seen as a process of embedding concepts within a student rather than a student's simply learning about the concepts, of grasping the significance and import not just the content and practices. "Students need to understand the concepts and principles rather than the mechanics of liturgy." One recommendation was the enhanced use of *in situ* and other forms of experiential learning with ongoing critical reflection, which would help the students to develop a greater ability to synthesise all the aspects of their learning. While suggested means were vague, the desire for an integrated person as a graduate was common.

These issues raised with the leaders proved interesting as they touch on the very essence of graduate outcomes: what should a theological graduate look like? While most respondents generally affirm that their schools are producing effective leaders, this assessment focuses on the traditional base of producing a theologically and biblically well informed graduate and not so much on the emerging need for the development of an engaging practitioner. The primary focus on biblical and theological knowledge is affirmed, but the narrow or even exclusive singularity of that focus is seen by many as a contemporary shortcoming. The strengths of graduates are similarly noted as sound theological scholarship and biblical fidelity: the *sine qua non* of theological education. A recently emerging note is the development of some practical ministry skills, but a caution is sounded as to the need for such skills to be contemporary not dated, flexible not rigid, applicable to tomorrow not yesterday. There is a growing recognition of the need for graduates to add the skills of appropriate leadership and social engagement to their knowledge base. This is seen in conjunction with the revised role and status of the minister, no longer necessarily viewed as the sole repository and exponent of biblical authority, but needing to manage people and society (both in and beyond the church) in a more dialogical manner. This will require more than a knowledgeable theologian and more than a skilled practitioner: it will also need an integrated person who has appropriated theological concepts and mastered principles of practice in a holistic expression of ministry in a variety of modern and often unpredictable contexts.

6. What are the Opportunities for Transformative Learning?

The issue of transformational learning is elusive in description and vague in attainment. Most parties strongly desire it as an aspirational outcome, but great variability exists in its implementation. The terminology is used variously (priestly formation or personal development or radical change?), there is uncertainty as to whose role it is (academy or seminary or church?) or how it is to be facilitated (in class or in community?) and, even more so, how it is to be authenticated (by measurement or demonstration?). Consequently, there is a reluctance to grasp the nettle of transformative ideals in a structured and deliberate way, with few deliberately structured transformative elements within the formal degree program (beyond the limited Supervised Field Education units and a few practical elective units), with this element left largely to informal extra-curricular activities loosely based around campus life and college missions. However, despite this overall vagueness, there is a strong and clear expression of the desire and need of an integration of learning and life during the course of theological study, not just the production of a graduate who is theologically informed or ministerially skilled. Even where the focus is on producing ministers, there is a general sentiment that effectual leadership flows out of transformed lives.

Some recent curriculum developments have incorporated transformative learning strategically in the degree, by placing intentionally transformative units within the degree curriculum at strategic points, by the use of integrating exit projects, the involvement of more than one lecturer in a unit delivery to engender diversity, and by incorporating learning methods such as appreciative inquiry, collaborative learning and educational field trips with appropriate educational supports. However, these efforts remain relatively few in number and tentative in application, with the main avenues of transformative opportunities depending on the lecturer's informal interaction and dialogical teaching style within an open and safe yet challenging atmosphere in which growth may occur. The importance of appropriate complementary co-curricular programs is commonly stressed as a vital means of promoting transformative experience, yet rarely is there any sense of cohesion, comprehensive inclusion of students, or evaluation of outcomes of such activities. If these are authentic parts of the transformative agenda, then there is a case for their more formal inclusion in the program.

A strong motif was the desire for holistic and integrated learning to replace the traditional compartmentalised approach to theological instruction, based on the transmission of a pre-determined and controlled corpus of specialised knowledge, with a more open-ended system of theological discovery which generates an authenticity of experience for the learner rather than a detached mastery of content. The two elements of legitimate content and authentic experience are not incompatible, but the connection between them is causative rather than casual, that is, the mastery of content has a purpose of (trans)formation or else it risks becoming an exercise of limited if not dubious value. A number of recent graduates reported that, along with the legitimate quest for biblical and theological advancement which they value highly, there is also the less tangible but earnest desire for authentic personal spiritual growth, expressed in the plea that all knowledge could be transformative.

The particular difficulty of noting and reporting the results of transformative learning requires that some means of demonstrating transformation be established. There is a prevalent academic suspicion of anything that cannot be assessed in numerical or grade terms, so how does one "measure" transformation? Similar questions are asked (and similar suspicion exists) about any such skills or personal development units (eg SFE and Guided Spiritual Formation). The answer may lie in a re-definition of assessment, with a shift away from purely quantitative markers (such as percentages – themselves a dubious measure of any theological unit) to qualitative markers, which will provide *demonstrability* rather than *measurability*. However, extreme care is needed to generate adequate and authentic qualitative markers and valid accountability instruments.

Over all, there is a high level of consensus that theological education needs to incorporate the whole life of the student and that there is a need to anchor theology in the faith tradition which has given rise to it. The real need is therefore to bring these two aspects together in an integrated and authentic way. The challenge for theological curriculum designers is to move deliberately towards the aim of theological education as transformative rather than merely cognitive.

6 | WHERE DOES CURRICULUM FIT INTO THE JOURNEY?

1. Why Curriculum?

As reported in chapter 2, a recent UNESCO manifesto lamented the general lack of attention given to tertiary curriculum over the years. As also noted in chapter 3, perhaps nowhere has this curricular conservatism been more evident than in theological education, which has undergone minimal development in the past thirty years in Australia, beyond some structural changes in semesterised delivery and internal assessment. There has been very little development in actual curriculum design and virtually none to do with the intentional and strategic incorporation of transformative concepts into the philosophy, aims or design of that curriculum. The recent workshop noted that theological curriculum has been basically modelled on the humanities, with its generalist approach to introducing students to classical scholarship, whereas a more suitable model for transformative learning could well be that of other service-oriented professions such as medicine, nursing, teaching and social work, a point also illustrated in some recent curriculum developments in these latter fields (see chapter 3).

That current curriculum design is in need of considered re-orientation in this regard is attested by the evidence of students in focus groups and surveys, which indicated that the pressure and academic orientation of units at times limited or truncated the opportunity for personal development. Students reported some important challenges which they encountered as they entered theological study, the most profound of which was that of being confronted with the need to question academically their held belief systems. The critical study of scripture was particularly unnerving, especially early in the course. Many students reported that their study had caused some disruptions to, or even negations of, previously held views or perspectives, including some previously held "foundational" doctrines and understanding of scripture and the importance of denominational distinctives. On the other hand, when students were asked to indicate what stood out as most important and most positive in their experience of theological education, their responses centred on the need for the application of theological knowledge to (their) real life rather than the mere development of a set of propositional truths and the importance of the educational process and community in which the education occurred.

Since such challenges exist in a great majority of situations, they need to be considered not only pastorally but also in curriculum, since it is the very content, volume and detached critical analysis of such curriculum material that provide the bulk of the concerns. Opportunities for students to assimilate the wide array of new theological concepts into their existing frames of reference or to revise those frames of reference to accommodate the new knowledge need to be factored into the curriculum. While transformative learning will require far more than a mere re-writing of curriculum documents, if it is to be taken seriously, then the construction and delivery of the curriculum have a major role to play in the facilitation of such learning. If the theological program is to be conceived of as a part of the life-long journey of the student, it will need to have integrated connections with those parts of the journey which both precede and extend beyond the formal educative program. Thus the curriculum will need to be constructed with such connectedness in mind, to incorporate structured opportunities and experiences that will promote transformative development.[1]

As with many other traditional areas of knowledge, Christian theology has a long history of received wisdom and scholarship. Indeed, as revealed in the wide range of surveys, focus groups and interviews, it is the stated mission of most theological providing bodies to safeguard and to perpetuate this sacred knowledge and it is the desire to engage this vast body of knowledge that motivates most incoming theological students.

---

1 The terms "facilitation" and "promotion" of transformative learning should not be confused with a "guarantee" of such learning. However, while no educative program can guarantee any stated objective, an intentional approach to curriculum design and delivery is needed to establish an operational framework in which the desired objective may be strategically pursued by all parties.

Consequently, there is a long-standing tradition of theological educational curriculum being organised in ways that will systematically introduce students to this body of classical Christian scholarship and, at a tertiary level, to teach ways of analytical interpretation and communication of this material. However, given the noted typical lack of connecting this knowledge to prior life experience and the declared aspirations of graduates and, particularly, the employing stakeholders and church leaders for a more personally integrated graduate, there is clearly room for curriculum development which packages and delivers this sacred knowledge in ways that will be more effectively engaged by the learners.

So then, the traditional base of theological curriculum has been the content deemed by teachers (and their owned tradition of scholarship and/or ecclesiology) to be important for students to engage. The base of transformative learning is the centrality of the student's continuing life and experience. The major challenge identified for theological curriculum is that of preserving the high value placed on the historical and creedal bases of traditional theological teaching, while adding value to the development of practical skills as a legitimate component of contemporary theological education, and yet at the same time expanding its pedagogical horizons to take seriously the responsibility for the formation of people and the transformation of both individuals and society. This challenge comes by way of reaction against the dissatisfaction with the limitations of the knowledge transmission philosophy of modernism and it seeks to re-locate the person as a legitimate focus in the educative process. This placing of the learner at the centre of learning – in course aims and curriculum design as well as delivery methods and desired outcomes – is fundamental to the philosophy of transformative learning. How to do it without sacrificing (or, preferably, with enhancing) the valued theological content is the next frontier for theological educators to cross.

2. Developing the Curriculum

In addressing the issue of curriculum development, there are several interwoven issues that emerge, which can loosely be arranged under "process" (the *how*) and "agents" (the *who*). Questions of process include just where do we start in curriculum development. With the accreditation focus on benchmarking, it seems that most curriculum development has been initiated by either "what we have always done" or "what everyone else is doing." Many faculty and stakeholders referred to the impositions of accreditation regulations (of government, university or church) as significant inhibitors of curriculum development and, particularly, of innovation. However, as noted at the workshop, although there may be some apparent regulative blockages to the implementation of transformative learning, they are not as restrictive as often perceived and are often overcome by sound argument and active pursuit of the sector's goals. Questions of agents include identifying and collaboratively incorporating those parties who have both a vested interest in the programs and a capacity for informed and constructive input into curriculum development. While the traditional emphasis has been on faculty working within their specific discipline areas, there are other considerations which can productively contribute to enhanced curriculum development.

The process of curriculum development requires the consideration of a variety of needs and expectations, which are not always the same, for example, student expectations, teacher expectations, unit/course/graduate outcomes and attributes, and expectations of churches, agencies and accrediting bodies. There needs to be effective dialogue amongst all parties and balance among the competing requirements. This sentiment is widely expressed by faculty and all other stakeholders, yet the research was able to detect very few mechanisms in place for such wide-ranging effective dialogue in the development of curriculum. The dominant driving forces of curriculum development seem to be the accreditation cycle and in-house faculty determinations. This was indicated strongly in the interviews, with faculty and academic chairs overwhelmingly attributing major curriculum influence to the teaching faculty, driven often by one dominant individual within the faculty, typically the academic leader of the School (Principal, Academic Dean, Director of Theology, etc) who exercised a top-down authority within curriculum decision-making. While a significant number of responses identified the church which stood behind the college or university department as a significant influence in curriculum shaping, only a very few stated this influence to be normative and dominant. Input from the workshop reinforced this since, while colleges which are primarily ordination-focused have their general requirements stipulated by a national or international central body, the prescription regarding the very content of units is not stipulated, and even the scope of units across colleges in the same ecclesiastical tradition can be quite varied. Similarly, members of a university department or a teaching consortium commonly made reference to the influence of the institutional regulations as a limiting influence. However, all such responses acknowledged that, while these regulations constitute a significant framework in which they are obliged to operate, none the less they are not dominant in that individual colleges have considerable flexibility in their selection, specific content and delivery of units within the general regulations. That is, the regulatory structures and protocols were seen to have a relatively minimal impact on actual curriculum decisions.

That dialogue with parties beyond the faculty is very limited was also attested by the observations of these other parties. Some references were made to the informative and generally informal input of students (via Course Experience Questionnaires) and stakeholders (via occasional meetings and conversations), but such input was always expressed as relatively tangential and rarely did it comprise a formal part of the decision- making processes. The workshop acknowledged the need for networking between all stakeholders, especially among the churches, and observed that stakeholders can have somewhat unreal expectations, which highlights the need for effective dialogue to educate the stakeholders as well as to help the stakeholders to define their aims and needs regarding formative and transformative aspects. However, the workshop also noted that sometimes the key fundamental stakeholders are not represented on boards, councils and committees, which makes such dialogue difficult to manage. Most church leaders and employers indicated that they had no direct influence in shaping the curriculum. Some indicated that, by virtue of their senior status within the state or national governance of the church, they had considerable oversight and approval authority, and therefore potential to influence the curriculum. However, this was generally exercised in matters of vision, trends and overarching policy rather than any hands-on curriculum engagement, that is, "broader oversight at a bit of a distance." Only one interview with a missions agency state director described a system of annual meetings of missions personnel with college faculty to discuss issues pertinent to graduates and to improve the shape of missions units, with encouragingly satisfactory outcomes. Generally, the typical stakeholder response was, "I have reasonable access to the college, but limited capacity to change anything. The Principal and Chairs are open to discussion and give opportunities for this (but) over all, my influence on the curriculum is not significant." In terms of graduate and student input into curriculum, very few colleges reported having a student or graduate member of academic boards and responses by the graduates indicated that there was effectively no formal student or graduate voice in curriculum matters.

In summary, the current situation of curriculum development is one where the teaching faculty, especially the dominant academic leadership of the faculty, play the most significant role in determining the shape and delivery of curriculum. Whether this be done by top-driven means or by more collegiate methods of faculty engagement, it is clear that if any curriculum is to be developed or enhanced, the impetus for and implementation of such will come from the faculty. There are various levels of external influence, especially where the teaching institution is closely aligned with a controlling church (and most particularly when that church operates on a nationally or internationally organized basis). Such church alignment typically requires the primacy of the ordination requirements of the church and, as seen in chapter 3, the larger the ecclesiastical organization, the more restrictive is the primary degree curriculum in its framework, with a consequent resistance to curriculum change. Conversely, the more autonomous the teaching institution, the more it is open to local initiative and more direct implementation of change. Such external restrictions are noted more by faculty than by the church leaders, who typically put more distance between themselves and curriculum matters, preferring to allow the appointed faculty to take the responsibility for such issues, with general oversight rather than management by the church leadership. Since external engagement with curriculum is largely restricted to feedback and approval, there is virtually no effective forum for non-faculty to have a proactive voice in curriculum design or development.

In general, there was a high level of satisfaction expressed across the board with the *status quo*. However, within this, there was a frequently perceived need for a more comprehensive and accurate knowledge of stakeholders' needs and the need to go beyond the faculty to achieve more flexibility in the face of the strong received traditions of the institution which militate against change. Most faculty suggestions for improvement centred on the formal and effective inclusion of students and recent graduates in curriculum development deliberations, in order to achieve greater ownership of the course by students (who were commonly said to be resistant to imposed curriculum changes) and to hear more voices in the process. Other suggestions were the involvement of more external representatives in the process, which included more market research to learn of current needs and developments elsewhere, as well as more strategic partnerships with the churches. Church leaders' suggestions centred on improving the formal communication structures between colleges and stakeholders, which would give the stakeholders a more effectual voice in curriculum matters. The most commonly expressed element of dissatisfaction was the lack of any structured forum for stakeholder dialogue. Even among those who praised the dialogue with their colleges, the suggestion was made that such formal structures would provide not only better pastoral education information to the stakeholders (seen as valuable in itself) but also the opportunity to provide proactive input by the stakeholders into curriculum rather than simply being occasionally and informally reactive as is generally the case now. Other changes desired included a greater and more formal integration of college and church in areas of pastoral units and field education training, with a significant call for the more effective training of field education supervisors by the college to ensure appropriate reflective practices, and the inclusion of some student voice or advocate in curriculum committees to ensure consideration of student pastoral and vocational needs.

While there is a high level of satisfaction expressed in this regard by all groups of stakeholders, there is yet room for a more inclusive approach to the incorporation of key stakeholders. In particular, faculty need to have a mechanism by which they can be consistently informed by the contemporary needs and issues of both students and stakeholders, especially with regard to contemporary issues in education and ministry. This will involve strategic and effective faculty engagement with a wider sector of tertiary education, with current ministry practitioners and with current students or recent graduates. In particular, there is a strongly voiced desire for more effectual two-way communication between teaching institutions and stakeholders, on a formally structured and regular basis, offering proactive developmental opportunities rather than merely reactive assessments. Within the bureaucratic organizations of universities and the international hierarchies of some churches, there is limited if any opportunity for local forums, while the more loose regulatory nature of the major theological consortia allows for much more local initiative. In autonomous colleges, such expanded communication is probably more urgent, given their lack of organic support by larger bodies.

All categories of respondents engaged in the research presented a consistent picture of the centrality of the faculty in curriculum design and implementation, within the context of dialogue with significant stakeholders. Such dialogue needs to be genuinely two-way dialogue, incorporating all interested parties: faculty, stakeholders, students, graduates and yet-to-be students. The primary onus of and opportunity for curriculum development lie clearly with the teaching faculty. However, the warning needs to be heeded that a teaching institution that is not connected organically to its community runs the risk of delivering a curriculum which is a product of insular in-breeding and which may lapse into mere self-perpetuation with its ultimate implosion born of isolation and irrelevance.

3. Designing the Curriculum

An aim of transformative classroom teaching is to create students who are agents – in the classroom, in the world – who know how to learn and who take a role in their own transformation. Therefore, before proceeding to a detailed consideration of curriculum design, it is well to consider perhaps the most salient of all preliminary questions, namely, the issue of what graduate outcomes and attributes are meant to be produced. What should a theological graduate look like? Should the principal product be a well formed church leader with effective ministry capacities and leadership or a transformed life exhibiting commendable qualities and personal attributes? Most stakeholders ideally seek a balance of the two elements of leadership formation and personal development, but there is a growing realisation of the diversity of clientele and stakeholders in most institutions, with a resultant tension of needing to serve multiple masters and an emerging need for institutions (especially small colleges) to re-define their core objectives and to establish viable parameters of operation. As well as such vocational objectives, some schools are reviewing their philosophical objectives. For example, one college recently abandoned a unit in spirituality and made spirituality the centre-piece of the curriculum that was explored in every unit. Another workshop participant challenged us to think about transformative learning as a uniquely Australian experience and to consider how that curriculum might look. Similarly, others challenged us to consider how the curriculum might look if we took seriously the cultural backgrounds of Asian, Islander, Australian Aboriginal students. Such prior vocational and philosophical re-definition will have a significant impact on the design of the curriculum.

The main focus of the theological and Bible colleges is training for ministry, with personal growth viewed as a secondary and supporting element of that training. This ministry focus is achieved by formal curriculum shaping (in the choice and arrangement of units offered), encouraged in the various extra-curricular programs and structures of colleges, and strongly influenced by the lecturers, whose personal examples, teaching methods, relations and attitudes do much to affect the shape of the ministry persona resulting from the study program. A noted characteristic suggested by many graduate surveys is the relative weakness of theological programs in developing the students' capacity for effective teamwork. Among church leaders and more so among graduates, there is a growing requirement for graduates to be competent in areas of leadership, social engagement and holistic ministry. The role of transformative curriculum design is integral to the pursuit of such institutional objectives. For the purpose of this discussion, approaches to curriculum design can be understood as "traditional" or "transformative."

Traditional curriculum design is essentially content-centred and starts from the question, "What do you need to know?" As detailed in chapter 3, most theological courses present a first year of introductory overview units in the major sub-disciplines of scripture, theology, history and some combination of biblical languages, philosophy and practical ministry. Thus, in the case of a student going no further, a sound basis of a theologically informed person has been provided. Alternatively, a general "big picture" has been provided as a basis of a closer scrutiny of sections of that picture in later years, which comprise a set of advanced more specialised units, covering a selection of biblical books for in-depth exegetical study, a series of systematic theology units covering all the major Christian doctrines, and further history, philosophy and ministry units. A concentration in one or more of the sub-disciplines is considered a "major" study.

Transformative curriculum design is learner-centred and starts from the question, "Where are you?" To resume the theme presented in chapter 2, the first year starts from identifying the existing frameworks of commencing students and structures content to facilitate the continuous critical review of those frameworks as students encounter new theological knowledge. Advanced units of study continue and intensify this process with the objective of a holistic integration of units taught within the expanded or revised frameworks of the students, resulting in the articulation and/or implementation of a coherent theological world view. It is the role of curriculum to establish an operational framework for the attainment of such integration.

Chairs of academic committees were asked to indicate what they considered the most significant recent curriculum improvements in their schools. By far the main area of improvement has been the course structures and content. Within this category, the main trend has been to rationalisation of offerings, especially but not exclusively in the universities. There have been some reviews of course structure in terms of majors and minors, with further defining of streams within the degree to provide a clearer focus, and some significant reduction of the overall number of units offered with a greater degree of prescription and direction of learning pathways available to students. The aspects of perspectives and approaches were less frequently mentioned. The broadening of learning horizons was limited, with one university listing the initial exploration of dual degrees within its university and one college listing the use of special units delivered according to faculty research interest, especially by overseas visiting lecturers. There were several reports of improvements in terms of learning approaches. One reported the development of its own unique degree which allowed it to stress its focus on social engagement. One reported the development of a critical thinking unit as a first year unit and one reported the intentional attempt to integrate academic biblical study with practical field education. Two schools reported the strategic review of Learning Outcomes to establish Academic Links within units and to integrate the Learning Outcomes with a revised set of institutional Graduate Outcomes.

In the area of improvements still needed, there was, however, a shift in emphasis from content to approaches to learning, with numerous responses stressing this area. Several advocated the introduction into the formal degree structure of first year units to develop the necessary academic and critical thinking skills to facilitate effective theological study. Some suggested the development of more intentionally integrative units and the involvement of more than one teacher in a unit to provide greater expertise and wider perspectives. A couple of schools are considering the need to be more contemporary in learning styles, including the adoption of online learning and adapting practical ministry units to align with contemporary contexts. Another is planning to develop new Graduate Outcomes to inform the Learning Outcomes of all units. In general, the academic chairs' emphasis for future improvements is moving away from content revision to considerations of learning approaches.

Over all, the movement in curriculum design has been towards a rationalisation of awards with a higher degree of precision in offerings, with a consequent defining of streams and reduction in total units. This can be seen as a distinct moving away from a previously popular notion of being "all things to all people," with its unrealistic tendency to add more content by way of additional available elective units, which were often not viable because of small enrolments. The recent trend has been towards developing a clearer focus and greater definition of the study program, with a reduction in content coverage (apparently) available in a comprehensive array of units to a smaller number of units which can deliver a more cohesive overall course. Where there have been some additional units offered, this has generally been as a somewhat limited response to identified stakeholder needs. The move towards rationalisation has been accompanied by a somewhat tentative approach towards the enhancement of learning by means of some additional study or critical thinking units early in the course and by a more strategic approach in some cases to integrating explicit Learning Outcomes of Units with the overall desired institutional Graduate Outcomes. Given that Graduate Outcomes are typically expressed in terms of personal attributes, this explicit integration of institutional and unit outcomes seems to suggest a fertile field for development in considering transformative learning within the curriculum.

The previous statement is reinforced by the aspirational comments made by the respondents. There seems to be an acceptance of the need to reduce overall content in the quest to consolidate a more defined and more cohesive overall program of study. Even in the relatively small number of places where additional stakeholder-serving units are seen to be needed, the challenge is what to leave out of an already crowded curriculum. Rather than the traditional specific content focus in curriculum, the emerging dominant sentiment is the desire to develop more generic skills within students and to achieve greater integration within the overall learning agenda. The suggested means vary from expanding cross- disciplinary perspectives to providing skills support to first year students, from using multiple teachers in a unit to crafting strategic units to facilitate development, from responding to contemporary stakeholder needs to the intentional integration of Graduate and Learning Outcomes within unit documents and implementation. Yet all these means have the same end in view: a cohesive course of study and an integrated and holistically developed graduate student.

The desire for flexibility that was commonly expressed centred mainly on opening up course structures or core requirements to allow for more focus to be given to the interests of students and the expertise of faculty. This involved the scope to add more specialist units (*contra* the recent trend to pare down units) to allow faculty to use their special expertise across more than generic units, but more significantly, it referred to the desire to connect more effectively with students in their real context. The desire to foster deeper personal growth in students was the major reason underlying this aspect. "It would be good if our formal academic subjects could give space to allow more emphasis on individual Christian and spiritual formation."

If "Where are you?" is the primary guiding question for transformative curriculum design, then there needs to be a fundamental shift from starting from the teacher's interests and expertise to starting from a student-centred focus. It was frequently observed by students and graduates that often it was the lecturer's personal research interest that shaped the content of units, an approach which was usually typified by personal lecturer enthusiasm but not necessarily by equally passionate student engagement. While it is obvious (and desirable) that any lecturer is going to utilise personal research and prized content, the challenge of transformative teaching is to ensure the effectual connection of that knowledge with the location of the student and its contribution to the student's growth. It was noted in the workshop that student-centred learning is admirable, but there are lots of learning styles and personal backgrounds in one room.

This is the first challenge of transformative curriculum design: to create structured opportunities to identify and to utilise this variety. This will require due consideration of variations in cultural and generational comprehension and the implications for resources (eg time and work load for staff and students). Such considerations need to be sustained at all points of the curriculum: where it starts, how it proceeds, how it is best rounded off.

The commencing phase of any program needs urgent attention, as this is the stage where the overarching approach to study and development is established – and where most attrition among students is experienced. This is the period when the most intense challenges of a personal, intellectual and faith-based nature emerge. As reported in student surveys and focus groups, it is a time of considerable loneliness and, at times, a sense of pastoral isolation and spiritual inadequacy, exacerbated by the perception of the need to present as spiritually, socially and emotionally well adjusted at all times within the college context. It is the pivotal time for a student to appreciate the need for critical review rather than to be thrust into the pressured processes of mastering vast amounts of new data. It is the time for the facilitation of reflection and re-orientation, of induction into new ways of thinking and performing, of practising new academic and performative skills and developing new understandings. Yet the traditional approach to curriculum presents a student with a suite of survey units or other introductions encompassing a large volume of detailed knowledge to be digested in what is widely acknowledged to be a time-pressed situation. "Good" results are obtained by those students blessed with a capacity for accumulation and retention of detailed data. The typically crowded first-year curriculum is one of the main impediments to the establishment of a climate conducive to transformative learning.

A transformative first-year curriculum will put less focus on comprehensive content coverage and more focus on the strategic provision of opportunities for students to identify, articulate and critically review their personal frames of theological and biblical reference as a starting point for their further development or modification. To do this, students will need to be provided with the skills of such analysis and review. At the same time, this will allow teachers the opportunity to discern the variety of cultural and educational backgrounds and to accommodate the range of existent learning styles within the class, and it will serve to overcome some of their possibly erroneous assumptions concerning student motivations, aspirations and needs. The whole focus of at least a first semester of theological study will be changed from an overload of content, based on a notion of a class of "typical" students, commonly presented as discrete fields of knowledge with little if any integration, to an introduction to and practice of the needed process skills for theological thinking and critical review, supported by the provision of appropriate processing opportunities within a safe climate and adequate processing time. "Core" introductory subjects will be defined not by the classical scholarship of theological disciplines but by the process skills that are essential to developing a theologically articulate student. In short, at least the first semester of the curriculum will focus on situating the study in the context of the student's ongoing life experience and providing the necessary resources and skills for the student to proceed to integrate new theological knowledge into that ongoing life experience.

This change of first-year emphasis from much content delivery to more student-focused development will raise immediately the objection of loss of valued content and/or the need to add a further year to the course. This is the perennial "quantity vs quality" tension; however, as canvassed in chapter 2, the claims to identifying just what is foundational knowledge and to achieving an effective and comprehensive coverage of all necessary content by way of lecturer delivery in a crowded curriculum are dubious at best. If the theological undergraduate degree is seen as a part of a life-long journey (which began before college enrolment and will presumably continue beyond graduation), then it is essential that all partners in that stage of the journey know and appreciate the context of the bigger journey. In so doing, they will participate in the formal program as an integrated section of that journey, with no delusion as to the all-sufficiency of any one stage.

Of course there is more to the process than merely setting up the initial climate and skills for transformative learning. It needs to be constantly kept in mind that the mastery of biblical and theological knowledge is fundamental in the motivation of the students and the requirements of the stakeholders. Hence the classical corpus of theological knowledge will provide the substance of the ongoing curriculum. However, the means of presenting and processing that knowledge need to be matched to the principles of transformative learning, which impinges on curriculum considerations. It is not appropriate to follow an introductory semester of "transformative" learning with five crowded semesters of "didactic" delivery of content. The basic tension of *work load vs processing time* needs to be managed in curriculum design. This affects decisions such as the number of units that constitute a full load as well as the amount of content and the number and weight of learning and assessment tasks included in a particular unit. As students are introduced in a systematic way to the broad range of new knowledge, they will need to continue the *transformative processes* initiated in the early stages of the course: processes of analysis and interpretation, assimilation and accommodation, review and critique of personal frameworks, connecting with real-life experience (of themselves and of society), and progressive articulation of developing world views.

There is also the need to present a *holistic picture of theological knowledge*, which brings into question the whole issue of fields and majors. Some universities which house the theology degree within an Arts or Humanities faculty treat Theology as one field and so avoid the traditional separation into theological disciplines such as Old Testament, Systematic Theology, Church History, Philosophy etc. Yet even here, the idea of Theology as separate from, say, Literature or History or Science tends to establish a disconnection of disciplines rather than the integration of learning. A prevalent sentiment expressed by academic chairs was the desire to expand the intellectual and experiential horizons of students, which would include the intentional exposing of theology students to a broader suite of disciplines, especially philosophy, ethics and history. This would allow and encourage students "to see our own moment as one part of the whole of history." However, this sort of disconnection is commonly even more pronounced in theological colleges, with divisions (and, as not uncommonly reported, inconsistencies) between such clearly associated areas as biblical studies, theology, church history and philosophy, with an even greater gulf between the theoretical "academic" subjects and the pragmatic "practical" units. This sort of disconnection of studies into component parts is a major concern expressed by graduates and church leaders, which needs to be addressed as part of the overall transformative goal.

This need for greater cohesion of curriculum was particularly prominent in the observations of recent graduates, whose most common suggestions for the improvement in courses were in the area of curriculum content and management. Some suggested the inclusion of more specific ministry skills units to complement the strong theological base, with greater attention from the college faculty rather than leaving it to external supervisors, since students at times felt they were left to fend for themselves in confronting "life pastoral situations." Others called for a greater sense of curriculum management and co-ordination, including more effective inter-relation of units in the course. The other significant suggestion was for the more intentional and cohesive integration of college and local church in the overall training program, with more work done in and with the churches. One respondent summed up the thoughts of several in the following statement:

> There could be significant improvement in the matter of integrating the local church and the local pastor into your studies in a more effective way with more accountability. Theology is always in the context of the whole community, not just college. The college community is a bit contrived. A tertiary institution should also be dealing with not just the head and grades, but it should be more of an apprenticeship model, with on the job engagement. This is a big challenge, and it requires more mentoring.

The final stage of curriculum design consideration is the matter of how to round off an effective transformative learning program, which is just as vital as establishing the suitable starting point. The key word in this consideration is *integration*. Throughout the course of study, learners have been led through a process of continual encounter with and processing of new knowledge, incorporating regular personal reflection and critique. To complete this process, they will need to have a structured opportunity to formulate, articulate and where appropriate activate their developed and cohesive world view in relation to their own life situation. In this way, their total learning experience will be grounded in the reality of their life, it will serve to give more meaning to that life, and will provide a base for their ongoing development – a desired outcome expressed almost universally by all participants in the research. Transformative curriculum design will strategically provide such integrative opportunities.

If analysis, interpretation and reflection typified the developmental stages of transformative learning, then the final stage will be marked by synthesis, conceptual appropriation and active application. The curriculum will structure opportunities for students to produce their own syntheses of studies. For example, a study of the New Testament would not necessarily start in semester 1 with an exposition and a scholarly resolution of the Synoptic Problem, but may well have provision in semester 6 for students to develop their own construct of the problem and its resolution, in ways that are meaningful to them in their own context. Comparable exercises could apply in all other fields. Yet more significant than such sub-discipline studies are the possibilities for integrating the whole spectrum of studies. As acknowledged in the workshop, capstone units are an important aspect of transformative learning, especially when the student has a large hand in shaping that unit. Such individual units will allow the student to bring together the various strands of the study program in an integrated application to real life and in so doing will provide a vehicle for the articulation of an integrated, personally owned and dynamic world view which has resulted from the course of study. Wherever possible, opportunities for the active implementation of a program based on such personal development in some service provision are an excellent avenue for transformative action. While such implementation is obvious in practical ministry situations, it is also possible in other areas, with such things as group projects, teaching projects, social engagements and community-based projects. Biblical, theological, philosophical and historical units have just as much potential for active implementation as the more obvious practical ministry units. As the first semester de-emphasised new knowledge in favour of developmental processes, so too the final semester could well de-emphasise more new knowledge in favour of students' personalising the totality of their discovered knowledge.

4. Delivering the Curriculum

Of at least equal importance with curriculum design is the matter of curriculum delivery. It is commonly acknowledged that it is the quality of the interaction between teacher and learner that most profoundly influences all good education, a point voiced universally and enthusiastically in this particular research project. So too with transformative learning, the relation of teacher and learner is vital. As noted in the workshop, the teacher is neither the agent nor a guarantor of transformation, but is certainly a facilitator. So it is important to understand the nuances for transformative learning of the roles of teacher and learner and the methods of curriculum delivery which facilitate such desired transformative outcomes.

A common reservation expressed about student-centred transformative learning is the loss of the teacher's control of the educative experience. Within the research interviews, many teachers, students, graduates and stakeholders expressed the thought that the teacher is the professional who knows what is best for the delivery of the program. The high degree of trust afforded the teachers in matters of curriculum was impressive and widely held to be justified. An outstanding note within the interviews was the emphatic description of the centrality of the lecturer in the effective educative process, not only because of subject expertise, but more particularly because of the essential personhood of the lecturer. It is in light of such observations that the role of the teacher needs to be affirmed. Yet such affirmation does not exclude the refinement of that role as it seeks to enhance the quality of the educative process.

The most significant nuance in refining the role of the transformative teacher is not in terms of responsibility but in style. Even in student-centred transformative learning, the teacher remains the director of the process. The change comes in that the teacher does not have so much control over the *limits* of the knowledge communicated to the learner, since the teacher is not seen as the sole or even the main source of information. Rather, the teacher assumes the role of enabler and facilitator – as well as process controller. The teacher is there to structure knowledge, not to be a fount of information. This does not suggest that the teacher does not need to know the subject matter well. On the contrary, it calls for greater expertise in a wider range of pertinent knowledge, since the teacher's task is not to deliver a pre-determined and pre-limited set of information, but to be a manager of that quantity of information as well as the wide range of information that will potentially be accessed by the students. Creating and managing the processes by which the learners will access and process information become paramount in the transformative teacher's role. As well as expertise, the character of the teacher also features strongly in transformative learning. In terms of character, the "transformative" teacher presents as a model of formation: learned but co-learning, both with and from the students. Among other things, this will be manifest in the teacher's desire to develop an openness to learn from others (faculty, students, "outsiders") and to be prepared to change as required. Thus the learner will see the teacher as an embodied model of transformative learning.

The focus of transformative learning is on the learner. Therefore, the role of the learner needs attention. Since tertiary students in general, and theological students more significantly so than most undergraduates, are adult learners, they need to be able not only to connect their learning with their life, but also to take progressively increasing responsibility for the design and execution of their learning. Such an approach will create a greater sense of ownership and relevance of their studies. This is not to abandon students to their own ignorance, but it is an emphasis that will shape the direction provided by the teacher-facilitator working collaboratively with the student. One college has a policy of individual tailoring of the course of study to match a student's prior learning and desired post-study pathways, with regular monitoring of progress and amendments needed along the way, and the creation of learning tasks that will suit the individual. Reports from graduates and church leaders strongly endorsed the outcomes of this approach, in terms of both personal fulfilment and ministry readiness. It requires more intensive inter-personal relations between teachers and learners, but it exemplifies a fundamental tenet of transformative education: the investment in learner development not just knowledge transmission.

Of practical interest is the matter of teaching and learning methods that contribute to the facilitation of transformative outcomes. The key distinctive here is the shift in emphasis from *teaching* methods to *learning* methods. A summary of methods can be grouped under the headings of knowledge transmission, data processing and concept appropriation. In the primary domain of knowledge transmission, while the teacher remains a pivotal agent in the process, the role has changed. The classroom and the teacher need not be the sole or necessarily the major locale and source of information transmission, since there are many contemporary means of knowledge transmission, especially the multitudinous electronic resources available, that are more efficient and allow more legitimately educative learning to take priority in the classroom. The need to facilitate learners' access to knowledge beyond the classroom (including before, during and after the class meeting times) by contemporary communication means is simply a fact of modern educational life.

In light of the increased and rapid access to vast stores of information, the skills of processing that information assume heightened significance. This processing requires both analysis and evaluation, both of which require expert direction and effectual practice. The methods of data processing include discipline-specific research and analysis skills and vocational or performative applications and critique. The statements of systematic theology are examined within the historical context of their originators and the philological and philosophical systems in which they were composed. It is not just the content that is analysed, but also the contingent factors which have led to the texts. Real-life ministry scenarios (actual or simulated) and observations are analysed and evaluated. Students are encouraged to present arguments about causes and consequences on the basis of demonstrable evidence and logical development rather than simply present the formulated conclusions of scholars or lecturers. Some criticism was levelled by church leaders at graduates who "presented as summaries of others" at the end of their study. Mastery of critical analytical argument leads the learner to clearly formed evaluations of ideas, events and practices. The emphasis is always on the development of research and reporting skills, how to access and evaluate information, and ultimately a connection to personal contexts, in both doctrinal expressions and performative situations.

Transformative learning will be seen to have taken place when the learner has demonstrated a significant shift in perspective, which may be a progressive development or a radical change. In any case, learning methods that encourage the personal appropriation of vital concepts in shaping a coherent theological world view need to be intentionally cultivated if such a demonstration is to be enabled. Methods that promote skills development, proceed to critical and reflective processing of content in various areas, and lead on to educing overarching principles of understanding and living will be more likely to facilitate the personal appropriation of concepts that typifies integrative learning. In line with previous statements about curriculum structure and design, the delivery methods need to be consistently connected with the learners' situation. Such obvious but rare things as the need to identify and utilise various learning styles within a class are a starting point. During the delivery of the course, there needs to be the consistent provision of authentic opportunities for critical review of held positions and formulation of learners' "owned" positions. Such opportunities should include the recognition of the need for the "deformation" of some prior positions, since many learners will have barriers of fear, prejudice or false humility that resist integration in learning. Each person in the learning community potentially holds or is held by such "distorting perspectives" that can change and be healed through learning. Towards the end of a course, there is the vital need for students to reach their own holistic and synthesising integration, by means of some significant capstone exercise. Finally, for integrative learning to be concretely actualised, there needs to be opportunity for some genuine enactment of the perspectives attained. While such opportunities may involve a host of possible classroom delivery or field-based action programs, they must include the freedom for a student to express authentically and without recrimination the holistic concepts that have been personally appropriated.

An interesting note has emerged from various items in the research with regard to the role of community in transformative education. Some colleges hold strongly to the philosophy that it is in the residential community of a theological campus that transformation occurs most effectively, especially within the informal co-curricular activities of the campus. However, most students taking a theology degree do not experience such residential life and even among some who do, the perception is of a sometimes contrived college community, which can be remote from other significant elements of life. Yet most students spoke warmly of the "theological community" of which they were a part, a community defined not so much by local residence but more by a sense of theological cohort. While transformative learning can arise from any number of disorienting events out of which arises critical reflection that can lead to perspective transformation, it was generally recognized that transformative learning in a theological education context is often facilitated by interpersonal relationships built within a community of trust. The workshop noted that this applies to online learning just as much as to classroom-based learning, with many successful accounts offered of the formation of strong on-line communities, typically generated by a dedicated distance education coordinator with whom the students were able to build a long-term relationship. As a co-curricular element of transformative learning, the building of a conducive theological community was seen to have a vital role to play. There is then a need for the climate in which the formal curriculum is delivered to be consistent with the co- curricular community climate, or else a deleterious dissonance will result.

There is one final evident challenge: how do we *assess* integrative learning within a typical semester structure, especially since such learning is clearly a cumulative process? As well, the very intangibility of personal formation – let alone transformation – defies any notion of quantifiability. This presented as a significant issue at the workshop as well as in the interviews, with concern expressed that transformative learning is incapable of measurement, with significance for assessment. To an educational mindset (among both educators and students) that consistently commodifies learning in terms of percentages and grades, it seems impractical to suggest any kind of measurement of integration, yet without such "results," the whole undertaking seems at risk of losing credibility. There is therefore a need to review those transformative outcomes that are measurable, such as the degree to which a student's perspectives have been expanded and applied, via skills of critical reflection, identification of issues, etc, which are progressively facilitated throughout the course. The aspect of the extent of personal difference undergone by a student may not be measurable (or may not need to be measured) but there should be indicators that emerge from the development of specified skills such as critical reflection that typically contribute to such difference. Thus some legitimate markers of transformative development can be generated. There may also be a case for transforming the standard numeric (or grade) approach to registering the outcomes of an educative process. While the obsession with numerical results may well be challenged, that does not mean that integrative attainment may not be valued and legitimately registered. Items such as progressive individual interviews, students' personal documentation, journals and portfolios, as well as the carefully constructed learning tasks within the formal curriculum, can be used to compile a cumulative register of development which can demonstrate to a third party that formative and transformative learning has taken place. Significantly, it was observed at the workshop that of the different parties that need this feedback on the transformative nature of the educational process (external accrediting bodies, lecturer assessments of students, students' self-understanding), it is the student who most benefits from the insight that transformational learning has taken place. While this aspect may not be subject to precise measurement, it is surely subject to demonstration and thus legitimate validation. This will require a clear definition of integration, the establishment of appropriate criteria or markers of integration, and the observation of the articulation and enactment of the personally integrated perspective. Such things are attainable and demonstrable, even if not numerically measurable.

5. Results of a Transformative Curriculum

When various stakeholders' "wish lists" for institutional development were collated, three areas emerged most clearly. The first area was that of curriculum, with an oft-expressed desire for a greater sense of curriculum management and co-ordination, including more effective inter-relation of units in the course. This extended to a desire for practical field education to be enhanced by the establishment of more efficient and more accountable supervisor training and the development and coordination of authentic field experiences, critical reflection and practical improvement processes. These elements were associated with the acknowledgement of the need for learning to constitute an authentic experience for the student, for theological teaching to connect with the real life of the students in some genuine way, and for students to discover rather than merely to receive theological truths. The second area was the enhancement of functional ministry capacity, to include effective experience in a wider range of ministerial duties, learning how to master not only time and program management but also people management, and the ability to assess ministry and personal practices in terms of biblical and theological processes. This could be assisted by incorporating more intentional and cohesive integration of college and local church in the overall training program, with more work done in and with the churches and more experimental and creative approaches to liturgy to facilitate a more contemporary expression of church worship. There was a strong desire expressed for the integration of a theological world view and contemporary social action. The third aspirational area was the need for theological education to be holistic and integrated rather than teaching just theological data. This need was commonly expressed in more innovative colleges, is emerging in universities, and remains somewhat cautiously approached in more traditional colleges. This requires the personal and strategic integration of cognitive, practical and affective elements of the theological development of the students, including those students who are not specifically ordination candidates. It involves the development of character and values as well as knowledge.

Put simply, there are three levels of experiential application which may be used to guide the teacher in the development, design and delivery of integrative transformational curriculum. At the *intellectual* level, there is the need to integrate learnings with learnings. That is, the student needs to have guidance in how to integrate various learnings across the curriculum and structured opportunities for doing so. The "silos" of compartmentalised subjects need to be blended together in a holistic way so the student may be allowed to "make sense of it all" rather than simply have a sound knowledge of the disparate disciplines. This may involve curriculum re-design or team teaching or other creative approaches, but when the focus is put on a student's holistic development, content cohesion is more likely to be a factor. At the *vocational* level, there is the need to integrate learning with life and work. The nexus between underlying principles and operational practices needs to be clearly understood and activated. The commonly lamented disconnection between theoretical learning and vocational skills and inter-personal relations is not limited to theological education, but an intentional and strategic focus on integrative transformational learning will ideally express itself in a congruence of learning and life, where principles and practices cohere. Finally, at the deeply *personal* level, integrative learning will involve the need to integrate learning, life and a coherent world view, whereby all of a person's life – the theory, the praxis, the values and the relationships – will be shaped around a coherent central and dominant life principle. While not restricting the range of different roles a person may be called upon to enact, such a coherent integration will dispel variability of character, fragmentation of identity and incongruity in life. The ideal result of an effectively designed and skilfully delivered transformative curriculum will be hopefully a well-formed, sometimes even a transformed, but always a truly integrated graduate.

7 | THE CURRENT STATE OF PLAY

SOME GOOD EXAMPLES

1. Who Does What?

The research has focused on listening to a multitude of voices to discern what is understood and desired in the areas of student life experience and transformative ideals. At the same time, it has also uncovered many good examples of such elements currently in play, even though at times the conceptual framework for them has not necessarily been specifically articulated. These examples occur at the levels of both principles undergirding the delivery of theological education and practices which are employed in the actual design and delivery of the curriculum. While this account of the research has often avoided the naming of specific institutions so far, it seems appropriate in this chapter to acknowledge at least some of the places where these positive principles and practices are operating, not so much for the sake of commendation (though that may well be in order), but rather to facilitate ongoing dialogue among partners who might find such dialogue helpful. The illustrations that follow, of course, are not meant to be exhaustive, but they are indicative of some of the significant observations made during the overall investigation.

2. Good Principles

The first notable principle for the generation of a cohesive program of teaching and learning is that of *philosophical coherence* of the institution. A number of colleges attributed their successful teaching of an integrated world view to such a coherence embodied primarily in the faculty and infused into the students. That is, the philosophical ethos of the curriculum stems from a consistent and coherent hermeneutical, ecclesiastical and overarching world view held and promoted by the faculty. In the case of Moore Theological College, this was managed by the staff selection policy, with all teaching appointments coming from their own graduates, thus ensuring a continuity of the institutional philosophy, albeit at an acknowledged cost of some lack of openness to new traditions. In Christian Heritage College, *Christian Worldview* was placed as a core unit which laid the basis of later philosophical teaching. In Sydney Missionary and Bible College (as in several other places), an explicit commitment to an evangelical tradition and the priority of the Bible as transformative pervaded all teaching and community life in the college. In Nazarene Theological College, the faculty commitment to the Wesleyan ideal of all theology being practical theology characterised the teaching of all units. Negatively, there were some (few) instances noted where such congruence among faculty was noticeably absent, with a consequently detrimental and fragmenting impact on students. In general, there was a strong indication that the consistent, coherent and explicit philosophical approach to teaching, learning and curriculum design and delivery was an important element in achieving successful integration in learning. Associated and to a large degree shaped by such a philosophical commitment was the relatively recent focus on unit outlines which have clearly defined learning outcomes, including practical and/or personal applications which stem from and are associated with the explicit philosophy of the institution. The formulation of such clear learning outcomes led on to learning and assessment tasks which featured the philosophical "So what?" type questions.

A second and associated principle that promotes coherent and formative outcomes is that of clearly *defining the institutional purpose*. Since most theological degree providers are effectively quite small numerically, they cannot realistically attempt to be "all things to all people." Even in the public universities, where service provision of theological units is sometimes prominent, the actual Theology degree cohort is small, with university deans and heads of school often noting the small class size of specialist classes which are often the subject of rationalising scrutiny. So, in order to do a job well, it seems necessary to define precisely and realistically just what that job is. Colleges where such definition is in place report much more satisfactory and coherent outcomes. Ridley Melbourne has strategically designed its learning pathways and limited its unit offerings to ensure a ministry focus, a policy that has carried over to its extra-curricular programs and guest speakers as well. While this limits the elective offerings available, it marks a clear line of development that features in all college activity. The Adelaide College of Divinity Bachelor of Ministry degree (largely delivered through the Uniting College for Leadership & Theology) is based on a philosophy of practical ministry preparation and engagement. "Pedagogically, the BMin places the learner, the learner's ministry context and the practice of ministry at the centre and introduces theology progressively into this nexus, emphasising hand-on or experiential learning."[1] The teaching faculty have been strategically appointed to promote such a commitment, which is well known and endorsed by all parties. Whitley College places an emphasis on what it means to be Christian and church in the unique context of Australia, and to reflect theologically on this in conversation with Australian cultural forms (essentially non-theological forms), using methods that see culture and experience as theological sources in conversation with Scripture and tradition.[2] These are a few of the institutions that have defined their focus and reports of stakeholders indicate a high degree of integrated world view identity in graduates.

The third principle that has been identified is the emerging emphasis being placed on *locating theological education in the context of community engagement*. Interestingly, it is the universities which are leading in this area, although some independent colleges are also developing this concept. Australian Catholic University has recently developed a university-wide innovation that is still a work in progress, namely, the incorporation of a core unit *Community Engagement and Transformation*. Every enrolled student will undertake a supervised community placement, which may be in settings such as a church, a youth program, an aged care facility, a refugee centre and so on. This development has emerged partly from the Catholic ethos of the university's mission and partly from the identified strengths of other disciplines such as education and nursing. A similar concept, though not as well developed yet, is expressed in Murdoch

---

1   Adelaide College of Divinity, "Application for Accreditation: Attachment 2.3a" (2010), 1.
2   Darren Cronshaw, "Australian reenvisioning of theological education: In step with the Spirit?" *Australian eJournal of Theology* 18:3 (December 2011), 233-34.

University's *Work Integrated Learning*. While philosophically driven as a part of the universities' charter, and as yet still early in development, these units are an explicit recognition of the value of grounding academic programs in a real world context, not as an extra-curricular adjunct but as an integral part of the academic program itself. Alphacrucis College's defined Social Engagement Stream, with its mandated community engagement, concretises this principle. While theological colleges often incorporate field work for ministry candidates alongside the formal curriculum (or to a limited extent within the electives of the curriculum), Alphacrucis College has strategically committed to social engagement and some universities are also starting to incorporate into the overall university charter the areas of community engagement and integrated experiential learning.

The fourth principle is not totally distinct from the previous one, namely, *intentionally connecting with the students' life experience*. As has already been reported, very little is done in this regard in theological institutions. However, one emerging area is perhaps showing the value of making more concerted efforts here. For nearly twenty years, some colleges have offered theological degrees in Chinese or Korean language medium, to connect with the increasing Asian Christian population. However, more recent efforts have sought to express the education in terms of the cultural forms of the student sector. Whitley College has a large *TransFormation* program, which brings creative forms of theological education to Non-English Speaking Background or refugee people. In several other colleges, there have been a number of tentative attempts to teach some units beyond the college walls, for example by offering some units *in situ* in Aboriginal settings. More systematically, Alphacrucis College has an intentional policy of scaffolded learning, which begins from the student's prior experiences and understandings and grows upon such a foundation. However, while in many colleges such a principle is generally viewed as desirable, there remains little convincing evidence of its effectual implementation.

The fifth principle embodies a quite commonly expressed concern, namely, *proactive consultation with stakeholders*. Many stakeholders are concerned at their lack of opportunity to have a formative voice in curriculum development; many faculty speak of the need for stakeholders to be educated in the realities of theological education; some institutions are actually managing worthwhile dialogue between interested parties.

Australian College of Theology conducts a regular national Consortium Conference which engages with college principals and heads of college councils for communicating and developing both administrative and pedagogical processes. Adelaide's Uniting College for Leadership & Theology indicated a significant involvement of stakeholders in curriculum shaping, in a total curriculum review and implementation. The Principal's acknowledgement that he was the main driver of the reforms was supplemented by the comments offered by the church's ministerial placement officer, who related the involvement of a church-appointed review team including the Principal, thus establishing an effective partnership of church and college in the reform process. At Sydney Missionary and Bible College, a major missions agency state director described the system of annual meetings of missions personnel with college faculty to discuss issues pertinent to graduates and to improve the shape of missions units, with encouragingly satisfactory outcomes. The role of a regular Student Representative on the Academic Board at Melbourne's Catholic Theological College was reported by the representative as an effective means of providing a student perspective on such things as the impact of proposed revisions and work load. Most institutions reported merely *ad hoc* arrangements or, more typically, simply occasional personal conversations as the means of stakeholder connection. However, there are some instances where such consultative arrangements are more structurally systematic and more effectual in curriculum development.

The remaining principles are more to do with faculty functions. Principle number six is to incorporate the *concept of deep learning* in all learning and assessment tasks. Charles De Jongh of Malyon College has analysed this concept, showing that deep learning is concerned with the quality of the relationship between the learner and the object of learning. The learner makes a choice with respect to an approach influenced by an internal (personal) motivation and an external (learning environment) impetus. It is essentially motivated from within the learner and results in learning that has deep consequences and significance. The process is internal: the students are concerned with integrating the new material with their personal experiences, knowledge and interests. It embraces a sense of the student's *intention* in taking up a learning task as well as *how* he/she goes about the task (processing it). A key motivation is the belief that the studies are an opportunity to learn about reality and to develop one's way of thinking about reality.[3]

The seventh and final principle is perhaps more of an ideal aspiration, but it bears noting, namely, the *expansion of faculty horizons*. Some are deliberately working on the enhancement of pedagogical perspectives. Brisbane College of Theology had a system of encouraging its faculty to undertake a Graduate Certificate in Higher Education, a practice elevated to a requirement for all Australian Catholic University new staff. Such a policy was supported by several at the recent workshop, with particular application to newly appointed academic staff. Tabor Victoria has instituted a process where, at each Academic Board meetings, one of the four Heads of School brings a one hour presentation to the Board on how transformative learning is being implemented in their school. Similar faculty processing is envisaged at United Faculty of Theology and Catholic Institute of Sydney. Numerous faculty in many institutions are undertaking broader higher studies (both theological and non-theological) at secular universities in order to expand their own world views, rather than rely on their established theological education which may well be dated (to some degree) or limited (to a particular tradition). Active conference involvement, international and inter-denominational connections, wider fields of study and research are evident in many ways, but even more can be done to expand this approach from the general base of individual initiative to institutional encouragement and facilitation.

3. Good Practices

It has been both informative and encouraging to note the wide range of potentially transformative practices being progressively implemented in a variety of teaching settings. While such practices seem to be generally driven intuitively as an outcome of individual teachers' initiative rather than as a systematic and strategic approach by the institution, their growing presence is symptomatic of an impulse in contemporary theological education in Australia. Because of this generally unstructured approach, it is not easy to categorise the practices, but for purposes of this analytical

---

3   *Transforming Theology Newsletter*, Issue 5 (January 2012): 1. See also chapter 2.
    Dr De Jongh's Doctor of Education thesis is entitled "Theories of Multiple Intelligences and Learning Assessment for Deep Learning in Higher Education" (University of Johannesburg, 2010).

report, they can conveniently be arranged under the headings of curriculum design and teaching/learning methods, both of which are integral to the attainment of transformative goals.

*(a) **Curriculum Design***

The first and most wide-spread emerging practice in curriculum design aimed at integrative ends is the incorporation of special introductory units designed to facilitate effective learning rather than to introduce students immediately and systematically to classical theological content. These units have one of two foci (which are not necessarily mutually exclusive): study skills or world view. Such units de-emphasise specific content and focus on a broad spectrum of skills or world view issues. The study skills units are geared to practising the analytical and processing skills of various aspects of theological inquiry and typically include materials from all (or at least many) of the traditional sub-disciplines of theology. Commonly delivered by a team of teachers, such units seek to introduce theological studies as a less fragmented field of inquiry and learning and to equip learners with the tools for deep learning as they engage the later and more detailed content of theology. Murdoch University has a core introductory unit *Thinking Theology* which offers students "an opportunity to encounter the various disciplines within Theology that are taught here in the Theology Program and to discover ways in which they all contribute to the work of theological studies … taught by all the members of the academic staff."[4] The unit takes a centralising theme of the images of God as discerned in the various fields of biblical, theological, historical and practical expressions, and in so doing sets up a coherent frame of reference as well as the tools for analysis. Thus it intentionally provides a common base of theological understanding to balance prior experience, wherein the focus is on what are the specific ways in which each topic transforms the student's theology and relationship to God. Whitley College has a not dissimilar unit *Beginning Theological Studies* which incorporates a series of individual journal exercises, a variety of primary document analyses and a significant essay as students explore the means of processing theological thinking. As a part of the review of their Philosophy offerings, Catholic Theological

---

4   Murdoch University, THE107 Thinking Theology: Internal and External Unit Information and Learning Guide, 1.

College has implemented an introductory credit unit *Analytical Skills* which incorporates critical thinking, logic and academic skills. There is a discernible trend towards including such skills units as a core introductory component of a theological degree, in a strategic bid to develop more critical and expert processing of theological knowledge. In some significant ways, this is changing the focus of introductory study units from comprehensive surveys of content to the setting up of a base of deeper and more integrated learning.

The other objective of special introductory units is that of establishing a philosophical or hermeneutical base on which to ground the course of studies. Sydney Missionary and Bible College has a Core First Year unit *Thinking Theologically*, which is designed to de-construct students' assumptions and to develop an openness to theological processes in five fields (biblical, systematic, etc), not just one theological model. Tabor Adelaide has recently introduced a new Core Unit *Christians in a Multicultural World*, designed to encourage students to engage, from the beginning of their studies, the cultural dimensions of the ministry, theology and culture dialogue in which they are now participants. Christian Heritage College has introduced a core unit *Christian Worldview* which sits a little later in the course, but which has a similar objective. The placing of such philosophical units at or near the beginning of the course, especially when in conjunction with specific skills elements, establishes a sound platform for the facilitation of cohesive and integrated learning. Such integration can then be developed in terms of both avoiding the common fragmentation of theological sub-disciplines and reviewing and potentially transforming the personal philosophical and world view development of individual students.

A similar strategy of incorporating potentially transformative units within the degree has led some colleges to develop more such units at advanced levels as well as the introductory ones. While the practice occurs to a limited and unstructured way in such units as Australian College of Theology's *Guided Spiritual Formation*, it is more clearly developed and structured – and is particularly prominent – in some Pentecostal colleges. Tabor Adelaide's core unit *Theology and Spiritual Formation* is designed strategically to help students to process their own theology and spirituality and personality. The unit is staged over the three years of the degree and includes components in each semester drawn from a wide range of well structured and delivered Spiritual Formation Opportunities. These elements are specifically not academically, research or skills focused, but reflective in nature with an emphasis on facilitating individual reviews and charting of progress. The unit is graded on a set of qualitative criteria rather than a numerical percentage basis and forms a part of the overall credit for the degree. Tabor Victoria has developed a one-semester advanced unit called *Theological and Spiritual Formation* which, while introducing students to several approaches to theological, missiological and spiritual formation, puts an emphasis on the students' theological practice of such discerned principles and their reflection upon their practical implementation. Guided throughout by one well chosen key text book, the students are required to engage critically with that book, apply selected principles for personal use and active implementation throughout the semester, and critically review their progress in the semester. Assessment criteria are in place to ensure that it is the quality of the process that is evaluated, not the spiritual outcome itself. While the mere presence of such units does not guarantee personal formation – let alone transformation – the well structured and challenging nature of the units, with clear qualitative criteria of assessment, puts in place an effective element for the promotion and facilitation of such development.

While it has been widely reported that strategic connections with students' prior experience are quite limited, there were some specific examples of where the actual unit design and content has been amended to suit the prior experience of incoming students. Several colleges reported changing specific study topics in a unit to match them with students' backgrounds or ambitions. Vose Seminary noted the changing demographic profile of students taking the unit *Introduction to Ministry Formation*. Whereas previously, most students had been in the age bracket of 30-40 and had had considerable lay ministry experience, recently this had changed to a more youthful and more youth-oriented intake, which led the teacher to change the entire unit content, while maintaining the same syllabus document, to match the new demographic. At the same college, provision has been made for Non-English Speaking Background students to use the Bible in their own language for exegesis and to draw classroom comparisons with English versions, a practice which has added a new dimension to textual study for the native English speakers in the class as well.

This kind of initiative is once again generally a case of individual teacher initiative, but it is suggestive of creative practices which connect with a student's life experience and which thereby advance that life experience.

A more course-wide approach to connecting studies with students' individual backgrounds and aspirations is also emerging, albeit in relatively smaller institutions or with smaller groups within the overall student body. This is particularly noticeable in those institutions which have strategically articulated their institutional purpose and seek intentionally to match courses with students in order to fulfil that declared purpose. As noted earlier, Ridley Melbourne tailors its courses to match its pastoral training goal and establishes co-curricular groups of like-minded students, attached to a faculty member, to supplement their courses. The Uniting College for Leadership & Theology, with a similar purpose of producing reflective ministry practitioners, has a system of personal preliminary interviews with students to discern backgrounds and ministry goals and to plan an individual course of study to connect the two. For example, while preaching is normally a core requirement, if a prospective student has either a demonstrably effective background in preaching or has a vocational goal which does not need preaching, then an alternative is arranged. This is not just a case of granting credit for prior learning and thus shortening the course, but rather it is a matter of course planning to connect with actual experience, either past or projected. Throughout the course, students are matched with a particular faculty member who manages the progress of the course, with adjustments made as needed with changes of experience or objectives, with encouragement to experimentation and individual creativity in ministry, and with strategic placement and support in a field placement. Such an approach is obviously more manageable with a small cohort of students and is applied mainly with a denomination's approved candidates for ministry rather than with all students enrolled in a course. It is also noteworthy that it operates more successfully in those schools which have a defined and limited institutional purpose. However, the notion of knowing where students are coming from and where they aim to go as a consideration in the planning of course structures is well worth taking seriously. In general, the degree cohorts in Theology are not so large as to make such individual curriculum management untenable, if schools are willing to engage all faculty in the process rather than just the registrarial personnel.

The inclusion of potentially transformative units at strategic points within the degree structure and the matching of individual students' situations with course delivery and progressions are occasionally intentionally consummated by the use of capstone or other intentionally integrative units in the final stages of the course. However, while the workshop agreed that capstone units are an important aspect of transformative learning, there is no evidence to suggest their widespread use in undergraduate studies. Australian Lutheran College has an interesting Faith Life Program which progressively journeys with a student through the whole course, with increasing reflection, personal integration and accountability towards the end of the program. However, while this program has much inherently transformative value, it is limited to ordination candidates and is implemented as an extra-curricular component only. There were only few examples of such elements being programmatically included in the formal curriculum, but where they were, it was with enthusiastic endorsement of a strong integration of theology and continuing life and profession. Generally, these were taken by way of an elective Guided Independent Study unit, initiated by the student. One Sydney Missionary and Bible College graduate described how the third year integrative project had allowed him to establish an integration of the sacred and the secular in regard to his prior and ongoing profession, the real purpose in his coming to college, which had eventuated in his particular ministry beyond college. A Nazarene Theological College graduate particularly noted the nexus of theology and his secular specialist teaching profession, which provided a new framework to interact with his students. The innovative Bachelor of Ministry of Adelaide College of Divinity quite intentionally included a number of such independent and supervised Guided Studies in the final year as well as two *Integrative Ministry Practice* units. In these units, an attempt is made to model the process of transformative integration and so the focus is on the processes of inquiry and learning with the incorporation of significant journaling and critical personal reflection. So, although few, such capstone study opportunities were highly valued. The results of such units were strongly affirmed by recent graduates as having contributed to their overall frame of reference and their capacity to understand and to articulate their sense of ministry and personal identity.

A final comment on curriculum design is warranted with regard to the increasingly significant field of online or distance learning. Apart from considerations of philosophy and methods of delivery, the very question of online curriculum design has not been given much attention, although it is needed. It is virtually universally accepted that online education is not simply a matter of loading classroom-based lecture content onto a website but that a quite distinct pedagogy is required. This has significant curriculum ramifications, since the whole concept of an online community needs to be ensconced within the design of the course. Theological education involves more than cognitive learning: it also involves "affective" learning and practical elements. Balancing these various elements within the curriculum is a particular challenge for online theological learning. It was generally recognized at the workshop that transformative learning in a theological education context is often facilitated by interpersonal relationships built within a community of trust. It is in this area of establishing a trusting community that curriculum has a role to play. Important factors in building such a community included the early introduction of "getting to know you" kinds of forums in each unit and the need to structure into all units the opportunity for a student to take a much more central and interactive part in the learning process. Effectual learning also includes the sequencing of multi-learner activities rather than a reliance on the standard (and isolating) individual learning tasks. That is, online learning curriculum needs to structure ways in which learners are led beyond mere content knowledge and mastery to an engagement with their individual context and the community of co-learners. Ways in which some online providers have been successful include creating a safe, welcoming and hospitable environment; developing various forms of interaction in online learning; the sequencing of learning activities which involve groups of learners interacting within a structured set of authentic collaborative activities; giving greater attention to the relational and affective components of instruction; and deliberately structuring learning to include the affective as well as cognitive domains. In general, effective online learning design has developed the sense of community as a formative dimension and, while still transmitting coherent content, it does so in ways that strategically and more intentionally embrace the aspects of context and activity rather than simply content and absorption.

(b) Teaching and Learning Methods
Throughout the research visits and interviews, there were numerous examples noted of effective teaching methods which generate opportunities

for students to reflect critically on their own perspectives of understanding and values and to process their learning with reference to their own life experience beyond the classroom. While varied in nature and clearly emanating from the individual teachers' personal teaching styles, what they all have in common is their focus on the learner's learning rather than the teacher's teaching. As with the account of curriculum design practices above, this section offers a review of some of these teaching/learning methods. This review is not meant as an exhaustive list, not necessarily as a recommended list, but as a sample of some methods which seem well suited to the attainment of transformative goals by connecting with the life situation of the learner and in so doing facilitating the learner's integrated development or modification of personal perspectives.

Two pre-class considerations for integrative learning are common. First, as previously noted, a high work load is seen as a hindering factor for transformative learning. Schools which have incorporated special integrative and skills units into the beginning stages of a course recognise this and have consequently reduced the amount of classical knowledge content encountered in the first year. Instead, they focus on personal reflection, journaling and life applications rather than the systematic coverage of the biblical, theological and historical fields. Second, the setting of a text to facilitate the way students "read their worlds" also contributes to transforming perspectives. Tabor Victoria's *Theological and Spiritual Formation* unit has one set text which establishes paradigms of spiritual exploration and analysis framed around the title's centralising concept of being "Conformed in His Image." This becomes the platform for the semester's work, which requires learners to locate themselves squarely within the paradigms presented. Sydney Missionary and Bible College has a Church History text *Hitting the Holy Road* which provides a "guided tour of Christian history from the Early Church to the Reformation." The book is written in a way that connects the analysis of historical events with a contemporary tourist's personal encounter with the places and monuments of that history, thus drawing the readers into more of a living engagement with the history. The setting of such guiding texts not only provides a compendium of factual content but it also guides the reader in how to read the world of that content.

Two other general approaches are quite widely reported as methods of integrative learning. Contextual framing, with its explicit connection of each lesson to the wider goals of the course and other elements in the unit, is an effective cohering practice. With such framing, no unit is presented in isolation from its broader context and hence cohesion rather than fragmentation of learning is more likely to be achieved. As well, practices which consistently include learner engagement are becoming increasingly employed. The use of work-related or real-life issues, existent dilemmas or problems and contemporary social elements, is becoming more prevalent. The provision of regular opportunities for students to summarise succinctly their evolving perspectives serves a strongly formative and integrative function.

Several schools are intentionally employing graduated learning techniques. Murdoch University has a strategy of deliberately graduated teaching across the year levels. In first year units, there are mainly lectures and tutorials, with the emphasis on giving content.

Advanced units are based around student groups, with more focus on student input and discussion. Late third and fourth year units are predominantly seminars. That is, across the four years of the degree, students are required to assume progressively more responsibility for their studies. The scaffolded learning used at Alphacrucis is another version of such graduated methods. At Ridley Melbourne, the emphasis in the early stage of the course is on the delivery of content. Later, it is more process driven, with more collaboration with students and progressively more student control of the learning process. While these individual examples are different from those which reduce early content in favour of skills and world view units, they are not necessarily incompatible, as the underlying concept of progressively increasing the learner's responsibility for learning is equally applicable.

The issue of classroom relationships has been widely cited by various research respondents as a major facilitator of potentially transformative learning in the creation of a learning atmosphere of safety, trust and open inquiry. This was commonly expressed in the faculty interviews and strongly so in the focus groups of current students. Many students spoke of the positive transformative effect of small group tutorials or other discussion forums which provided structured opportunities for sharing personal stories which engendered a non- judgemental critique of variant views. In the process, students noted that they learned from one another as well as from the teacher, that their horizons of understanding were significantly expanded and, importantly, that they grew in tolerance, respect and sensitivity towards others' views, even if they did not embrace them. As one member of a focus group summed it up:

> There needs to be a willingness for people to listen to other people's stories. If we are being trained as people enablers/helpers, is there something we should be doing to invite people to share real stories without being judged or put down? If we are to be real, genuine people helpers, we need to be able to share our story at a very deep level because it's going to be our stories that affect other relationships with people in our ministries.

The relationship between teacher and learners is important to recognize and to cultivate, since it is in this relationship that much good – or much harm – will be done to the cause of personal engagement with the subject under study. Vose Seminary's adoption of the "Affirm-Stretch-Re-affirm" cycle exemplifies an intentionally transformative facilitation. There was widespread affirmation across the schools of such attitudes of the teachers to student inquiry, with numerous positive comments on their openness to discussion and questioning of views and the creation of an atmosphere which included challenges to views and practices within a climate of respect and generosity of spirit.

The "teacher-learner" relationship is not the only relational consideration within the classroom. There is also the "learner-learner" relationship which can be productively cultivated. Ridley Melbourne is piloting a scheme of Collaborative Learning, which is seen as a very important development, incorporating both individual and group learning with a greatly increased capacity to be transformational. This element of collaborative peer learning is significant for the development of team working capacity, a noted weakness reported in many recent graduate surveys. The use of group projects in many colleges, especially at advanced levels, is increasing as this outcome is actively pursued. When the group also assumes significant responsibility for determining the topic and parameters of activity and learning, then transformative outcomes are more likely. A warning is sounded here, however, as such processes require very clear articulation of expectations and criteria of performance, assessment and other operational details to ensure the project retains focus and legitimacy and does not descend into individual fragmentation or irrelevancy (or worse).

A less common consideration, but one which can possibly be enhanced as a potentially integrating strategy, is the "teacher-teacher" relationship. The principle of institutional coherence has been treated earlier, but in the classroom dynamic, it has an opportunity to be overtly manifest. This does not mean that all teachers must have identical views and approaches to all topics, since the honest and respected expression of differences that are sustainable within an overarching coherent world view can be a construc tive contributor to dialogue and to learners' development. Indeed, such a demonstration, where it is practised, is almost universally valued by learners, who are thus encouraged to think beyond simplisms and to reach for their own expression of a coherent world view. Brisbane College of Theology, a consortium of Anglican, Catholic and Uniting Church colleges, presented the first year unit *Introducing Theology* as a combined class taught by three lecturers (one from each tradition), which allowed the theological emphases of the three traditions to be aired and discussed openly, respectfully and yet within an overall framework of unity, an outcome highly valued by the learners. Nazarene Theological College teaches *Introduction to Worship* with the involvement of four lecturers, which not only utilises a range of expertise in a practical unit, it also presents a broader perspective of worship. The collaborative interaction of teachers in the delivery of units can also result in the teachers' expansion of perspectives, and so can be a powerful model of transformative ideals.

Student action and reflection typifies some learning practices. While it is common to associate such learning with supervised field education and other "practical" units, it has application across the board of theological units. Mention has been made of Ridley Melbourne's collaborative learning, which involves students in cooperative learning in various ways, both in and beyond the formal classroom. Church History students at Queensland Theological College have researched and written a history of their local church complete with reflections on the historical dynamics at play at pivotal junctures in that history and insights into how that history could be influenced for further development. Other Church History students at Sydney Missionary and Bible College and Malyon College have constructed and delivered teaching lessons on historical topics, either within the history class or as a practical component of an Education unit. Similar units have been constructed in biblical and theological subjects. Such exercises lead the student to a broader integration of the field of the topic itself and to connect that topic to a wider contemporary context. They have most impact on the learner when they are accompanied by opportunities for evaluative reflection on the significance of the teaching following the event.

A more holistic approach to action-reflection has been implemented by Forge Mission Training Network, which offers some units through Tabor Victoria and Whitley College. The Forge program places interns in an incarnational mission context designed to stretch them out of their comfort zone. Interns are supported by regular coaching and peer clusters to reflect on what they are experiencing in mission, and a number of teaching intensives. It is a "reflection-in-action" experience, focused on acting into new ways of thinking rather than expecting students to think into new ways of acting.[5] A similar internship system (though not as philosophically radical) is employed in Australian Lutheran College's Faith Life Program and in Alphacrucis' internship program for ministry candidates. Tabor Adelaide incorporates spiritual retreats as a component of its *Spiritual Formation* unit. Similar principles generally apply to the various Guided Spiritual Formation units in many colleges. The most significant developmental and potentially transformative aspect of such experiential learning practices lies in the capacity for ongoing informed critical reflection and personal evaluation, leading to perspective modification, articulation and, as appropriate, active implementation.

Supervised Field Education (SFE), whether within or parallel to the formal degree structure, is the area most commonly credited with opportunities for learners to grow through real-life experience and in personally integrative and transformative ways. However, there has been much criticism of the shortcomings of SFE in practice, in terms of its fragmentation, its "hit and miss" activity, the system and quality of supervision and its lack of overall coordination within a study program. Where SFE succeeds, there are several common contributing factors which are worth noting. First, SFE works best when it is integrated with the rest of the study program. This integration can be by way of curriculum design where SFE topics are specifically linked with other biblical, theological or ministry topics. Or it can be connected to the rest of the course by means of common faculty leadership. Murdoch University has shown that such

---

5   Cronshaw, "Australian reenvisioning of theological education: In step with the Spirit?" 230.

coordination is possible even when SFE is not part of the degree itself, but it requires good coordination between faculty and church leaders to formulate and deliver the parallel program. In any case, integration and transformative ends are fostered by means of structured reflection in individual and group settings. Some colleges, such as Malyon College and Crossway College, have dedicated Field Education faculty and SFE units incorporated into the degree, which feature regular timetabled sessions led by the Field Education Director where classes meet for interactive processing of ministry experience, as well as individual accountability through the Director. At times, other faculty are also involved in such group processing, which not only adds to the status of SFE but also provides a further dimension of overall integration.

The faculty's connection with outside personnel is also an important factor in successful SFE programs. Nowhere is this more important than in the second observed common factor in success, namely, supervision. Most SFE programs stand or fall on the basis of the quality of supervision, which is commonly not very well controlled by colleges. All colleges rely on external non-faculty supervisors, but the management of the supervisory system determines its quality. The Malyon College system of SFE, also employed by Nazarene Theological College and borrowed by some overseas organizations, is very coherently structured and supported by an effective system of quality control. Potential supervisors are accredited by the College, with accreditation requiring mandatory involvement in the College's supervisor training program. This program involves a day per semester attendance at the college (or equivalent sessions in regional locations conducted by the Field Education Director), wherein the requirements of supervisors' input, monitoring, professional guidance, regular reflection, evaluation and reporting are developed, and some input into contemporary ministry is provided. This is followed by regular contact among the Director, the supervisor and the student. It is a rigorous program of management, but the investment in personnel and energy has borne good fruit in both learners and supervisors, who themselves have received appreciated in-service value in the process.

The third factor contributing to the success of SFE is the school's partnership with the churches. Denominational colleges which have direct connection to a church system are well placed to develop a coherent formation program for ministerial candidates, especially when coordinated by faculty, although this is generally limited to specified ordination candidates. Bible College of South Australia, while not having such direct links, has a Partners in Training Program, which seeks to connect with the student's church to enhance the overall educative experience for the individual student. Vose Mission is a partnership arrangement with a group of missions agencies which facilitates similar coordination. In general, SFE works best when it is coordinated by the college working in close partnership with a dynamic functioning organisation such as a church or another ministry group. Again, this allows for greater cohesion of learning and practice, especially when quality supervision and rigorous reflection and reporting are also in play.

There is a growing recognition of the value of field experiences, not only in SFE but also in the more traditional literary units. Catholic Theological College uses a number of such experiences to help students ground their studies in a living context. In *Christian Spirituality*, the third hour of each week's session is devoted to "Experiences," a process of going out and seeing how the Spirit is working unusually, such as visiting a Benedictine monastery to see how such a community operates in its spiritual exercises. In *Australian Church History*, there is a day-long visit to historic churches in Melbourne to analyse the theology behind their construction. This sort of experience is aimed at helping to achieve an integration of the various fields. Australian College of Theology has a number of "In Context" units, involving a tour of Bible lands or Lands of the Reformation, where students visit the great sites of the Christian heritage to make a personal connection with these sites. Nazarene Theological College visits a mosque and interacts with the local Imam as a part of the World Religions unit. Australian Catholic University has a similar unit which involves multiple site visits. By going beyond the confines of the classroom and connecting directly with such places, students are encouraged to broaden the horizons of their world view.

While such "tours" are of inherent value in generating active interest in a topic, their value in potential transformation is not simply a matter of taking an excursion. Indeed, such experiential undertakings are optimized when they are grounded in appropriate theory and scholarship, so the student's experiential learning is well informed and facilitated by the lecturer, rather than simply being a case of asking, "What is/was your experience?" The transformative value of the Nazarene class's visit to the mosque lay not just in the visit itself, but in the class's prior articulation of their expectations and fears and their later review of those presuppositions and changes of understanding and values in light of the actual experience, consolidated by their reporting in chapel to their peers who had not experienced the visit. The Ridley Melbourne unit *The Reformation in Context* was successful when it incorporated significant pre-tour study of the Reformation, its main issues and events, its leading characters and major documents, all geared to the sites which were to be visited. Then, with clear directions for observation and analysis, the students' visit was informed and their analytical and reflective reports of the tour featured deep insights into the way in which the history was shaped and expressed in the churches, museums and monuments encountered as well as the deep impact the visit made on them personally. Experience needs to be located within an articulated frame of reference if that frame of reference is to be recognised, reviewed and modified. Uninformed experiences will be limited in their capacity to produce personal development or perspective modification.

A final observation should be made on a number of learning and assessment tasks that seem appropriate to the attainment of integrated transformative goals. While intentional linkages to students' prior life experience were quite limited in scope, there were some examples provided of how the consideration of prior experience has been constructively incorporated. Some noted the application of assignment topics to prior life situations, while others told of using some theological concept mapping and action reflection to review critically some previously held views and practices. At the workshop, it was suggested that every learning task should have a section that applies the research specifically to a student's life situation, which could facilitate an ongoing effective integration of life and learning some years later; however, there was little evidence of this being a widespread practice. The use of journaling of personal experiences and progression of spiritual or personal development is common in spirituality and ministry units, but has some application in charting progress in other units as well. There were many reports of teaching "in the moment" within the classroom, where simple techniques were used to help the students ground their new knowledge within their own frame of reference. Vose Seminary was one of many who related the importance of the "So what?" question in teaching, including biblical, theological and ministry units: "If you were to take this passage seriously, what difference would it make to the way you live your life?" Queensland Theological College reported, "We intentionally include moments in the classroom where students are asked to de-construct and re-construct their assumptions regarding Bible, theology and history. This has its moments!" Others made comments such as, "We always finish the lecture before the end of class time to allow reflection on how it impacts our life and to make regular pastoral applications." These are some of the simple yet effective ways of building into a regular class setting a pervasive ethos of continual and critical review of assumptions and attitudes, which can contribute to a cumulative re-shaping of the learners' understanding of knowledge encountered and appreciation of their own developing identity and role within their world.

4. The Need for a Strategy

This review of some of the prominent principles and practices prompts the "So what?" question. There are currently in evidence in theological providers throughout Australia a large number of good principles that govern transformative and integrative learning. There are also many current practices that intuitively facilitate students' critical self-evaluation and expanding world views. All of this supports the common claims of lecturers and the almost as common reports of graduates that theological education has produced some very effectual transformative outcomes. However, what is equally apparent is that such outcomes are the result of individual initiative and intuition rather than an institutional strategy or even a coherent policy. Some schools have some of the elements articulated as policy, but these are few and the implementation of the policy is piecemeal. While many schools have been cited as representative of good practices, even in those schools, the practices are not universally employed. If transformative principles and practices are to become an intentional feature of theological education, the sector will need to articulate such policies clearly and to disseminate and creatively develop more of the good practices. Heads of schools in particular and teaching faculty in general, who have all been entrusted with the primary responsibility for the quality of the education delivered, will need to put in place some strategic processes that will create a climate conducive to transformative learning and that will systematically educate teachers in the methods of attaining that goal.

8 | WHERE TO NEXT?

RECOMMENDATIONS FOR PRINCIPLES, PRACTICES AND CURRICULUM DESIGN

1. Where to Now?

Having analysed the findings of the research, it is now time to propose a number of recommendations for embedding certain elements into undergraduate theological curriculum design that will incorporate student experience and transformative learning. The recommendations all arise from the many forms of the research undertaken, with a heavy emphasis on the input provided by current faculty, students, graduates and other key stakeholders. The recommendations are not meant to be prescriptive or universal, but are offered as a compendium of what people have proffered as both desirable and possible, born of an impressive and candid aspiration to enhance what is seen as a good product but one which we all want to do better. While they are expressed mainly in quite general terms, the aim is to present them in ways which are readily translated into active implementation in a number of varied contexts.

In this attempt to discern some useful direction in a vast and varied field such as this, there are several inter-connected elements which need to be considered in the overall complex that is curriculum design. First, there is the issue of definition: both of context and of terminology. We need to have a clear understanding of what we mean by "student experience" and "transformative learning" and the ramifications of the varied delivery situations before we can proceed strategically to implement these things. Then, there needs to be the articulation of general principles which are common to all theological bodies and which will undergird and inform the development of curriculum. Finally, effective classroom practices which are suitable and possible need to be identified, since these will also have an impact on a legitimate curriculum design: it is pointless to construct a "model curriculum" if classroom practices are not available to support it. When all of these inter- woven and inter-dependent elements are brought together, some coherence may be attained in the production of a curriculum that will intentionally, strategically and effectively incorporate student experience and promote a potentially transformative agenda.

2. Defining Contexts and Terms

(a) Contexts

The provision of theological education is complicated by the wide variety of institutional contexts in which it occurs and the purposes for which it is delivered. There are large public universities and there are small private Bible colleges; there are global denominational controls and there is local church-based autonomy; there are different kinds of university, consortial and independent administrative systems. Where the institution fits will have a bearing on the nature and degree of incorporation of transformative goals. However, regardless of that fit, it is possible to incorporate some kind of transformative strategy to a significant degree. What is required is the clear identification and analysis of the institutional context and a realistic approach to the task.

The context of the public university is clearly different from that of the private theological college, primarily in its basic charter. The public universities, apart from Australian Catholic University, do not have a faith-based charter as the private theological colleges have and so their theology schools may not explicitly pursue faith development. The mission statement of Australian Catholic University clearly locates the university "within 2,000 years of Catholic intellectual tradition" and seeks to bring "a distinctive spiritual perspective to the common tasks of higher education." However, within this context, the stress of the mission statement is on what it shares with other universities, namely, "a commitment to quality in teaching, research, and service (as it) aspires to be a community characterised by free inquiry and academic integrity."

University of Notre Dame Australia, as a private university within the Catholic tradition, has a distinctive goal "to provide a forum where, through free inquiry and open discussion, the various lines of Catholic thought may intersect with all the forms of knowledge found in the arts, sciences, professions, and every other area of human scholarship and creativity." Again, as befitting the university ethos, the university requires "not a particular creedal affiliation, but ... a willingness to enter into the conversation that gives it life and character. Therefore, the University insists upon academic freedom that makes open discussion and inquiry possible." Hence the focus in these Catholic universities is more on studying the intersection of the faith with community issues of ethics, justice and equality than on adherence to the faith or the propagation of the faith *per se*.

In general, most university theology programs are geared largely to the notion of a liberal arts education, which in itself sits somewhat uncomfortably within the more dominant professional/vocational orientation of many universities. However, the universities have shown a recent move towards a more deliberate emphasis on the person at the centre of the learning experience. One prominent public voice in this regard is that of Macquarie University Vice-Chancellor Steven Schwartz, who maintains that for centuries universities understood their main job as being to mould the character of their students, a goal he would like to see re-established.[1] This trend is most manifest in areas such as nursing and teaching but, partially drawing from their strengths in these latter areas, it is also emerging as a part of the overall university charter. Among other things, this is being expressed in such university-wide concepts as community engagement and learning in the workplace. Within the framework of theological education, such person-centred and community-based approaches fit well into the transformative agenda. In theological and Bible colleges, the dual focus of a faith-based and person-centred learning program is clearly amenable to transformative goals.

Another often noted difference between university and theological college is that of size, both institutional size and class size. Most specialised theological colleges have between fifty and 100 students within the institution, with an institutional size of over 500 being rare, whereas

---

1   "Universities 'should trade in morals, not profits'," *The Sydney Morning Herald*, 6 June 2011.

all universities have thousands of students. Consequently, it is noted that the more individualised interaction with students so prevalent in the small colleges is not practical in the universities or the few very large colleges. However, institutional statistics can be misleading, since the degree of individual contact is not a factor of the overall institutional size but is related more to the course and class size. At the operational level, the university Theology schools are not large; in fact, they are typically smaller than the theological colleges. As well, it is common for the university Theology school to comprise or to be closely linked to a number of relatively small church-based theological bodies. In the matter of class size, theological classes, especially at advanced levels, are typically very small in universities as well as in theological colleges, with no discernible difference in the two types of institution. Indeed, the largest advanced classes are in a few quite large theological colleges. At this operational level of delivery, there seems to be no significant difference in size between universities and theological colleges, with the few large colleges being those who need to accommodate the larger classes. It is noteworthy here that these large colleges are the ones which seem to have in place some good systems for student management and personal care, involving the commitment of all faculty.

One area where large class size is a major factor is the provision of service teaching. Where the charter of a university or other multi-discipline college has a service provision of the inclusion of some (typically one or two, occasionally up to four) theological units either in all its courses or in a selection of vocational courses such as education, a particular introductory class in Theology may number in the hundreds. Thus individual contact with students is impractical, a situation exacerbated by the general lack of any ongoing contact beyond the unit and a generally reduced level of intrinsic motivation in the students taking the unit. In such units, it is agreed that individualised learning and development and the attendant transformative goals are not practical, although some of the classroom practices detailed below may still well apply. However, it should be noted that the purpose of this research project pertains to the curriculum of a theological degree, not to service teaching of a limited number of units in other courses. That is, the transformative agenda and processes are seen within the framework of an undergraduate degree program in its entirety, not in terms of an excised suite of units taken elsewhere.

One concrete area where real differences exist is that of regulatory administration. Simply put, the larger and more complex the institution, the more cumbersome are the systems of review and development. University regulatory frameworks tend to sit somewhat uncomfortably with theological delivery, not just because of an inherent suspicion of a faith agenda but also because of the need to accommodate generally small specialised units within the Theology degree. Such units have little attraction for non-ordination candidates and so are subject to continual rationalising scrutiny with regard to viability. It is therefore difficult for a church to introduce new units or to influence the cycle of offerings. To a lesser degree, membership in a large private consortium also has regulatory inhibitions, although most member colleges agree that they have quite effective input into and opportunities for development of their own offerings within the consortia. Autonomous colleges, while still subject to broad governmental regulation, have far more direct control over their reviews and developments. While there are various levels of convenience in regulatory development, it is universally true that the teaching faculty are the ones whose initiative drives any curriculum reform, whether that reform is at a structural level or at the level of unit content and delivery or at the level of teaching/learning methods.

The other major contextual consideration is the basic purpose and ethos of the institutions, although this has more to do with the nature than the possibility of a transformative agenda. At one end of the spectrum is the secular public university, with its commitment to a secular liberal education; at the other end is the theological college driven largely by the need to provide priests or ministers for the global church by which it is established and ultimately controlled. While both ends of the range have similar regulatory inhibitions, they differ greatly in their purpose. The college aiming at priestly formation will focus on just that: providing the theological base required by a priest, with other formative elements developed elsewhere. Hence its theological program will be more limited and focused. On the other hand, Bible colleges with no specific church affiliation will have a broader world in view as their contextual ambit: a general evangelical ethos with practical skills for laity as well as potential clergy, but without an emphasis on the specific ordination or liturgical requirements of a particular tradition. So, the differences between preparing ordination candidates and developing general laity, between projecting a strongly denominational framework or generating a broad ecumenical world view, between providing a liberal arts education and promoting a spiritual or faith development: these are significant differences which need to be identified and which need to inform the degree and nature of any transformative thinking.

(b) Terms

The language of transformative learning presents as a vexed issue and one which needs clarification at the outset. As reported in chapter 2, Mezirow's pioneering use of the term focused on the critical reflection on and review and modification of values, beliefs and presuppositions, occasioned by some discomforting disorientation, resulting in the transformation of meaning perspectives. The discomforting disorientation may result from a specific moment or event or from a cumulative accretion of events during a person's development towards more inclusive, discriminating, and integrative frameworks. A key element in this thinking is the process of change, which dominates other traditional understandings such as the acquisition of knowledge and vocational skills. Transformative theory since Mezirow has developed a more integrated or holistic view of transformative learning, which incorporates dimensions of personal and spiritual development.

Despite the progressive refinements in such theory, there is still a lack of consensus on what constitutes transformative education. In particular, there is in Australian theological circles a lack of clear distinction between "formation" and "transformation." Is there a difference? Are they simply interchangeable terms? Do we want one but not necessarily the other? Is it even possible to orchestrate either? Whose job is it anyway? Such questions consistently circulate around almost all conversations in the field. Hence it is important that we seek some workable consensus on the meaning of the terms for our particular sector.

"Formation" is a term generally associated with priestly formation (especially in Anglican, Catholic, Uniting Church and similar traditions). Thus understood, it includes theological, spiritual, priestly and personal formation, with theological formation being the province of the academy; priestly and spiritual formation the task of the seminary or the church beyond the academy; and personal formation being a somewhat more vague ancillary to institutional programs. Formation therefore presumes a pre-determined shape, a priestly persona, that a student is to be formed into in order to fulfil the role of a priest or minister, which is generally shaped by the needs for the performance of ordained ministry. In traditions where such formal priestly formation is not so articulated (eg Baptist, Bible Colleges, Pentecostal), formation is commonly associated with the growth of Christian character, along the lines of some generally quite vague existing concept of what is authentic Christianity, typically associated with the habitual performance of revered practices of individual piety. In either case, there is the basic notion of knowing what shape a student should be moulded into and the program of formation is aimed at such a moulding.

"Transformation" carries the connotation not just of being "formed into X," but rather of being "changed from A into B." It is generally associated with the notion of a significant change in world view or intellectual or social perspective. "Formation" requires a starting point of knowing what the desired outcome X looks like, with a program designed to lead the student into that particular shape. On the other hand, "transformation" requires a starting point of knowing just who and what A is, that is, an awareness of the two personal dimensions of the identity ("who") and role ("what") that shape the individual student who is about to engage theological study. The subsequent program will then lead the student to review that shape and take on another but not initially delineated form as the product B. That is, transformation is not predictable, it does not have a pre-determined shape that will be assumed by the graduate. Rather, the change process is the focus, with the outcome demonstrated in the articulation and/or enactment of a significant change in world view, of self-understanding, of role or social interaction. Saul of Tarsus had his Damascus Road experience; Ignatius of Loyola famously declared that he had become "another man" at Manresa following a moment of spiritual enlightenment. This is the language of transformation which, in its desired positive form in our context, leads to a creative and productive life in godly ministry in ways previously not known or possible. However, a major concern to Australian theological education – whose main *raison d'être* is the provision of ordained clergy and informed lay members of the Christian community in the service of the churches – is the implicitly anarchic open-endedness of transformative experience. When a church licenses a priest, it wants to know that the priestly formation is appropriate to the mission of the church, not an inappropriately radicalised identity. So, there is a degree of understandable disquiet about a commitment to transformative learning ideals.

Such problems of definition show that there are many good aspects but also many negative connotations in both "formation" and "transformation." Formation, while providing a proficient priestly or admirable spiritual persona, has a propensity for fragmented moulding. Transformation, while generating exciting and potentially world-changing outcomes, has the potential for chaotic radicalisation, or even radical chaos. Within the Australian theological sector, there is clearly a desire to have the best of both worlds: a well- formed priest and Christian character who can reliably perpetuate the received Christian heritage as well as an impressive individuality engaging creatively with a changing contemporary world, with a capacity to influence that world not just preserve a traditional expression of its heritage. At the risk of adding to the semantic melting pot, but prompted by the dialogue within the research, I suggest the use of the term "Integrative Learning" as a means of incorporating all the positive ideals of formative and transformative learning while retaining the integrity of the valued theological heritage that is central to the whole theological enterprise.

Integrative learning treats formative and transformative learning as not mutually exclusive but as complementary attainments. The concept emerges from the noted gaps and aspirations of many stakeholders. There is a noted need for the integration of all strands of learning in place of the currently decried "compartmentalisation" and discrete "silos" of theological subjects. There is a noted need for the integration of theological learning with vocational practice, in place of the oft lamented practice of resorting to pragmatics in times of pressure rather than working from a theologically principled base. There is a noted need for the holistic personal appropriation of theological concepts and principles to govern the values and relationships of Christian people (ministers and laity) in place of the inconsistently presented characters sadly observed all too often within the Christian community. "Integrative learning" in Christian theology can be understood as that style of education that strategically embraces and promotes the characteristics of the holistic congruence of all fields of learning, imbuing life practices with theologically formed principles, and the cultivation of a holistically consistent person whose values and relationships embody the ideals of the Christian heritage. In this way, both formation and transformation can be blended, with the resultant well formed minister possessed of a transformed and enlarged world view, engaged in productive and generative activity beyond what was initially thought of or thought possible.

3. Governing Principles

There are various approaches to the formulation of principles and associated practices. When an institution has been in existence for a long time (as is the case with many theological institutions), a common approach is to start from current practices and derive principles and policies from them. This leads to policies that are effectively a retrospective validation of what we currently do and thus tends to concretise those practices. Consequently, such derived principles are governed by the practices. However, if a transformative paradigm is to be developed, it needs to be based on principles which govern practices, not the other way round. Therefore, before proceeding to recommendations for implementing effective practices and designing appropriate curricula, there needs to be some articulation of the governing principles of integrative and transformative learning. This section suggests four such governing principles as an appropriate starting point for such curriculum review. As with the previous section of this chapter, these principles have been educed from the research dialogue – in both the literature and the field – in an attempt to capture what the wide range of stakeholders have contributed.

Principle 1: The Primacy of Biblical and Theological Knowledge

The acquisition and mastery of biblical and theological knowledge is clearly the main motivation and most valued outcome of theological education, which has been affirmed strongly by all categories of stakeholders. Teaching the Bible and its associated theology is the core business of theological education. Students overwhelmingly report that their main motivation in enrolling and the main benefit they derive are both related to the acquisition of such knowledge. Faculty report that this is their chief aim and passion. Church leaders affirm this as a major and mandatory strength of all their institutions. The universal desire, affirmation and strength of the biblical tradition is at the heart of theological education. The faithful preservation, transmission and perpetuation of this tradition are the *sine qua non* of the enterprise. While placing a corpus of knowledge at the primary position in learning does not fit easily with Mezirovian transformative theory, it can readily be accommodated to a concept of integrative learning within a given tradition. Given the historical and creedal bases of Christianity and its theology, this is the first and most fundamental principle of theological education.

The substance of biblical and theological content – the *what* – is thus seen as sacred and not negotiable. However, while sustaining this emphasis – indeed, to execute it with authenticity – there is a need to review the ways of conducting the enterprise, that is, the *why* and the *how* of the process. To ensure an authentic and relevant handling of the sacred content of the Christian heritage requires both a willingness for and a commitment to a reconsideration of the purpose and means of theological knowledge transmission and processing.

Principle 2: Contemporary Engagement of Theology with Society and Culture

There is a growing cry for a more comprehensive educative experience for equipping people for the mission of the church as theological graduates. Although theological graduates are generally regarded as being well versed in scripture and systematic theology, questions are asked as to whether they have a suitably wide world view or are adequately equipped for effectual dialogue with a contemporary world. While the focus on biblical and theological knowledge is affirmed as necessary, the very singularity of that focus is not of itself a sufficient preparation of graduates for "real-world" ministry. Graduates need to have the capacity to engage effectively with lay people in the church and secular people beyond it, as integrated persons rather than as esoteric professionals. Thus they need to be integrated people who can think, relate and live theologically and skilfully in a contemporary world context, rather than simply to present as informed and articulate theologians.

This principle presents a challenge to traditional theological education as it requires the development of a much wider world view than that of the theological world alone. To engage the wider contemporary world requires an understanding of that world as well as the theology of the "Christian" world – and how and where the two intersect. It requires that both learners and teachers have the ability to communicate and act in terms that transcend traditional limits. It requires that theology be connected with lived experience, both within the constantly changing landscape of the churches and beyond the churches in an increasingly disconnected world at large. The social and cultural contexts in which theology is to be expressed beyond graduation need to be integrated into the curriculum if theology is to be treated as a living organism and not an archival fossil.

Principle 3: Holistic Integration of Learning and Life
There is a widespread and strongly expressed desire for theological education to be holistic and integrated rather than being based on sets of content that are often disconnected from one another and from life beyond the classroom. Such integration will combine cognitive, practical and affective elements and will involve the intentional development of character and values as well as knowledge and skills. It is acknowledged that theological graduates need to have more enhanced skills of appropriate leadership and social engagement. This will require an integrated person who has personally taken ownership of governing theological principles which will be determinative in all of life's activities and relationships. This will allow for greater flexibility in practices in response to unanticipated contexts without compromising core theology.

Such integration will have two dimensions: vocational and personal. The vocational dimension will require the development of performance skills grounded in theological principles. The personal dimension will require the development of a consistency of character and a coherence of world view, values and conduct. In total, it aims at a congruence of creed, conduct and character within the person of the graduate. As a base, this principle will require holistic and integrated learning to replace the traditionally fragmented approach to theological instruction with a more inter-connected and yet potentially open-ended system of theological discovery. This will not dilute or debase the theological content, but it will facilitate a coherence that draws all the content together in connection with authentic experience. Legitimate content and authentic experience are not mutually exclusive: their integration enhances both in a potentially transformative way.

Principles 1-3 undergird the development and implementation of classroom practices (see Classroom Practices below).

Principle 4: Intentionality and Strategicality of a Transformative Agenda Expressed in Curriculum Design and Development

Given a commitment to the above three principles, an institution must develop a culture of intentionally and strategically incorporating those principles into a well structured curriculum designed to facilitate the attainment of the transformative and integrative goals. It is true that curriculum design itself will not ensure the attainment of goals, but it is also true that those goals are more likely to be attained if the curriculum is designed with a clear intent and strategy to achieve them.

Intention will arise from a shared institutional philosophy and articulated educational aims. Any coherent curriculum requires a governing philosophy as its starting point. Such a philosophy – what are we about as an institution – will drive the whole curriculum. If a transformative agenda is wanted, there needs to be a consistent and unified institutional commitment to that agenda, developed and owned by the faculty and the other key stakeholders. The translation of this shared philosophy into educational delivery will require a clear statement of educational aims developed within the ethos of the institution, with due regard to its own culture, skills and resources (but not necessarily limited to its customary conventions).

While transformative intention is expressed in various schools, its attainment is very often left to unstructured and somewhat wishful informal events and *ad hoc* personal contacts. Such serendipitous happenings are common and should not be downplayed. However, mere intention itself is not enough. The setting of goals is one thing, but the attainment of them will require a clear and realistic strategy to be formulated and executed. This will involve a deliberate pedagogic approach as well as the occasional personal interaction. As with the institutional philosophy, the institutional pedagogic approach will ideally be developed by the faculty informed by other partner stakeholders. It is only as faculty – the key delivery agents of the curriculum – take ownership of and have a commitment to such integrating philosophy and pedagogy that transformative goals will be strategically pursued and most likely be attained.

Principle 4 undergirds curriculum considerations which are connected to and facilitate classroom practices (see Curriculum Design below).

4. Classroom Practices

A review of effectual classroom practices will indicate some ways in which the above principles may be implemented in active delivery. As usual, this review is based on what has been gleaned from the research, as many examples of effectual practice are in operation. It is the aim of this section to bring them together as recommended ways in which a coherent approach to developing curriculum may be established and shown to be realistic and achievable.

(a) Implementing Principle 1: Primacy of Biblical and Theological Knowledge
As stressed above, the given understanding in this principle is that the sacred content of Christian biblical and theological knowledge must be retained as the *sine qua non* of the educational enterprise. The challenge here is to review the ways in which this can be done in order to enhance the educational experience of the learner and thus generate a transformative experience that will produce a more integrated graduate. This review is not of what content to include, but of what is the purpose of theological education and what are the best means of delivering it.

Any such review needs to start from a re-phrasing of the fundamental question we ask about the purpose of theological education. *Educationally, the question is not how does the learner fit into the world of theology but how does theology fit into the world of the learner.* Since learners will bring with them an already formed "world" of some sort, an acknowledgement of the principle of learning by assimilation and/or accommodation rather than by an encounter with disconnected new information needs to be made. This leads to the fundamental premise that, especially in an adult learning process, the learner is placed at the centre of that process. This is not an anthropocentric theology, where the learner is the subject of theological inquiry; rather, it is a learner-centred pedagogy, where the learner is the primary agent of educational inquiry. The key educational concept of the learner as the centre of the educational process addresses both the *why* and the *how* of the process. An integrated program will teach Bible and theology with a personal purpose of forming people theologically and will develop strategies to develop persons not just knowledge/skills. This changes the emphasis from "how I can teach" to "how can students learn".

The differences between a content-centred curriculum and a student-centred curriculum may be suggested graphically. In a content-centred curriculum (Figure A), the world of theology is seen as a known and defined corpus of content into which the learner is invited in order to acquire familiarity with that world. This views theology as a static fixed canon into whose limits the student must learn to fit. In a student-centred curriculum (Figure B), the world of the learner is seen as an ongoing journey into which we seek to introduce the theological knowledge required to make that journey more meaningful. This views the learner as a living organism to whose expansion theology is to make a dynamic contribution.

Figure A: Content-Centred Curriculum

Figure B: Student-Centred Curriculum

Such a pedagogical re-orientation leads to a review of methods of knowledge transmission and reception, the primary domain of any educational system, especially in a field where the preservation and perpetuation of traditional knowledge and wisdom are a large part of the institutional *raison d'être*, as in theological traditions. The traditional approach to such transmission of knowledge has been centred very much on the focal role of a master teacher, who stands before the class and delivers from the perspective of a subject expert to a group of more or less passive recipients. The teacher is the personal repository of special expert knowledge, who acts as the determinant of such important knowledge via the selection and ordering of significant content, and who delivers the content by means of well prepared lectures and communication and good classroom transmission resources. However, while the aim is to transmit to the learners the vital truths and wisdom of the tradition, in practice a lot of faith is placed in the person of the teacher to do that comprehensively, wisely and faithfully, in the relatively short space of time available within a class contact session. What is presented as the vital tradition of the community is in reality that part of the tradition which has been mastered and deemed important by the teacher, which may or may not be the full tradition that is claimed. Yet it is the teacher's pre-determined content and knowledge that set the scope and limits of the knowledge to be received by the students. Depending on the contextual resources available (eg extensive reference library, adequate time for full consideration of content within a commonly crowded curriculum), this classroom-based teacher-delivered content may well be the bulk of what the learner receives.

Within this approach, a basic assumption is that all students will benefit equally from this set corpus of knowledge, that they will be receptive to and appreciative of it, and that they will memorize and be able to reproduce it as required, typically by way of periodic examinations of various kinds. The student who manages to do this well will be considered a well-educated graduate. Yet generations of students through the ages have echoed the sentiments that, at the end of a degree program, they are left with screeds of lecture notes never re-visited after exams and a real-life vacuum which has done little to prepare them for life after graduation. In the best case scenarios, this accumulation of knowledge during the degree has provided a sound base for further learning, that is, more knowledge with life application, which will continue beyond graduation. Virtually no teacher or student would ever claim that a degree program has taught all possible knowledge, yet the emphasis on delivering a vast amount of knowledge content within the classroom seems to be an attempt to do so.

A contemporary approach to learning and teaching demands a critical awareness of the changing context in which education is delivered. In the last ten-twenty years, our generation has witnessed and participated actively in not so much a knowledge explosion but a *knowledge access explosion*. In 1995, a high-achieving Bachelor of Theology student would listen attentively to an expert lecturer for a three hour lecture, then proceed to ferret out further details by reference to the dozen or so reference texts in the library recommended by the lecturer. When time permitted, further browsing of journal lists held in the college's library would provide a useful adjunct to this research. Such diligent library research, duly recorded by means of hand-written notes, would ultimately generate a commendable research essay and provide some good information for exam purposes. A good result is obtained for the unit, but it is doubtful that these notes would be consulted again after the exam. In 2012, that same student may sit in the comfort of home, google the lecture or assignment topic and immediately have access to literally thousands of resources, many of which will open up a world of content far beyond the lecturer's knowledge or intended scope. It was only about five years ago that lecturers were warning about the unreliability of electronic sources, but today virtually all leading universities and publishers have embraced electronic resourcing, with a massive investment in and usage of such resources. With the infinite access to knowledge afforded by the Internet, the now common sharing of inter-library resources and vast electronic facilities, no longer is any undergraduate student limited to the hard copies of books and journals held in the local library: much less is that student dependent on the individual lecturer to provide all the knowledge needed in any field.

So, what is the role of the classroom teacher in this primary domain of knowledge transmission? While the teacher remains a pivotal agent in the process, the role has changed – and must change if it is to remain legitimate and relevant. Put simply, the classroom and the teacher need no longer be the major focus of information transmission. Indeed, to perpetuate such a classroom teacher delivery approach is to hold back the students from the vast resources of knowledge that are now available. Such an approach will not only put limits on the knowledge available, but at the same time it may effectively communicate a tacit message that the content of our course is not really a part of the contemporary world. Many students of my (older) generation recall university days dominated by massive content delivery to massed classes, with no provision for processing of that content, save for some occasional and often disconnected tutorials. Many teachers of my generation commonly bemoan the lack of adequate class time to cover all the necessary content. Others complain that the syllabus is so content-oriented that there is no real time available for developing important skills, a process that is often relegated to students' out-of-class trial and error. Such higher learning domains can, however, be readily accommodated if the methods of knowledge transmission are revised to exploit the contemporary means available instead of being locked into traditional transmission methods. That is, the essential knowledge can be delivered, but in ways that are more efficient and allow more legitimately educative learning to take priority.

There are simple methods currently being used in educationally progressive institutions which do not consume the bulk of the class meeting time with information transfer, yet do not lose integrity in delivering the essential knowledge content. For example, by using any of the vast array of electronic means commonly and cheaply available (group emails, message boards, Blackboard, Moodle to name a few), a teacher can distribute a bulk of lecture content in advance of the class meeting. Not only does this reduce the masses of paper handouts by the teacher, it also delivers the content in more manipulable form for the students and frees them from the onerous, distracting and generally inefficient task of lecture note taking while trying to comprehend the content. Nor does the pre-delivered content need to be comprehensive in its text coverage; it may well include various linkages to extra knowledge resources of many kinds. When the class assembles, having received the content in advance, they will need to have a teacher-led program that adds value to that content by various creative means. The scope for added interest, primary materials, multi-media resources, hyper-linked resourcing, cultural engagements, peer learning and in-class student activities is limitless, once enslavement to time-poor content delivery is removed. Pre-class content delivery of this nature has the obvious corollary of far greater post-class knowledge access, which will inevitably expand and enrich the content available. The concept of alternative pre-and post-class content transmission can be readily applied to any class situation, be that weekly classes, intensive blocks, weekend series, or distance or online learning. There is much to commend in this sort of "inside-out classroom" approach in terms of facilitating student transformation and integration.

Far from reducing the significance of the teacher or devaluing the teacher's expertise, the delivery of content by alternative methods demands a greater degree and mastery of contemporary as well as traditional knowledge by the teacher. It also requires a much more creative approach to facilitating learning by the students. It is a more challenging pedagogical role that the teacher is called upon to play, with a change from being a revered font of limited and controlled knowledge to being a director to vast sources of not always controlled knowledge, from being proudly didactic to being humbly facilitative. In reality, it requires the teacher to be an active participant in the process of constantly accessing more knowledge, with a real likelihood that the students will add to the store of the teacher's knowledge. It seems particularly pertinent to teachers of theology that such a model of humility and ongoing personal growth should typify the learning process. But regardless of any moral that may be thus drawn, it is in fact a poor use of limited class contact time to spend it on this primary domain of information transmission, since such transmission may be done far more efficiently in other ways. Using alternative means for such transmission has the added bonus of leaving scope for higher domain activity within the precious and limited resource of class contact time.

(b) Implementing Principle 2: Contemporary Engagement

"Engagement" requires people who are more than knowledgeably informed and articulate. It requires people who are capable of critical thinking and processing of issues, who can connect their theological learning with experience in a much larger world than their classroom, and who can adapt flexibly but authentically to a variety of situations and contexts. This is a higher level of operation than knowledge reception and it requires the strategic provision of significant learning opportunities for its development. The skills of engagement have more to do with the dynamics of learning than with the content of teaching.

An effective starting point for such development is the acquisition of generic process skills of analysis, critical thinking, evaluation and cogent argument. This requires a greater emphasis on the processing of information received, rather than the comprehensiveness of that information. The "learning what" progresses to the "learning how." This progression from content coverage to information processing has two aspects: the development of analytical skills of critical thinking that pertain to different disciplines and the application of that information to skills development associated with vocational utility.

To submit the sacrosanct tenets of belief to critical analysis is not an attempt to undermine or replace them, but it is an attempt to appreciate them more fully and in a more contemporarily relevant way. Such an approach asks hard questions: of the texts and of the learners. It acknowledges the historical and cultural provenance of the beliefs and movements, their core meanings as distinct from their cultural peripherals as well as their intersection with contemporary culture. It establishes principles and systems for the analysis of texts as distinct from simply absorbing the content of those texts. It sets theological texts and issues in the context of broader historical developments and global issues. It utilises the analytical methods of literary, philological, historical and social-scientific disciplines. Importantly, it connects the thought and action world of the church with that of the wider social and cultural world, including an interface with non-traditional bases. For example, Shakespeare, Dickens and the Simpsons may well be included in theological curricula, as their insights into popular theological concepts and the societal conditions in which the church has developed lend themselves to significant theological and ecclesiological analysis and evaluation. Such an approach places theological learning squarely within the realm of higher level humanities studies and fits theological discourse into the wider framework of contemporary thought and dialogue.

The methods of data processing common to the traditional areas are essentially those of the humanities and social sciences. Discipline-specific research skills are exercised. Rather than an expository reading of biblical books, an historical-critical (or literary, or socio-critical or other form of) exegesis is adopted, where the methods of exegesis are taught, practised and refined by means of a detailed study of a limited range of texts. The statements of systematic theology are examined not only as tenets of faith, but also in terms of their historical, philosophical and philological provenance. Coherent systems of analysis of primary historical documents are taught and practised, so that students may apply such methods widely. Students are encouraged to present arguments based on demonstrable evidence rather than simply to present second-hand scholarly summaries. The progressive development of such a faculty of critical analysis is basic to effectual personal evaluation as well as the evaluation of external issues and institutions.

In the area of vocational skills units, the need for attaining contemporary relevance via effective methods is a vital necessity in any vocational or professional role within a societal setting. The pragmatic needs of working in a competitive public arena demand such vocational utility. It is not enough, for example, to know the Bible, the theology, the history; what is important is to know how to communicate and to apply all that knowledge in real life working situations, both in and beyond the church. Common methods employed in the development of vocational skills within a prevocational course are practical exercises in or beyond the classroom, practical demonstration and experimentation, case study observation and analysis, and field placements or internships. Real-life scenarios (actual or simulated) and observations dominate. Problem-solving techniques are often employed, where a problem is identified (in a practice, a system, a context), the problem is analysed in terms of contributing factors, alternatives for action are investigated and likely outcomes are projected. The provision of such practical elements can often give impetus to and insights into a student's vocational strengths (or weaknesses) and future roles (or areas to be avoided).

It is in the area of vocational skills development and community interaction that significant attention is needed to promote effectual contemporary engagement. It is a truism that the contemporary world is marked by rapid even chaotic change, which means that so many skills and systems become quickly obsolete. It is also true that no training system can equip all students for all situations. However, if theological principles are to be effectively and dynamically transferred to new and unpredictable contexts, then broad principles and their connection to specific practices need to be analysed and understood. Unless the conceptual principles of utilitarian methods are absorbed by the learners, many learned mechanical methods will soon enslave rather than serve them. Only that which is "owned" by the learner will go with the graduate.

To maximise an individual learner's engagement potential, two key things are needed: a genuine connection with the student's own experience and the strategic incorporation of ongoing practical exposure to the community in action. A student's prior experience needs to be identified, assessed and built on with a view to furthering specific individual aspirations. Opportunities to demonstrate and to develop this experience may be provided in the relative shelter of the classroom or in the less controlled setting of a community placement. Utilisation of individual experience, skills and interests in a variety of learning and assessment tasks needs to be a regular part of curriculum delivery and classroom practice. In this way, the new theological knowledge and concepts encountered are more likely to become a part of the integrated person of the student.

There are some common means for incorporating practical experience and community engagement into the learning program, either in or beyond the classroom. In classroom exercises, be they individual or group activities, it is vital that all such practice is connected with the theory of theological learning, else they risk detached fragmentation. When reflective analytical critique including the evaluation of the theological ramifications of practical exercises is seen as a normal part of praxis, it is more likely that such an integration of theory and practice will become a norm for the graduate. This need for practical experience to be informed by theological theory, within a theological framework, is central to experiential learning with a view to formative development and the cumulative development of a transformed theological world view. The same rubric applies to all educational field trips and external field placements, the latter being a matter of considerable challenge, but a challenge for which the teaching institution must take responsibility.

The most common provision of experiential learning and community engagement is the external field placement, typically associated with Supervised Field Education as a limited part of the degree program or as an extra-curricular component. Such placements are usually in a church setting and often under the supervision of a non-faculty practitioner, but effective contemporary community engagement will need to expand this horizon considerably in terms of location and management. Placements need to be sought in locations beyond the traditional church bases, such as is currently being done in some universities, despite the huge logistical exercise involved. It is a standard requirement for professional accreditation in many programs such as nursing and teaching, which have much in common with the human service aspect of theology. Placing a learner in the best location for individual development will greatly enhance the overall learning experience, whether that location is in a church, in the wider Christian community, or beyond the Christian community. There is a strong case for having some placement, even for potential ministers, in a secular setting, since most of the world encountered beyond graduation will be so located.

As well as the location of placements, there is a lot to be done in the area of placement management, since this directly affects the quality of the learning experience. The common practice of arranging a placement and leaving it to the local supervisor's initiative to manage, without any significant input from or relationship with the college faculty, is perhaps the main issue of negative comment encountered in the research. The propensity for disconnection, fragmentation and a lack of theological integration of informed theory and practice is widely noted. This is most pronounced when the placement is extra- curricular and especially when managed by a body other than the college. For a field placement to be a genuinely transformative opportunity, there must be a genuine sense of partnership not just placement. This partnership between college and placement institution will involve the college's taking responsibility for supervisor training and quality management as well as the integration of field experiences with classroom theory and critical reflection. The management of practical experience must be primarily the task of the teaching body, with the placement to serve the overall goals of the curriculum rather than simply being a placement with insufficient pedagogical quality controls.

Finally, the role of the teacher in this area needs to be reviewed. Such skills mastery – of critical thinking, vocational praxis and community engagement – requires a knowledgeable and skilled teacher-practitioner-demonstrator. The teacher is responsible for the selection and ordering of content, exercises and placements with variant facets to facilitate the expansion of horizons, critical analysis and evaluation of arguments. The teacher must be sufficiently knowledgeable to identify and analyse a wide range of disparate views, positions and approaches, and be capable of treating such variant views with empathy and integrity, including those views and approaches which are not personally held. The transference of principles needs to be not only espoused and professed but also demonstrated and facilitated by the teacher. Biblical teachers need to be able to apply biblical principles to non- biblical contexts; historical theologians need to be able to analyse not only creedal documents from history but also emerging documents from today's church and non-church sources; homiletics teachers need to demonstrate not just describe good preaching in variable contexts. As well as this demonstrability, the teacher requires an awareness of and an ability to construct effective situations for the students' own practice, which will allow for appropriate and authentic experience in ways that will not jeopardise the students' welfare or development. In this domain, the demand on the teacher escalates in the same way as it does on the learner.

(c) Implementing Principle 3: Holistic Integration
Historically, the main objective of theological education has been the training of clergy for ministry within a largely Christianised social context. Consequently, the formative component has generally been geared to the formation of a priestly persona, not to transform the individual or society, but rather to conform both to a model of Christian belief and conduct as understood by the traditional sages. Yet the destinations of and demands on today's theological graduates are far more diverse and a broader concept of personal and social transformation is being embraced as a desirable outcome of theological education. Often, transformative experience is promoted as a distinctive of theological education; frequently, it is reported as an actual experience of a graduating student; yet rarely is there any evidence that it is an intentional and strategic element in the curriculum.

Such holistic personal development occurs only when the higher domain of concept appropriation comes into play. Since this is the least tangible and measurable domain of learning, it is not surprising that it is the most neglected.

This domain of holistic concept appropriation is grounded on a basic assumption, namely, that integrated learning derives from what a learner absorbs into his or her own person, the concepts that become a part of a person's identity and thus shape the whole of one's life. It is far more than the acquisition of much knowledge and far more than the attainment of skills of thinking or performing. It is a way of holistic thinking and living, a way of perceiving one's self and the world, a way of *becoming*, not just knowing or doing. Such development is manifest not just in a discipline-specific way but in a holistic integrated life. It is in the development of a holistic world perspective that it occurs. It is in the articulation and implementation of an "owned" position that mature personal formation is observable. In short, this domain is concerned not just with what the learner does in processing received knowledge, but more with what the processing of that knowledge does to the learner.

In keeping with the major theme of this research, the starting point of such holistic integration is the acknowledgement of the centrality of the learner in the educative process and the accommodation of the individuality of each learner within the process. Such a focus on the person of the learner has several practical ramifications. First, it is necessary to establish early in the process the stage of the learner's journey, so that the theological study may be integrated into that journey. This includes the early obligation to know the learner's background, motives and aspirations. *It is worth noting that, in the Graduate Surveys, the institutional provision of meaningful personal support which accommodates individual personal and learning needs is one of only two areas that rate quite poorly across many theological colleges*, despite the good *ad hoc* provisions made by individual faculty. While this has implications for the amount of content that can be incorporated in the early units, far more work is needed to identify and to encourage different learning styles, an issue which needs considerable attention especially in the early stages of a course. A working knowledge by faculty of the background, experience, aspirations and learning styles of the students will foster a climate in which learning of content and skills can be effectively related to a personal situation within a broader theological framework.

Classroom practices which promote personal integration must include regular strategic opportunities for critical reflection, review and modification of held positions. These opportunities need to be orchestrated to ensure valid critique, but critique conducted in a safe environment for such reflection, wherein the learner has a sense of freedom to express and to experiment but also to grow without recrimination or devaluation. Such opportunities should include the recognition of the need for the "deformation" of some prior positions, since many learners will have barriers of fear, prejudice or false humility that resist integration in learning, and such "distorting perspectives" need to be processed and repaired through learning. There are three basic dimensions to such review processes. The reflective review may be done at an individual student's level, by means of personal journaling, either private or for reading by the teacher for comment and supportive guidance. In this way, a progressive narrative of individual development may be constructed throughout a course. It may also be done in a peer situation in seminars or discussion groups. This has the bonus of enhancing a team process as a part of personal growth: the capacity to contribute to the development of a peer is a valued quality of a theological graduate. In such situations, the individual's story needs to be viewed through an appropriate biblical/theological lens to promote an ongoing sense of theological reflection not just anecdotal story-telling. More formally, such reflection may also be facilitated by intentionally designed assignments processed by the teacher. Such formal work has the capacity for mature self-analysis and articulation of a coherent world view in reference to a personal context and it allows for the intense theological synthesis so important especially (though not exclusively) in the later stages of a course.

The practice of collaborative learning is an effective means of facilitating holistic integration. While inadequate institutional attention to personal support structures was mentioned above as one of two areas of relative weakness noted in Graduate Surveys, *the weakest feature noted by a wide cross-section of respondents was the lack of development of the capacity for teamwork*. This was also noted adversely by many church leaders and other employers, and it is particularly noteworthy in light of the fact that most post-study work will involve much such activity. This is very much an area of relational development, where relational integrity as well as conceptual and enacted integration may be promoted. It has several tiers of relationships, all of which may make a significant contribution to transforming the persons involved. First, there is the obvious learner-learner relationship of peers; then, there is the teacher-learner relationship as co-learners; finally, there is a teacher- teacher relationship which not only serves as a model of cooperative endeavour, as in team teaching or faculty forums, but which also serves to demonstrate how divergent views can be held within an integrated cohesion. Peer learning has numerous forms, ranging from group discussion and presentations to more extended projects (in virtually any field) and to individual tutoring of students by students. Progressive responsibility for not only one's own learning but also for that of one's peers may not be traditional, but it does sit well with concepts of integrated service within a social setting. At the level of both teacher and learner, it also involves an ongoing broadening of horizons in terms of both theological understanding and relational development.

As always, the role of the teacher is pivotal to holistic concept appropriation. It makes increasing demands on the teacher, in that it involves a fundamental re-orientation of the teacher's skills and perspectives. As well as having a wide knowledge of the subject field, with all its variants, and an empathetic approach to conflicting positions, the teacher requires the additional elements of flexibility and creativity in generating the students' individual processing and evaluation of data and concepts. As well, there is a need for genuine humility on the part of the teacher. No longer is the teacher the sole purveyor of knowledge or determinant of conclusions; rather, the teacher is now a facilitator of others' learning, which requires a genuine sense of humility before both content and learner. The teacher will intentionally be a humble risk-taking co-learner: humble in the recognition of the limits of one's own knowledge and the acceptance of the fact that the student may well transcend the teacher's knowledge in some ways; risk-taking in that the ultimate outcome may be beyond the teacher's control or even predictable knowledge; and co-learner in a readiness to allow students to critique the teacher's held positions, which are also subject to transformation in the overall learning process. However, far from allowing the teacher to be an ill-informed non-specialist, this approach requires a teacher who is so well-versed in the subject area that there is a well-formed conceptual grasp of the area of teaching accompanied by an articulate confidence that allows for fresh and constantly developing expansions and applications of that coherent world view.

In summary, the delivery of integrative learning needs to be guided by three levels of classroom application: the *cognitive* integration of all areas of learning; the *skills* required to integrate learning and practice; and the *personal* coherence of learning, practice and character. The challenge for theological curriculum design is to develop a curriculum that will best facilitate such integrated learning.

5. Curriculum Design

There are many challenges confronting the contemporary Australian theological scene in taking seriously the task of integrative learning within its curriculum. The first level of challenge is in the very structure of any curriculum, which would need to be designed to allow time for and to factor in strategic opportunities for integrative development. The prevailing structure is generally premised on a standard corpus of introductory material which is deemed to be equally significant for all beginners but with no cognizance of the commencing students' prior life experiences ("it is assumed that we are all starting from the same page and that page is zero"). This runs counter to the fundamental concept of integrative learning, which takes as its starting point the life situation and existing frames of reference of the learner. A syllabus that lays early bases for skills development before proceeding to critical processing of content and the formation of ultimate guiding principles is more likely to generate transformative outcomes. The culmination of such a process will ideally be demonstrated in significant capstone exercises and/or involvement in an active project of some sort.

(a) *Prior Considerations*

Before venturing into the specifics of recommended curriculum structure, there are several prior decisions and commitments that need to be in place in order to design a curriculum that facilitates the progressive and consistent implementation of the classroom practices presented in the preceding section. First, clear institutional goals need to be articulated. This will commonly require the defining of a limited overall purpose, a commitment to a pedagogical philosophy that will lead to the attainment of that purpose, and the setting in place of staff likely to achieve that purpose. Then, the institution will need to establish a clear set of desired graduate attributes in a realistic generic statement and set of characteristics of a graduate of the institution. These overarching philosophical elements should be the beginning of any curriculum process rather than being the product of a retrojected statement of philosophy drawn from conventional practices. Once such clear elements are in place, they will serve to inform and to shape the development of a progressive and integrated process leading from desired graduate attributes through a set of key performance indicators to specific learning outcomes, learning tasks and assessment tasks that will validate attainment. It is important that such a progression is in place to avoid the all too common trap of falling into the rationalisation born of pragmatism rather than the attainment of philosophically desirable transformative goals. Figure C gives an illustrative example of how such a generic guiding statement could be expressed. Working from such a base can lead to the development of progressively more specific course aims and unit learning outcomes that will be explicitly shaped by and organically linked to these guiding attributes. The teachers and learners can then work collegially in shaping learning and assessment tasks that cohere with these statements of goals. An illustrative example of such a progressive expansion with respect to one of the graduate attributes in Figure C is provided in Figure D. Of course, it should be stressed that these two figures are provided merely as an indication of how the whole process can be articulated to show the links in a connected progression from desired graduate attributes right through to specific learning tasks. The illustration draws on actual practices currently in use and so does not constitute any radical departure from practice; rather, it seeks to coordinate such practices in an explicit way. The illustration is meant to be neither comprehensive nor definitive, but to prompt further thought on the process.

The other prior decision to be made concerns the issue of the content of the course in total. This is a contentious issue, since it is one of the major points of tension in the entire consideration of transformative learning. The tension between the quest for comprehensive content coverage and the facilitation of skills and personal growth needs to be settled at the outset. Since any course involves a selection of content, and an additional strategic focus on transformative learning will necessitate a limitation of the amount of content to be included, especially in the early stages, the judicious selection of necessary and representative content is required. Content selected for transformative learning will thus be representative rather than comprehensive or exhaustive; it will be based on the need to eliminate fragmented "silos" of discrete learning, duplications and/or contradictions and significant omissions; and will be geared to a sequencing leading from skills development to personal integration. It is not sufficient merely to allocate certain quotas to various fields of study within the degree in order to achieve a mathematical balance in the award. Every item of content should be included on the basis of its explicit contribution to the attainment of the global objectives. It is thus necessary to consider the content in relation to its inter-connectedness and its complementarity in the attainment of desired ends within the context of the whole degree.

Figure C: Sample Statement of Graduate Attributes

1. Statement of Graduate Attributes

A graduate of (xxxxx) College of Theology will have a broad and deep cognitive knowledge of the classical fields of theological thought and scholarship, will have the process skills to evaluate and to communicate such knowledge in a variety of social and ecclesiastical contexts, and will demonstrate a personal integration of theological concepts within the conduct of vocation and life.

2. Characteristics

2.1 The acquisition of broad and deep cognitive knowledge is marked by the ability
- to *collect information* (in various ways)
- to *recall that information* on demand (by examination and other assigned tasks)
- and to *present that information* in an orderly and articulate manner (in various contexts)

2.2 The development of process skills involves both the evaluative skills of analysis and interpretation of material within specific disciplines and the vocational skills of communicating theological knowledge to others. These skills are marked by the capacity
- for *critical analysis* (of documents, systems and situations)
- for *evidence-based argument* (concerning ideas and practices)
- for *cogent evaluation* (of philosophical and practical movements and structures)
- and for *experiential performance* of a variety of ministry or other service functions

2.3 The personal integration of theological concepts is marked by the capacity
- for *synthesis* of disparate and wide-ranging perspectives
- for the *integration* of such perspectives into a holistic world view
- and for the *active implementation* of such a conceptual integration.

Figure D: Sample Process: From Graduate Attribute 2.1 to Learning Tasks (applied to the statement of Course Aims and Learning Outcomes of ACTh BTh 2012)

Graduate Attributes	Characteristics	Course Aims	Learning Outcomes	Key Performance Indicators	Some Representative Learning Tasks
Cognitive Knowledge	• Collection of information • Recall of information • Presentation of information	The aim of the degree is to guide students in a systematic manner to the acquisition of the body of coherent knowledge that is the classical discipline of theology as a means of preparing men and women for the responsibility of communicating Christian knowledge as leaders in the church.	• ability to interpret the biblical deposit, especially those books which have played a crucial role in the development of the Christian tradition, with a knowledge of their original context and their major themes and ideas, • knowledge of the major theological tenets of the Christian faith which underpin any coherent theological world view and philosophy of ministry.	• accurately locate key elements of (bible, doctrine, history, etc) • clearly explain key bib/theol/ hist/min principles to emerge from the study • present clear statement of major bib/theol/hist/min doctrines and practices	• textual survey • explanatory essay/seminar • time line • quiz • examination

(b) Curriculum Structure and Sequence

The desire to craft a curriculum that strategically facilitates integrative transformative outcomes presents some significant challenges but at the same time constitutes a creative opportunity. The challenges are in some ways confronting, as they fly in the face of some fundamental conventional practice. However, if a paradigm is to shift (or even progress markedly), it will necessitate a sometimes courageous willingness to address such challenges and, where necessary, to draw a bold line under some conventions in order to pursue refreshed objectives. The recommendations offered in this final section are presented not as an exercise in iconoclasm but in the hope of providing a spur to such transformative thinking about theological education.

The first structural recommendation is to consider a Social Sciences or a Social Work structure, which typically incorporates integrated practical placements, rather than a Humanities structure as being more facilitative of a transformative goal in place of the more fragmented liberal arts approach commonly associated with a Bachelor of Arts degree. Basic to such a reconsideration is a review of the concepts of "Fields" and "Majors." Most BAs are structured around the concept of majors, which allows for a more limited focus within a vast offering of otherwise disconnected units. These majors have typically been arranged around a structure of departments or fields within the overall Arts domain, with no interaction between those fields. In Theology degrees, this has typically led to the creation of Fields within the overall domain of Theology, commonly designated by such terms as Biblical Studies, Christian Thought and Practical Ministry, and incorporating sub-fields such as Old Testament, New Testament, systematic theology, history, ethics, philosophy, pastoral studies, missiology, Christian education, youth ministry and so on. While the intention of the fields in an undergraduate Arts degree is to allow for expertise in a designated field such as French or History as distinct from Geography or Philosophy, it is questionable if a parallel intention exists in an undergraduate Theology degree. The allocation of fields in Theology seems to be an attempt to maintain balance rather than to generate specialisation, with an equal share being allocated to the various fields. Some allowance is then made for a slightly increased selection from one field as a "major," which in some limited circumstances opens a way for post-graduate study in the field but hardly constitutes a deep specialisation. This is very much a content-centred approach, which seeks to ensure the exposure of all students to a wide suite of subjects, but it lacks any sort of cohering principle and generally militates against the integrative and transformative goals of student-centred learning.

A major problem with majors is that they foster undesirable compartmentalisation rather than holistic integration. Indeed, if fields themselves are to be retained, then consideration needs to be given to how they may be fashioned to fit into a coherent learning strategy and not be just constructs of convenience for organising content. There is a strong traditional attachment to fields and majors, although it is noteworthy that some universities consider Theology as simply one major within their humanities program. This attachment is not always a matter of conservative pedagogy, but it is quite often the product of extrinsic forces beyond the college or university's direct control. Commonly, the regulatory ecclesiastical body mandates traditional fields of study, so overt structural changes are impeded. Even so, there seems to be no significant external pressure on faculty in terms of the specifics of required units or the pedagogy of their delivery. So, while the retention of fields and majors may at times be mandated, there is a pressing need to find ways to develop a greater sense of strategic and personal integration across the barriers if holistic integration is to be attained.

A curriculum structure that takes as its starting point the person of the learner rather than a commitment to traditional majors (or even within a framework of majors) will more likely be strategically concerned with levels of learning than with fields of study. This does not dispense with the required content, but it bases its course framework on the learners' level of operation rather than on discrete sets of content. In analysing and evaluating some of the most productive methods of transformative learning discerned during the research, it seems that Levels of Learning suggest a more fruitful structural base for curriculum than fields and majors. By way of illustrative recommendation, one way of promoting the desired personal goals of transformative learning is the structure of three defined Levels, as follows.

Level 1: Establishing a Hermeneutical and Skills Base
Level 1 introductory units within an undergraduate Theology degree will dominate the early stages of a course, such as in the first semester or distributed throughout the first year. The focus of units at this level is the creation of a platform for integrative learning. These units will introduce academic and research skills, initiate process and performance skills, and establish a philosophical frame of reference for the whole course. They will draw on a range of content from the traditional bases of theological learning, but not in a "compartmentalised" way. Rather, they will use such content in ways that show their complementary interconnectedness and their effective use in theological inquiry and personal application. Students will be encouraged to see the Bible and theology in a holistic light which will guide the whole course of study and personal development. The involvement of a wide range of senior teaching faculty in these units will reinforce the value of such an approach. It is notable that many colleges currently include such

units, but typically they are delivered as extra-curricular topics because there is simply no room for them in the crowded award structure. Given that so many personnel find these elements so fundamentally important to successful student development, that their extra-curricular inclusion creates an additional impost on a heavily burdened first year student, and that their current delivery is at best piecemeal, there is a strong case for their formal inclusion in the actual curriculum structure.

Level 2: Application and Development of Level 1 base

Level 2 units will comprise the bulk of the undergraduate Theology degree, occupying some two-thirds of the award, such as (the equivalent of) semesters 2-5 of a 6 semester program. The focus of these units is the development of mastery of the skills of inquiry initiated in the Level 1 units, with regular and consistent provision for experiential learning and critical reflection on and development of personally held views. The bulk of the theological content of the course will be transmitted in these units, as students progress in their analysis and processing of core content and their development of skills related to personal contexts and vocational areas. There will be a continuation of the prevailing motif of the interconnectedness of all units, in their historical development, their conceptual consonance, and their practical and personal application.

Level 3: Integrative Synthesis of Studies

Level 3 units will provide the final stages of the undergraduate Theology degree, especially in the final semester or distributed throughout the final year. The focus of these units is the students' individual self-location and expression of world view in theory and/or practice. These units provide the learners with an increased responsibility for shaping and conducting their own learning as the culmination of their study. These units will not involve the formal transmission of additional content, but will require the student to execute inter-disciplinary studies in order to link various strands of study already undertaken. Such inductive studies as synthesising personal biblical, theological or historical surveys (as distinct from having had these overviews given to them in first year), the creation of an individual ministry or other vocational philosophy, and the integration of any such concepts within an articulate theological framework are aimed at developing a well formed and integrated graduate. Capstone studies to personalise and apply studies, individually designed research studies to promote individual further in-depth inquiry and action projects to apply learning to a practical situation typify such units.

Such a curriculum design structure facilitates the progressive and consistent implementation of the classroom practices presented in section 4 above. However, two associated questions immediately arise. First, if we include these sorts of personal developmental units, does that mean we will need to double the length of the course? Alternatively, if we add these units without extending the time for the course, does that mean we will need to dispense with important content? One answer suffices for both these questions, namely, neither of these negative implications needs to follow. Such a review as suggested does not mean abandoning any sacred content or taking extra years. What it does require is a thoroughgoing review of why and, especially, how we do what we do. What is needed is not an expansion of the curriculum but a smartening of it. As much content can be delivered in the same time, but in more efficient ways that utilise contemporary means rather than "stand and deliver" modes of lecturing. Thus the content delivered is actually intensified not diluted. Integrating the curriculum will lead to removing the inordinate overlaps that currently exist in the compartments of discrete fields that do not inter- communicate. For example, such major topics as Christology, ecclesiology, ethics, Reformation issues, missions and pastoral issues recur in so many units across the fields (New Testament, Theology, Church History, Pastoral Studies etc) that there is surely a great deal of duplication or, even worse, potential for inconsistency in what the students are required to learn. Again, all units in any system must and do make a limited selection of content (textual exegesis units engage a very limited amount of actual text, historical units cover a selection of issues only) and what is inevitably omitted negates any claim to comprehensive treatment. Since the quest for comprehension of content is arguably as futile as it is flawed, it makes good sense to ensure a mastery of the skills of learning and personal development, so that a lifetime of effectual learning and development may be generated rather than seeking merely to transmit a limited corpus of knowledge.

But even above all such arguments, the quest for genuinely formative, transformative and integrative learning will surely be enhanced by an appropriately constructed and philosophically driven curriculum. Such a curriculum will be based on the principles of student-centred learning and will intentionally and strategically incorporate an engagement with the learner's personal stage of life. It will thus provide means and opportunities for learning that will not only encourage the learner to grow in knowledge and skills, but will also provoke the learner to a holistic and authentic integration of theology, praxis and personhood.

6. Theological Transformation

At the end of all the research, a final question remains. To what degree – or, probably better, in what way – is transformative learning consistent with biblical and theological principles? There has been justifiable criticism levelled at Mezirow's rationalistic bases of transformative learning. However, the concept of holistic transformation effected through biblical theological education is well grounded and indeed may well extend and enrich our theological understanding of humanity and personal development. The imperative injunction in Romans 12:2 exhorts a continuous process of personal transformation (conveyed by the verb *metamorphousthe*) by means of the progressive renewal of the mind (*anakainōsei tou noos*). "Renewal" implies not merely a filling of the mind but a change of perspective of some kind. As Stephen Haar has lucidly expressed, such transformation finds expression in character and conduct and involves the alignment of a person's moral and spiritual vision and thinking to the mind of God.[2] As well as such individual development, the notion of the corporate and communal nature of Christianity requires a communal and relational expression of theological understandings and principles, within a holistically integrated world view. In light of such injunctions, the task of theological education is more than the responsibility to preserve and perpetuate theological dogma (though it surely does include this). Along with such a role, it needs also to see the person of the learner as a central focus in the overall theological process, since it is in the dynamic embodiment of theological understandings in the theologically integrated person that genuinely relational biblical transformation is manifest.

---

2   Stephen Haar, "Enhancing the Capability of Theological Schools in Becoming Agents of Change and Transformation in Civil Society" (Consultation on Establishing a Regional Network of Lutheran Theological Institutions: Bangkok; 18 March 2010), 3.

Postscript: *My Personal Research Journey*

The field research was an exercise in collecting, collating and analysing the input from hundreds of key stakeholders in theological education across Australia. However, it seems fitting to add a few words by way of a personal postscript to relate from my own perspective some of the stand-out features and special moments I encountered and some of the personal lessons I learned during the whole undertaking. These are offered not as definitive statements but as an indication of some of my own recent journey as a researcher and teacher.

What I Encountered

As a researcher, I rather ambitiously sought to gain access to a wide range of key players across universities, denominational theological colleges and independent colleges across all States (with apologies to Tasmania) and ecclesiastical traditions. This meant having to organise numerous sets of meetings and interviews with a lot of busy people – university deans, college principals, students, external academics, archbishops and superintendents, ministry leaders and graduates – all to be available according to my personal fly-in timetable on one set day at their associated institutions. On top of this, since most of the required people had never met me and many had no idea who I was or what my project was about, I expected to meet with some natural resistance. My researcher's anxieties all proved totally unfounded since, in the event, I was afforded the most efficient and enthusiastic reception I could have ever wished for. The collegiate cooperation of each institution's central organiser – the principals, the registrars, the personal assistants, the individual faculty members – set up the interviews and meetings with expert efficiency (and impressive hospitality), so that I had full and free access to all my expert participants. This response was as appreciated as it was efficient. Then, in all the interviews and meetings, I was struck by the sincerity, candour and enthusiasm of all participants in sharing their thoughts, their practices, their experiences and their hopes. I came away from these encounters encouraged and confident that I had been given a genuine insight into the coal-face operations of theological schools across Australia.

As a teacher (still my primary professional identity), I came away excited by what I had heard. Hearing people's stories on such a scale was a genuinely uplifting experience. I have always enjoyed the process of engagement of people and ideas, but this was special, as so many professional peers and kindred spirits related so many encouraging and positive things drawn from their educational experience. I was delighted, though not at all surprised, by the observation of so many stakeholders that the teachers in their institutions are the most significant and most highly appreciated force for effectual education. I was encouraged to hear of the range of creativity and the depth of commitment evident in the teaching across the board. I was most encouraged by the realisation that so many participants are on the same page of values and aspirations in theological education – this gives me great confidence that we are well placed to make good progress in educational enhancement. But some of the most exciting moments for me came from hearing of the life-changing events in students' lives that had occurred as a direct consequence of their theological program. There was the professional musician who realised that professional musicians had working hours not conducive to church attendance, so he had come to college to learn how to minister effectively to such a group, and finished up establishing an unconventional church for professional musicians. For him, BMus + BTh = new church structure. There was the small world religions class taken to a mosque by the lecturer. Their pre-visit anxieties were real, but after the visit, they fully analysed their preconceptions and fears, their changed perspectives and reasons for both, and reported these personal developments to their wider community in a chapel service. Their faith had not been undermined: it had found a much wider world in which to operate. The one hour at the mosque, with appropriate critical reflection and open dialogue, had been worth more than ten hours in the classroom. There was the young woman who, while sensing a pastoral call, lacked confidence in her personal ability for the role. She related a breakthrough moment during Clinical Pastoral Education late in her course where she discovered, "I *can* do pastoral ministry," which led to a clear understanding of her ministerial identity. These experiences are momentous in a student's life and I felt privileged as an outsider to be allowed to share them.

What I Learned

There were some outstanding lessons which struck me personally as most pervasive throughout the whole sector. While the terminology of transformative education is often confused and confusing, there is clearly an underlying concept of the centrality of a transformative experience in the theological enterprise. Whether we speak of "transformative learning" or "deep learning" or "good learning," most Australian theological educationists hold to the notion that a student's life needs to be impacted not just informed by a theological course. This involves more than being theologically articulate or biblically astute; it requires an expanded world view in some way, a changed or significantly enhanced perspective in values and/or active expression, some sort of identity formation not just vocational formation. Personal integration of learning and life is at the heart of such transformative education.

In conjunction with this notion of integration, I have become aware of the need to trust experiential sources in the educative process. As a biblical and historical scholar, I have always been somewhat suspicious of the reliability of experiential anecdotes, preferring the more "objective" documentary and documentable sources. My engagement with people and their experiences during my research has led me to be more sympathetic to receiving and trusting experiential narratives. I have no doubt as to the authenticity of the transformative accounts supplied or of the educational validity of the experiential learning reported. My challenge as a teacher is to make coherent connections with such experience.

Following these insights into the transformative and experience-connected dimensions of theological education, I see quite clearly that there is a fundamental role to be played by curriculum design and development in the encouragement of experience-connected learning and the facilitation of transformative experience. While much such experience has been reported, not much has been done in terms of strategic facilitation of it. It occurs to me that there is no real need to change the content of our theological curriculum beyond the normal revisions we regularly make to update resources and alter some topics. However, there is much room to alter radically the way in which we package that "sacred and inviolable" content. For example, one school which has taken this seriously has re-named all its discipline departments to reflect its developmental educational philosophy rather than retain the traditional departments of Old Testament, New Testament, Theology, Church History, etc. It no longer has a department or suite of subjects called Theology: it has not abandoned any of its former theological substance; it has re-packaged it in ways that integrate its theology with all dimensions of its applied teaching. The ramifications for curriculum design go further than the introduction of a couple of specific formation units or an elective final project (though both of these are positive steps). They extend to a complete re-thinking of the nature, the structure and the progression of content, skills and formative elements, to facilitate a development in students from where they are before the course to where they may be as a well-formed theologically developed graduate person. Curriculum design that focuses on the needs of progressing a student rather than a comprehensive content-based structure will more logically lead to those transformative outcomes which characterise so many statements of Graduate Outcomes but which do not formally appear in many Curriculum Learning Objectives.

Finally, I have learned (again) that the standing of the theological teachers within their community is universally high and obviously merited. All parties agree and affirm that it is the role of the faculty to develop good teaching and learning, including all matters of curriculum within minimal external restraints. Certainly, wider dialogue with interested parties is desired, but the primary and ultimate responsibility for educational design and delivery rests with the faculty. This I find is good news, as it gives the faculty a great opportunity to make positive progress in educational enrichment. From what I have gleaned from my research, I sense that there is a real desire among faculty to make such progress. We have a good product, true; but as with all good products, there is room for more good to be achieved. The current cry is for a greater degree of holistic integration of students' learning and life. The faculty are well placed to work creatively and earnestly in taking our product to an even richer level.

Appendix A: *Data Sources*

1. Primary Sources
Institutional Documents
- Theological curriculum documents from the period 1973-2012, which covers the delivery of Australian bachelor degrees in Theology. The review included historical and current curriculum documents from Adelaide College of Divinity, Australian Catholic University, Australian College of Theology, Brisbane College of Theology, Charles Sturt University, Christian Heritage College, Flinders University, Malyon College, Melbourne College of Divinity, Moore Theological College, Murdoch University, Sydney College of Divinity, Tabor Adelaide, Tabor Victoria, The University of Newcastle.
- Non-theological current curriculum documents. The review included the undergraduate programs in education and nursing of Australian Catholic University, Curtin University, Deakin University, Flinders University, Griffith University, Monash University, Murdoch University, Queensland University of Technology, The University of Queensland, University of New South Wales, University of South Australia, University of Sydney, University of Tasmania.
- Graduate Surveys, Graduate Destination Surveys, Course Experience Questionnaire Responses from students in theological courses for the period 2005-2011, from Australian Catholic University, Australian College of Theology, Charles Sturt University, Melbourne College of Divinity, Sydney College of Divinity.

Stakeholder Sources
- Unstructured interviews with Principals, Deans and/or Academic Deans at Australian Catholic University (Brisbane), Australian Lutheran College, Bible College of South Australia, Harvest West Bible College, Malyon College, Murdoch University, Nazarene Theological College, Perth Bible College, Tabor Adelaide, Trinity Theological College (Brisbane), Trinity Theological College (Perth), University of Notre Dame Australia (Fremantle), Vose Seminary.
- Structured interviews of 90 personnel from 15 institutions (each institution represented by one senior faculty member, one curriculum manager, the academic board chair, a church leader responsible for ministerial training and placements, an employer of graduates and a recent graduate). Institutions involved in the interviews were Alphacrucis College, Australian Catholic University (Brisbane), Australian Lutheran College, Bible College of South Australia, Catholic Institute of Sydney, Catholic Theological College (Melbourne), Flinders University/Uniting College for Leadership & Theology, Moore Theological College, Murdoch University, Nazarene Theological College, Queensland Theological College, Ridley Melbourne, Sydney Missionary and Bible College, Tabor Victoria, Vose Seminary.
- National Church Life Survey Leaders Survey 2011, with 2235 responses from current ministry practitioner/leaders to a module investigating theological educational experience.

- National Workshop 2012. The workshop involved 73 delegates from 40 teaching campuses (including the Council of Deans of Theology, 7 Australian and New Zealand universities, 3 major consortia and 10 independent private colleges) as well as a small number of observers. Delegates were largely senior theological and/or educational personnel of teaching schools and were drawn from 15 ecclesiastical denominations or traditions.

Student Sources
- 2010: Initial Student Survey, involving 20 students currently enrolled in a bachelor degree in theology, drawn from Australian Catholic University (Brisbane), Catholic Theological College (Melbourne), Crossway College (Brisbane), Malyon College (Brisbane).
- 2010: Three Student Focus Groups conducted in Brisbane, Melbourne and Sydney, involving 20 students in the latter half of their theology degree at 16 teaching institutions representing 7 denominations/church traditions.
- 2011-12: First Year Student Survey, Final Year Student Survey, Longitudinal Student Survey in two Parts, involving a total of 596 respondents currently enrolled in a bachelor degree in theology in Australia, drawn from 35 university and private Higher Education Providers.

2. Select Literature

Ball, Stephen — "The Usefulness of Transformation Theory in Understanding Student Learning in the Innovative Field Education Program of the Queensland Baptist College of Ministries: A Pilot Study." MEd thesis, Queensland University of Technology, 1999.

Billett, Stephen — "Curriculum and Pedagogic Bases for Effectively Integrating Practice-based Experiences within Higher Education." http://altc.edu.au/resource-integrating-practice-based-experience-griffith- 2011.

Bushe, GR and AF Kassam — "When is Appreciative Inquiry Transformational? A Meta-Case Analysis." *The Journal of Applied Behavioural Science* 41:2 (2005): 161-181.

Clines, David JA. — "Learning, Teaching, and Researching Biblical Studies, Today and Tomorrow." *Journal of Biblical Literature* 129:1 (Spring 2010): 5-29.

Cranton, Patricia and Merv Roy — "When the Bottom Falls Out of the Bucket: Toward A Holistic Perspective on Transformative Learning." *Journal of Transformative Education* 1: 2 (2003): 86-98.

Cronshaw, Darren — "Australian reenvisioning of theological education: In step with the Spirit?" *Australian eJournal of Theology* 18:3 (December 2011): 223-235.

Dalziel, James — "Implementing learning design: the learning activity management system (LAMS)." https://www.lamsfoundation.org/CD/html/resources/whitepapers/ASCILITE2003%20Dalzie%20Final.pdf

De Jongh, Charles — "Theories of Multiple Intelligences and Learning Assessment for Deep Learning in Higher Education." EdD thesis; University of Johannesburg, 2010.

Dirkx, John M. — "Transformative Learning and the Journey of Individuation." *ERIC Digest* No 223. ERIC Clearinghouse on Adult Career and Vocational Education, 2000.

Dodd, Ted — "Sacred circle of learning: A Model of transformative theological education." DMin dissertation; Vancouver School of Theology, 2008.

Foster, Charles R, Lisa E Dahill, Lawrence A Golemon, Barbara Wang Tolentino *Educating Clergy: Teaching Practices and Pastoral Imagination*. San Francisco: Jossey-Bass, 2006. Gunnlaugson, Olen. "Toward Integrally Informed Theories of Transformative Learning."
Journal of Transformative Education 3: 4 (2005): 331-353.

Haar, Stephen	"Enhancing the Capability of Theological Schools in Becoming Agents of Change and Transformation in Civil Society." Consultation on Establishing a Regional Network of Lutheran Theological Institutions; Bangkok: 18 March 2010.
Jensen, Ben	"Catching up: learning from the best school systems in East Asia." Grattan Institute Report, February 2012, 14. http://www.grattan.edu.au/publications/129_report_learning_from_the_best_main.pdf.
Kalantzis, M.	"Elements of a Science of Education," *Australian Educational Researcher.* 33:2 (2006): 15-42.
Kitchenham, Andrew	"The Evolution of John Mezirow's Transformative Learning Theory." *Journal of Transformative Education* (2008), 6:104-123.
Knowles, Malcolm S.	"Preface," in *Developing Student Autonomy in Learning.* David Boud ed; London: Kogan Page, 1981.
Long, Jude	"Teaching Adults: Insights from Educational Philosophy." *Journal of Christian Education* 53:1 (May 2010): 49-60.
Marmon, Ellen L.	"Cross-Cultural Field Education: A Transformative Learning Experience." *Christian Education Journal* 3:7 No 1 (Spring 2010): 70-84.
Mezirow, J.	"An Overview of transformative learning," in P Sutherland and J Crowther eds, *Lifelong Learning: Concepts and Contexts.* New York: Routledge, 2006, 24-38.
Mezirow, J.	*Learning as Transformation: Critical Perspectives on a Theory in Progress.* San Francisco: Jossey-Bass, 2000.
Mezirow, J.	*Transformative dimensions of adult learning.* San Francisco: Jossey-Bass, 1991.
Mezirow, J.	"Understanding Transformation Theory." *Adult Education Quarterly,* 44:4(1994): 222-232.
Mezirow, J, E Taylor and Associates	*Transformative learning in practice: Insights from community, workplace and higher education.* San Francisco: Jossey-Bass, 2009.
Newman, Michael	"Calling Transformative Learning into Question: Some Mutinous Thoughts." *Adult Education Quarterly* 62:1 (2012): 36-55.
Nichols, Mark and Rosemary Dewerse	"Evaluating Transformative Learning in Theological Education: a multi-faceted approach." *Journal of Adult Theological Education*, 7:1 (2010). http://www.equinoxjournals.com/index.php/JATE/article/view/9429.

Roberts, Nella Ann — "The role of spirituality in transformative learning." EdD dissertation; Florida International University, 2009.

Sadler, D Royce — "What it means to teach." Paper presented to Australian College of Theology Faculty Colloquium, Brisbane, 20 October 2008.

Sherlock, Charles — *Uncovering Theology: The Depth, Reach and Utility of Australian Theological Education*. Adelaide: ATF Press, 2009.

Taylor, Edward — "Building Upon the Theoretical Debate: A Critical Review of the Empirical Studies of Mezirow's Transformative Learning Theory." Adult Education Quarterly, 48:1 (1997): 51.

Taylor, Edward W (ed) — *Teaching for Change: Fostering Transformative Learning in the Classroom: New Directions for Adult and Continuing Education*. No 109; San Francisco: Jossey-Bass, 2006.

UNESCO — "Curriculum Reform Manifesto: *Principles for Rethinking Undergraduate Curricula for the 21st Century*." 15 August 2011. http://curriculumreform.org/curriculum-reform-manifesto/.

Weinski, Marie-Claire — "An inquiry into the transformative learning of evangelical theological students in Germany." PhD thesis; Trinity Evangelical Divinity School, 2006.

White, Roger — "Promoting spiritual formation in distance education." *Christian Education Journal* 3:2 (2006): 303-315.

Williams, Rowan — "Theological Education in the Anglican Communion." TEAC Principals Address, London: 11 May 2011.

Winkelmes, Mary-Ann — "The Classroom as a Place of Formation: Purposefully Creating a Transformative Environment for Today's Diverse Seminary Population." Teaching Theology and Religion 7:4 (2004): 213-222.

Appendix B: Denominational Variations

While overall patterns of student responses have been reported in the chapters of the book, there were noticeable variations in terms of the denominational background of students. The main issues are presented in the following charts from those denominations where statistically significant responses were received.

B1: Student Profiles

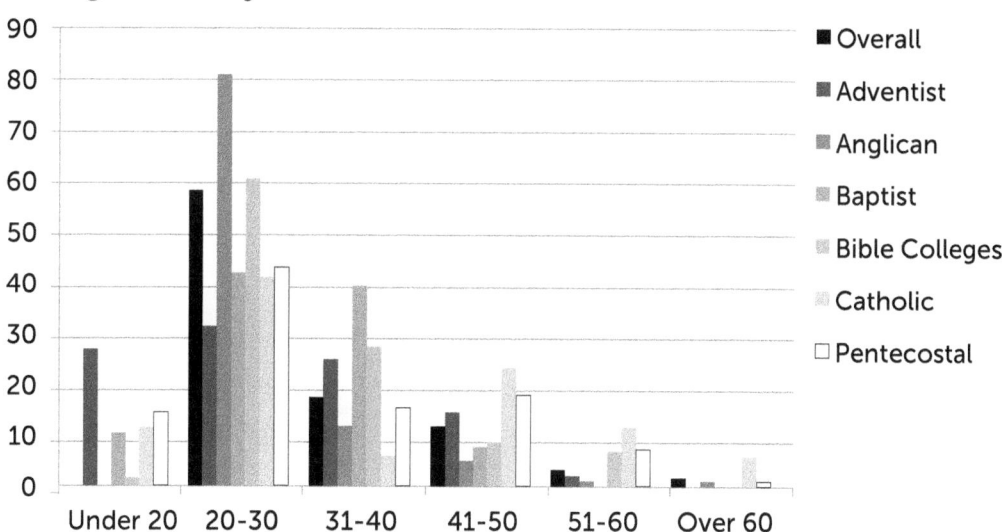

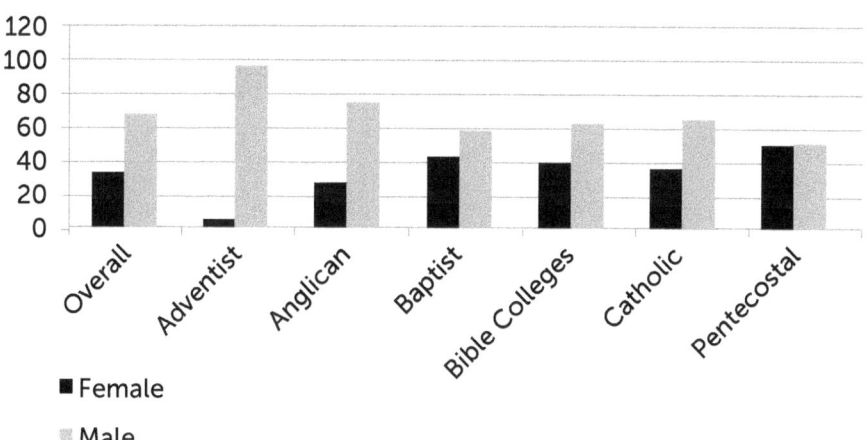

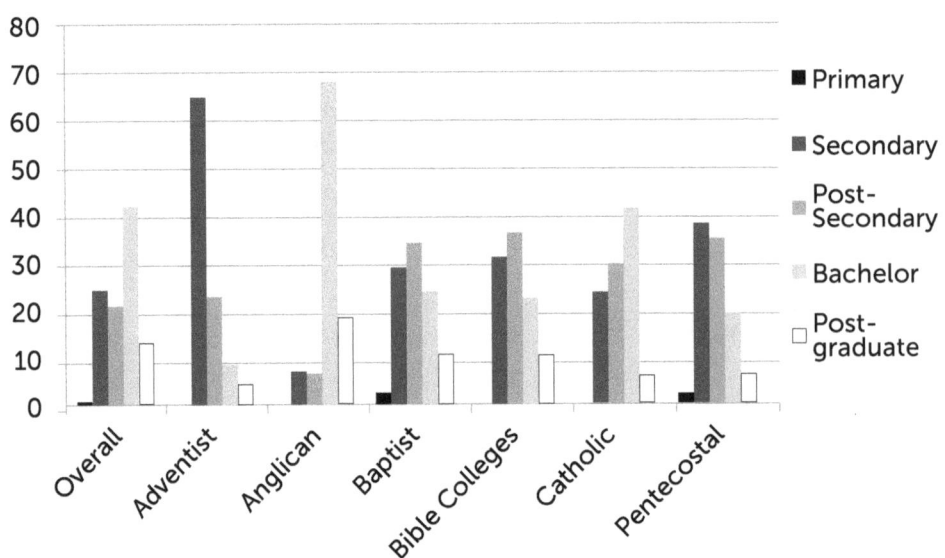

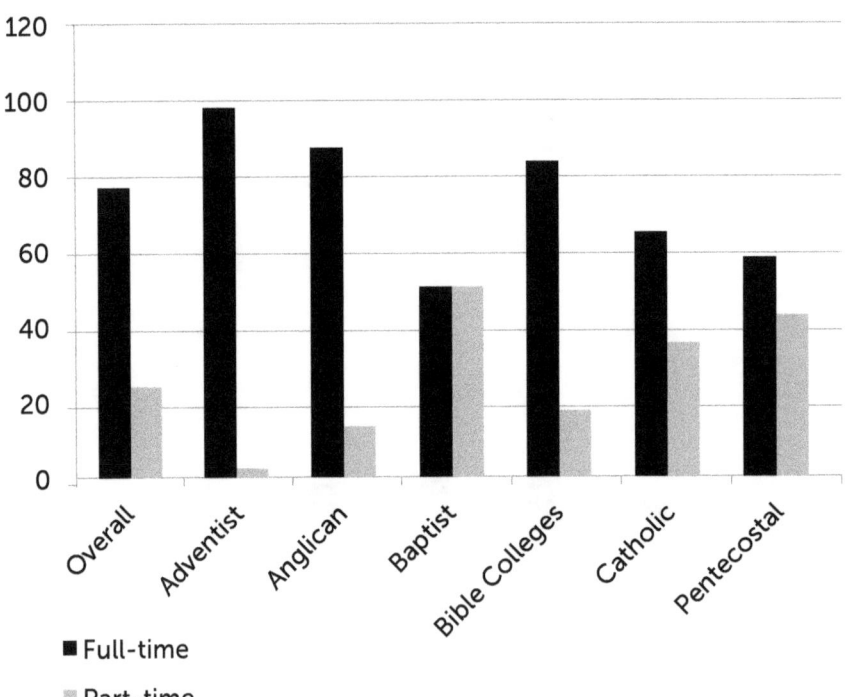

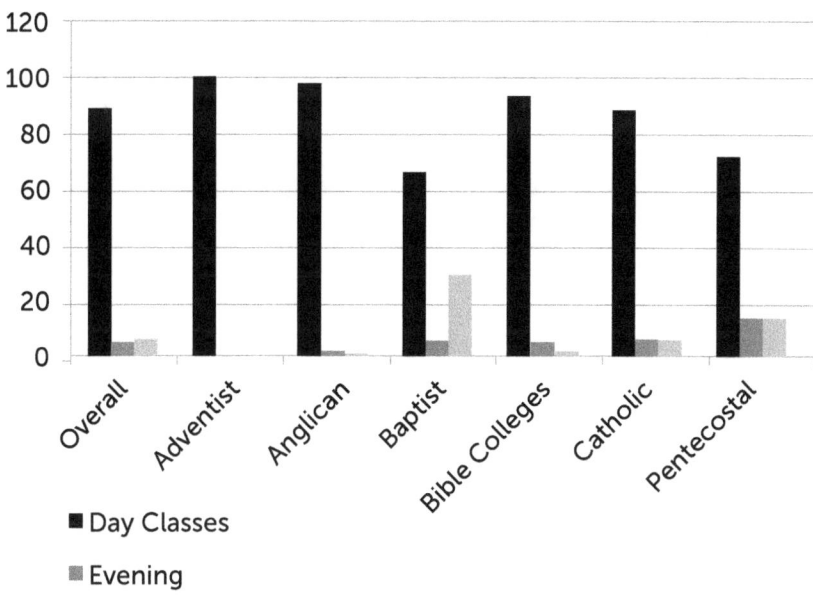

B2: *Student Experiences*

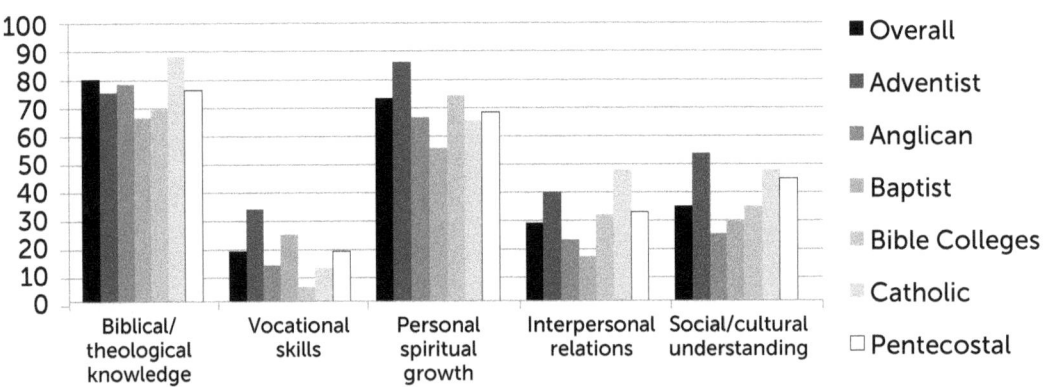

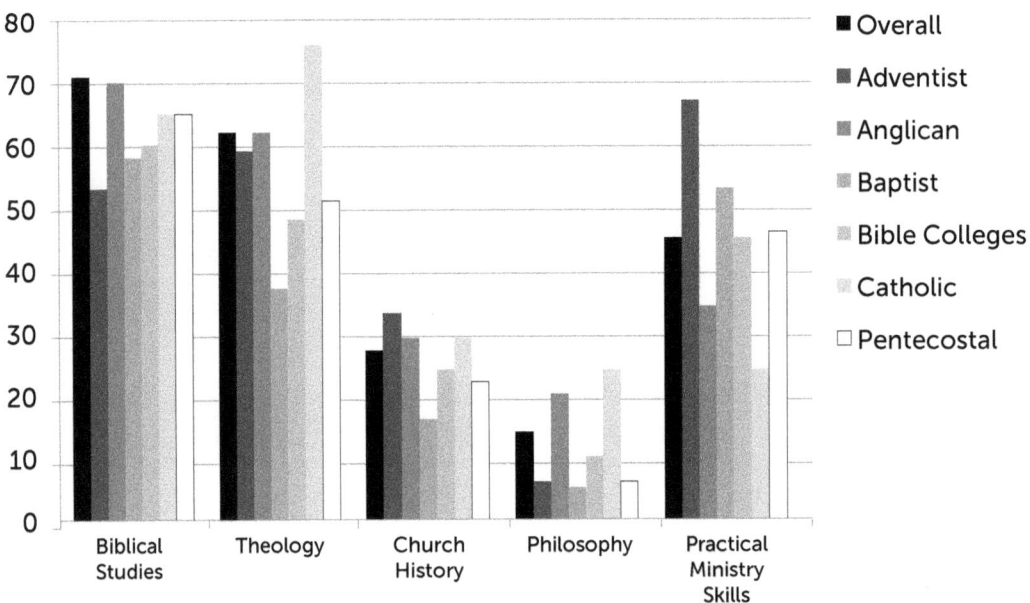

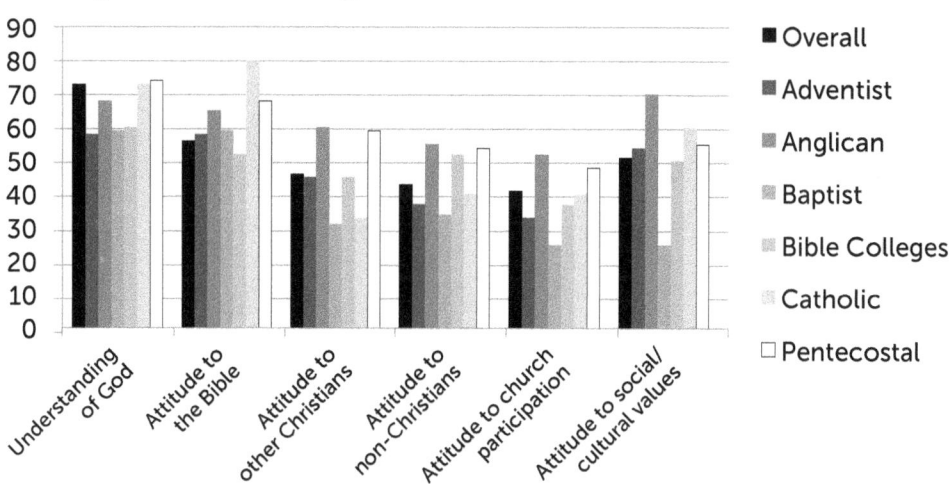

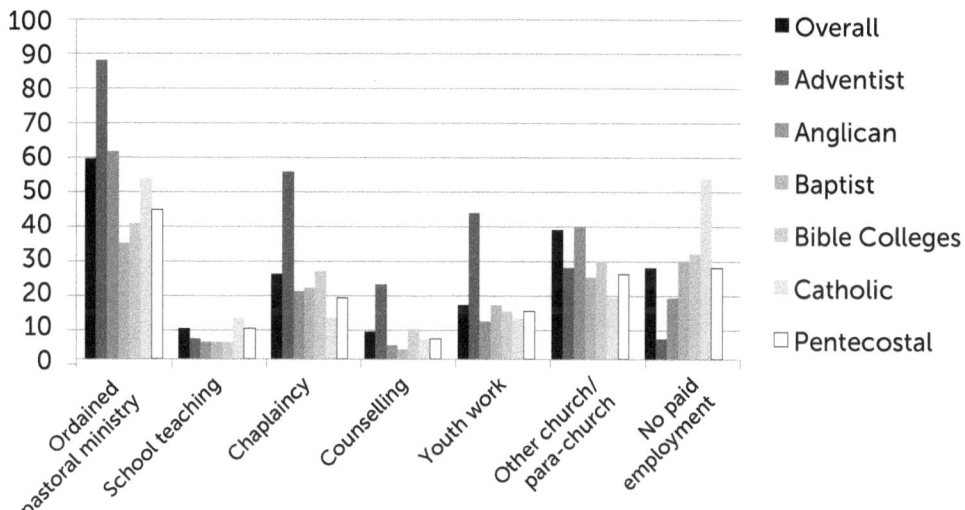

8 | WHERE TO NEXT?

Appendix C: Analysis of Graduate Surveys

Graduate Destination Surveys and Graduate Surveys related to the period 2005-2009 were reviewed from numerous institutions. The analysis of these surveys is summarised below.

Religious/NFP positions:	47%
Social Welfare/Health:	7%
Education:	7%
Private Sector/Other:	12%
Further Study:	2%
Not working/No return:	22%

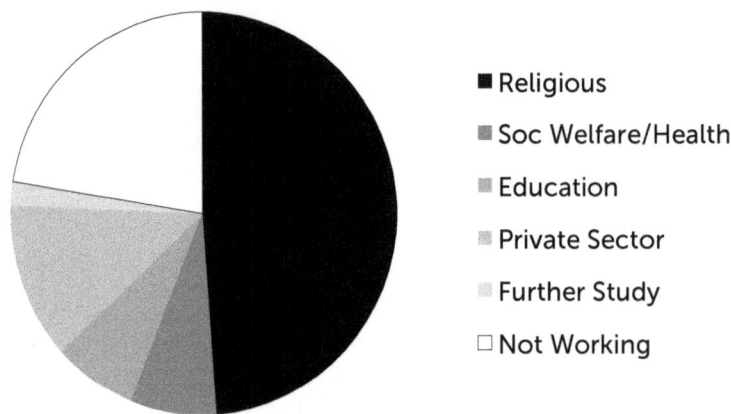

Comments

While ordination requirements of churches dominate curriculum construction and delivery, only half the graduates enter religious occupations, including non-ordained positions. Therefore, while such religious occupations remain the major destination of theology graduates, there is an equally numerous proportion of the student body who do not enter such vocations. This has a three-fold ramification.

- Given that religious service (including ordained ministry) remains the main vocational destination, there is a case for the greater and deliberate integration of theological principles and ministry practices within the degree itself.
- Given that a significant number enter (or remain in) human service occupations such as health, social welfare and education, there is a case for an intentional integration of vocational profession and theology.
- Similarly, since another significant number do not enter paid employment, there is a case for the intentional integration of theology and general world view within the degree itself.

Challenge

A major challenge is to construct a curriculum that incorporates flexible opportunities for students to have exposure to and develop mastery in ministry skills within a personally articulated theological worldview, while at the same time not limiting the scope for personal and other vocational developmental opportunities by imposing the narrowness of ordained requirements on students who are not heading that way.

Some Suggestions for Consideration
- Develop introductory units that intentionally allow and require students to begin to shape and articulate a theological framework for their own development. This will require a reduced emphasis on intensive content transmission in order to provide the opportunity for students to reflect on and meaningfully critique their own pre-suppositions and understandings and to refine them progressively in light of theological growth.
- Intentionally connect advanced units to this evolving theological world view by means of coordinated teaching (eg unit connections, cross-disciplinary units, team teaching, etc) and real-life assignments in individually pertinent contexts, group projects, peer learning and other student-based learning methods.
- Provide opportunities for capstone integrative study in the final stages of the course. This will ideally allow the student to formulate a coherent statement of personal theological understanding utilising the critical skills developed through all elements of the course (hermeneutical integration of theological learning), linked with an individually relevant ministry and/or vocational application (integration of learning and life)

expressed in terms of a person's individually formed values and perspectives (integration of learning and personhood).
- Incorporate relevant and effectively supervised field experience placements within the degree structure, to include individually relevant goal setting, critical reflection, journaling, and action observations, plans and critiques. This will require the establishment of legitimate theological and practical criteria for implementation and evaluation.
- Focus on learning and assessment tasks that promote deep learning rather than simply the surface learning of knowledge recall and collation.

Appendix D: *Focus Groups Analysis*

Three Student Focus Groups were conducted (in Brisbane, Melbourne and Sydney). The groups addressed a number of questions aimed at identifying student perceptions and experiences of their undergraduate degree in theology. The groups comprised students who had completed at least half of their undergraduate degree in either a Higher Education theological college or a university.

D1: In your course of study to date, what subject have you personally found most worthwhile?
Biblical Studies (including hermeneutics and languages) was by far the dominant response in all groups (55%), followed by Christian Thought (especially Christology) (25%). Others mentioned were Worldview Studies (10%), Spirituality (5%) and Philosophy (5%).

D2: Remember back to when you first decided to take up theological study. At that point, what did you expect to gain by doing the course?
In the Brisbane and Sydney groups, the dominant prior expectation of the course was the attainment of practical ministry skills which would equip for vocational or other serious ministry, though this was not mentioned at all in the Melbourne group. In the Melbourne group, the emphasis was on the attainment of a systematic and coherent understanding of the Bible and theology: answers to all the big questions to make sense of personal experience. In the Brisbane and Sydney groups (but not at all in the Melbourne group), there was an occasional reference to the development of a deeper personal knowledge of and relationship with God.

D3: Right at the beginning, what did you expect would happen to you as a person during your study?
Commonly, there were no clearly defined expectations, but there was a commonly expressed general sense of personal challenge which would result in becoming a more deeply thinking person on theological/spiritual/personal issues. Some of the younger members (mainly those entering theological study directly from school) indicated the expectation of some personal clarification of identity and/or life direction. There was no expressed sense of any expectation of essential difference as a person.

D4: You have all had certain life experiences before and during your theological study. Has your study program connected with these life experiences in significant ways?

With regard to prior life experience, there was very limited connection expressed between the theological study and such life experience. What was mentioned was stated as incidental only, with some empathy with and expansion of prior experience (especially noted by mature-aged part-time students), but there was no report of structured or intentional engagement with prior experience, even in Field Education units.

With regard to current life experiences, especially ministry situations, the studies were reported as intersecting more clearly and intentionally. The integration of theology and liturgy with life issues was commonly noted. Some reported changes in jobs and family conflict management as a direct result of their theological progression while others noted the impact of theological studies on their personal and public ethics, where previously held moral absolutes were commonly replaced with a more pluralistic perspective. The integration of study and ministry was particularly noted within Field Education placements in those colleges where such units form part of the actual degree.

D5: Has your study program offered you opportunities for personal growth or change?

All respondents reported a significant growth in terms of an expanded world view occasioned by their theological studies, with concomitant recognition of the need to grow or change in order to respond to that enlarged perspective. This led to a growth in personal understanding of self, God and the world, which in turn led to a widespread rejection of dichotomous and judgemental absolutes regarding God and the world. The main element of personal growth was expressed in terms of a greater sense of God's being in control rather than oneself. One person put it as, "The language of 'me' has disappeared from my vocabulary;" another expressed it as, "Previously, I was telling God what to do in me; now, it is God telling me what he is doing in me." This growing sense of God-dependency in place of self-sufficiency resulted in a vastly expanded understanding of the nature and various expressions of God, in terms of both individual mystical contemplation and a pluralistic community.

While not widespread, some limiting factors on such personal growth were noted. The pressure and academic orientation of units at times limited or truncated the opportunity for development. Some lecturers' attitudes (requiring conformity) and personal engagement (especially by way of negative off-handed comments) at times hampered growth. (However, generally, lecturers were praised for their openness and helpfulness in creating a "safe" environment for personal inquiry.)

D6: Throughout your course of study, has your understanding of the world changed in any way?
Given the weight attached to an emerging world view expressed in the previous question, responses to this question tended to amplify earlier comments. All respondents reported a greatly expanded view of the nature, diversity and value of variant cultures and people. This resulted in greater tolerance towards and genuine respect for others' views and cultures and an increased openness to dialogue. The world was now seen not as a dichotomous "opposite" to the church, but as the locus of God's overarching creativity. Hence it is essentially good, although damaged and in need of restoration to God's image. Similarly, the view of creation had become more holistic, going beyond mere humanity and the church and embracing the totality of God's creation(s). Within this perspective, there was noted a greater sense of the lostness of people combined with love and respect for them. In light of the greater sense of confidence in God, his world and his justice, there was a greater willingness to take a counter-cultural stand.

D7: Has your understanding of yourself changed during your course of study?
The dominant response was that of a growing sense of one's personal identity in Christ. This had the double effect of a growth in both humility and confidence, as they became less self- focused and more God-dependent. The increased awareness of personal weaknesses was accompanied by an increased confidence in God: "my frailty; God's 'bigness'." Increased understanding of doctrines of grace, justification and sanctification led to greater acceptance of oneself as identified with Christ, with more courage to enter new fields and "to run with a vision."

The other outcome of this personal growth was expressed in terms of a less judgemental attitude to others. There was a removal of the previous sense of superiority towards non- church people, now seeing all God's creatures as equals. There was now an understanding of their role as being to reflect Christ positively in the world rather than to judge the world, with a desire to care deeply about people and to relate to them at a deep level, with a view to improving the world.

D8: *Would you say that your theological degree has been about forming a person into what they should be or about transforming a person into what they have the potential to be?*
This question brought the most diverse responses. The Brisbane group strongly expressed the view that a theological degree is more about developing an environment that facilitates growing into the person God has created you to be, to discover and confirm gifts, rather than shaping a person into a pre-determined mould. The Melbourne group equally strongly expressed the view that the main objective of a theological degree is the formation, in terms of the tradition and requirements of the relevant institution, of a graduate with the appropriate graduate outcomes of a theologically articulate person, prepared for ministry within that tradition. (A minority of non-ordination candidates expressed the view that the attainment of personal fulfilment should take precedence over institutional tradition.) The Sydney group held both aspects to be important, but with a leaning towards the personal transformation. In particular, they stressed the value of transferable attributes such as critical thinking and new ways of thinking and the attainment of personal potential, but not in a *laissez-faire* manner.

All groups noted that the impact of lecturers was probably more significant in the matter of personal (trans)formation than the actual content of the units.

While there was no general agreement on this question, two points seem worth noting. First, in general, the students responded in terms of what they thought a theological degree *should achieve* rather than what they had *actually experienced*. However, from the general tone and interaction of participants, it was quite apparent that their responses were to a large degree a reflection of their experience, which was one that they endorsed. Second, the composition of the three groups may be pertinent. The Brisbane group was dominated (numerically) by an evangelical presence of people not all heading towards ordained ministry (Bible college, Baptist,

Pentecostal), which may have influenced the individual basis of their observations. Conversely, the Melbourne group was numerically dominated by a Catholic presence, along with many who were ordination candidates, which may also have influenced their tradition- oriented responses.

D9: Can you suggest ways in which students' life experiences could be more intentionally and effectively incorporated into the study program?
Participants offered numerous suggestions for incorporating students' life experiences strategically into the curriculum. Most were positive and proactive suggestions for consideration; some were negative and reactive ways of highlighting perceived shortcomings of current practice.

Positive suggestions mainly centred on the intentional inclusion of opportunities in various units for life application, by way of structured tutorial/seminar or other group discussion and by set assignments, either essay or project based. The sharing of personal stories with critique of variant world views was seen as a positive thing, provided it was facilitated in a non-judgemental way. Such personal experiences, while being respected in themselves, should also be filtered through the lens of the Bible rather than be automatically received as authoritative.

The more reactive commentary centred on the need for more consideration of and support for contemporary theological students and the elimination of presuppositions concerning who such students are and what their needs and motivations are. Issues highlighted include the danger of assuming common prior experience and motivation of all students and the need to recognise the shift in the composition of the student body from the former tradition of full-time males gearing for vocational ministry to the current preponderance of part-time female students not heading for ordination. This has ramifications in areas of delivery such as what load is a realistic "full-time" load; what hours of access are available (for classes, libraries and lecturer consultation); mode of delivery (day class attendance, evening classes, timetabling, weekends, vacation periods, online etc). There was also significant concern at the lack of support services typically available (or not available in most non-university colleges). While much praise was expressed concerning lecturers' general helpfulness, the lack of formal student centres, academic development support, chaplains and other personal support personnel and resources was seen to be in stark contrast with the provisions of most universities. Consequently, suggestions for catering for individual students' life experiences and situations included the provision of chaplains; the implementation of introductory programs in theological language and thinking as an orientation element; the development and implementation of student support and learning management systems; flexibility of delivery times and modes and access to lecturers; and a commitment to the valuing of all students' experience (including that of youth in a generally older cohort and of part-time women in a male-oriented institution) rather than merely the "traditional" or lecturer's personal experience.

Two other observations made in the context of this topic are worth noting. First, it was noted that, commonly, ordination students have a parallel formation program for practical ministry development and, while this is generally integrated with academic studies when the formation program is intentionally linked to the degree (by virtue of curriculum design or by common lecturers), when the formation program is quite separate from and independent of the delivery of the degree, such integration, even compatibility, is not always evident. The second comment came from a member of a larger institution, where individual connections between lecturer and student are not as close as is commonly the case in smaller colleges. It was stated that it is not the college's responsibility to integrate study and life, which is not individually practical in a large and varied institution. Rather, it is the institution's role to deliver knowledge; it is the student's role to apply that knowledge appropriately.

D10: *Of all that we have discussed about your theological education, what one thing stands out as the most important thing to you?*
The main responses to this question were two-fold. First was the need for the application of theological knowledge to real life rather than the mere development of a set of propositional truths. Second was the importance of the educational process and community in which the education occurred. These two elements came together in the willingness and openness to learn (even when this is discomforting) with a resultant respect for diversity and acceptance (of the people studied with, of churchly expressions, of the world at large), with an attitudinal development growing from exclusion to inclusion.

D11: In summary …
In general, prior expectations of students entering theological studies centred on the acquisition of deeper biblical and theological knowledge, the development of enhanced thinking processes and the attainment of practical ministry skills. There was little if any expectation of personal change, although personal challenges and some sense of deepening one's relationship with God were vaguely anticipated. While these expectations were largely borne out by ensuing experience, with a heavy focus on the value of the Bible as the basis of authoritative knowledge, the most profound development reported was in a vastly expanded (rather than radically different) world view which necessitated at times significant personal changes. Growth in theological knowledge and understanding led to a greater degree of simultaneous humility and confidence as one's identity in Christ became more fully understood and appropriated. At the same time, concepts of God and his creation were enlarged, leading to a far more defined recognition of and more inclusive respect for the diversity of creation (including people, cultures and churches) and an accompanying diminution of judgementalism towards others' thoughts and praxis. Personal development was seen more in terms of growing into the person one is capable of being – not necessarily a different person but possibly a hitherto unknown person.

The matter of any nexus between theological study and prior life experience was virtually a non-issue, as there was no report of any intentional connection, with only occasional and incidental intersection having been experienced. There was much more intentional linkage with current experience, especially in areas of ministry, most particularly associated with field placements which were integrated with or parallel to the degree program. Experiential application happened more via the community of theological education than by the content of the curriculum, with both lecturers and student cohort being noted as very significant agents.

D12: Have we missed anything important?
Many voices echoed the appreciation of the maturing of their theological understanding and personal growth during their degree program. Three things stood out. Theological education involves many unique personal challenges for students, which can even be damaging, so support systems

need to be carefully managed and structures for hearing the voice of students need to be authentically developed. Second, the changing world of education needs to be considered, with traditional assumptions as to clientele, content, aspirations, modern pedagogy and associated assessment being constantly reviewed. Third, a constant refrain through all group discussions was the significance of the educational community in the theological process, with particular importance attached to the role and personal modelling of the lecturer in areas of personal growth and development. While the theological content of study provided the authoritative base for an emerging world view and an enlarged understanding of the people in that world, it was the lecturers who provided the inspiration for the personal appropriation and activation of the theological principles so learned.

Appendix E: *Stakeholder Interviews Synthesis*

Stakeholder interviews were conducted with four discrete groups (faculty, academic chairs, church leaders, recent graduates), with sets of questions designed to provide a cross-sectional view of several key themes. In general, respondents in a particular institution presented a consistent set of responses to the various questions, which suggests a reliable overall picture. As well, across the range of the fifteen institutions, there was a high degree of consensus in most areas, with any significant variations noted below. A synthesis of the analytical conclusions of the various groups provides some thematic generalisations which may be drawn.

E1: Who has the capacity to shape the curriculum?

It is very clear that the teaching faculty, especially the dominant academic leadership of the faculty, play the most significant role in determining the shape and delivery of curriculum. Whether this be done by top-driven means or by more collegiate methods of faculty engagement, it is clear that if any curriculum is to be developed or enhanced, the impetus for and implementation of such will come from the faculty. There are various levels of external influence, especially where the teaching institution is closely aligned with a controlling church (and most particularly when that church operates on a nationally or internationally organized basis). Such church alignment typically requires the primacy of the ordination requirements of the church and the larger the ecclesiastical organization, the more restrictive is the primary degree curriculum in its framework, with a consequent resistance to curriculum change. Conversely, the more autonomous the teaching institution, the more it is open to local initiative and more direct implementation of change. Such external restrictions are noted more by faculty than by the church leaders, who typically put more distance between themselves and curriculum matters, preferring to allow the appointed faculty to take the responsibility for such issues, with general oversight rather than management by the church leadership. There is virtually no effective forum for non-faculty to have a proactive voice in curriculum design or development.

While there is a high level of satisfaction expressed in this regard by all groups of stakeholders, there is yet room for a more inclusive approach to the incorporation of key stakeholders. In particular, faculty need to have a mechanism by which they can be consistently informed by the contemporary needs and issues of both students and stakeholders, especially with regard to contemporary issues in education and ministry. This will involve strategic and effective faculty engagement with a wider sector of tertiary education, with current ministry practitioners and with current students or recent graduates. In particular, there is a strongly voiced desire for more effectual two-way communication between teaching institutions and stakeholders, on a formally structured and regular basis, offering proactive developmental opportunities rather than merely reactive assessments. Within the bureaucratic organizations of universities and the international hierarchies of some churches, there is limited if any opportunity for local forums, while the more loose regulatory nature of the major theological consortia allows for much more local initiative. In autonomous colleges, such expanded communication is probably more urgent, given their lack of organic support by larger bodies.

All categories of respondents presented a consistent picture of the centrality of the faculty in curriculum design and implementation, within the context of dialogue with significant stakeholders. The primary onus of and opportunity for curriculum development lie clearly with the teaching faculty.

E2: What is the major focus of theological education?

The acquisition and mastery of biblical and theological knowledge is clearly the main motivation and most valued outcome of theological education, which has been affirmed strongly by all categories of stakeholders. This is both the primary *raison d'être* of the teaching institutions and their most successful and most valued outcome. It is consistently asserted by faculty, demanded by church leaders and appreciated by graduates in all institutions. While connecting theological knowledge to ministry performance is attempted in some schools (especially those specifically serving State-based churches) and the personal growth of individual students is commonly desired (especially in smaller and generally autonomous colleges), these areas are neither the major focus nor the strongest outcome. Teaching the Bible and its associated theology is the core business of theological education.

Opinion is mixed as to the place of ministry skills and personal growth within the formal curriculum. Some traditions see the locus of these elements in extra-curricular contexts, such as the church, the seminary, separate ministry ordination programs and campus-based community life. Others lament the absence of these elements from the curriculum, but acknowledge that a small school cannot be all things to all people and that theological knowledge is primary, so the lack of other elements is an inevitable cost. Some recent positive developments in the area of practical ministry skills are noted, but the dimension of personal growth and spiritual formation, while also acknowledged as supremely important, especially for ministry preparation, is consistently neglected in formal programs in the vast majority of institutions.

Emergent questions arise. First, although theological graduates are well versed in scripture and systematic theology, do they have a suitably wide world view, are they adequately equipped for effectual dialogue with a contemporary world, do they have the ability to integrate their learning and their life and ministry? That is, while the focus on biblical and theological knowledge is affirmed as necessary, is the very singularity of that focus a sufficient preparation of graduates for "real-world" ministry? Second, when the extra-curricular formative programs are typically restricted to ordination candidates, what means are there for the formative development of non-ordination candidates, who commonly constitute the majority of students? These questions arose time and again in all forms of institutions.

While theological expertise is seen to be in good shape, there are calls for the enhancement of both practical ministry skills and personal growth within the formal curriculum, with the aim of producing more integrated persons who can think, relate and live theologically and skilfully in a contemporary world context, rather than simply to produce informed and articulate theologians.

E3: What is the place of experiential learning?
There is very little formal incorporation of structured experiential learning opportunities within the curriculum, with such learning being very limited in extent and narrow in scope. Any life-based connectedness within the curriculum is typically *ad hoc* and intuitive rather than intentional or strategic. The classroom is seen as the place to transmit information rather than to engage students in learning activity. Occasionally, some pastoral ministry units have a small practical project component and, even less frequently, some history and missions units incorporate experiential field trips. Supervised Field Education is the one significant area which features

experiential learning, but this is commonly (though not universally) limited to a small component of the course, commonly taken by the minority ordination candidates only, and commonly conducted in external church placements and not under the direct supervision of teaching faculty, thus reducing the integrating connections that may be made between "academic" and "field" work. There are but few examples of intentional and strategic curriculum planning that incorporates significant and well planned experiential learning by way of community engagement, involving both unit design and creative learning and assessment tasks. Apart from these curriculum elements, most experiential development is associated with extra-curricular activities, especially the separate Formation programs and the highly valued (though limited and at times seen as contrived) campus community life. While many endorse the value of experiential learning, there is little evidence of any expertise in designing or implementing specific programs for its attainment. This suggests an area in need of significant attention and development, if experiential learning is to be seen as an authentic element in theological education.

While there is a common recognition of the value of the diversity of students' life experiences and backgrounds, both before and during the study program, there is an equally common exclusion of those experiences and backgrounds from the teaching/learning enterprise. Field placements are rarely integrated with classroom curriculum and it is only by way of informal class discussion that connections are made. Any such connections (with a few notable exceptions) are incidental and at the student's initiative. This is an area where faculty generally seem to have a lack of either capacity to initiate or confidence to implement, despite the good results noted in those few cases where connectedness occurs. There are very few examples of an institutional approach to tailoring individual study programs to connect with prior and ongoing life experience and goals, accompanied by strategic field placement and support, recognition of different learning types and encouragement of creativity in learning and assessment tasks. Generally, there is no formal connection with a student's life beyond the course, with college seen as a discrete time out to study rather than a part of an ongoing organic life process. There are a couple of interesting innovations in universities, who are increasingly seeing their mission within the context of community engagement and integrated experiential learning rather than in social isolation.

The general disconnection between theological studies and life experience is seen as a limiting feature of the programs, and one which has significant room for enrichment.

E4: *What are the opportunities for transformative learning?*

The issue of transformational learning is elusive in description and vague in attainment. Most parties strongly desire it as an aspirational outcome, but great variability exists in its implementation. The terminology is used variously (priestly formation or personal development or radical change?), there is uncertainty as to whose role it is (academy or seminary or church?) or how it is to be facilitated (in class or in community?) and, even more so, how it is to be authenticated (by measurement or demonstration?). Consequently, there is a reluctance to grasp the nettle of transformative ideals in a structured and deliberate way, with few deliberately structured transformative elements within the formal degree program (beyond the limited Supervised Field Education units and a few practical elective units), with this element left largely to informal extra-curricular activities loosely based around campus life and college missions. However, despite this overall vagueness, there is a strong and clear expression of the desire and need of an integration of learning and life during the course of theological study, not just the production of a graduate who is theologically informed or ministerially skilled. Even where the focus is on producing ministers, there is a general sentiment that effectual leadership flows out of transformed lives.

Some recent curriculum developments have incorporated transformative learning strategically in the degree, by placing intentionally transformative units within the degree curriculum at strategic points, by the use of integrating exit projects, the involvement of more than one lecturer in a unit delivery to engender diversity, and by incorporating learning methods such as appreciative inquiry, collaborative learning and educational field trips with appropriate educational supports. However, these efforts remain relatively few in number and tentative in application, with the main avenues of transformative opportunities depending on the lecturer's informal interaction and dialogical teaching style within an open and safe yet challenging atmosphere in which growth may occur. The importance of appropriate complementary co-curricular programs is commonly stressed as a vital means of promoting transformative experience, yet rarely is there any sense of cohesion, comprehensive inclusion of students, or evaluation of outcomes of such activities. If these are authentic parts of the transformative agenda, then there is a case for their more formal inclusion in the program.

A strong motif was the desire for holistic and integrated learning to replace the traditional compartmentalised approach to theological instruction, based on the transmission of a pre- determined and controlled corpus of specialised knowledge, with a more open-ended system of theological discovery which generates an authenticity of experience for the learner rather than a detached mastery of content. The two elements of legitimate content and authentic experience are not incompatible, but the connection between them is causative rather than casual, that is, the mastery of content has a purpose of (trans)formation or else it risks becoming an exercise of limited if not dubious value. A number of recent graduates reported that, along with the legitimate quest for biblical and theological advancement which they value highly, there is also the less tangible but earnest desire for authentic personal spiritual growth, expressed in the plea that all knowledge could be transformative.

A particular difficulty in this consideration is that of noting and reporting the results of transformative learning, which requires that some means of demonstrating transformation be established. There is a prevalent academic suspicion of anything that cannot be assessed in numerical or grade terms, so how does one "measure" transformation? Similar questions are asked (and similar suspicion exists) about any such skills or personal development units (eg Supervised Field Education and Guided Spiritual Formation). The answer may lie in a re-definition of assessment, with a shift away from purely quantitative markers (such as percentages – themselves a dubious measure of any theological unit) to qualitative markers, which will provide *demonstrability* rather than *measurability*. However, extreme care is needed to generate adequate and authentic qualitative markers and valid accountability instruments.

Over all, there is a high level of consensus that theological education needs to incorporate the whole life of the student and that there is a need to anchor theology in the faith tradition which has given rise to it. The real need is therefore to bring these two aspects together in an integrated and authentic way. The challenge for theological curriculum designers is to move deliberately towards the aim of theological education as transformative rather than merely cognitive.

E5: What Graduate Outcomes and Attributes are produced?

What should a theological graduate look like? Should the principal product be a well formed church leader with effective ministry capacities and leadership or a transformed life exhibiting commendable qualities and personal attributes? Most stakeholders ideally seek a balance of the two elements of leadership formation and personal development, but there is clearly a growing realisation of the diversity of clientele and stakeholders in most institutions, with a resultant tension of needing to serve multiple masters and an emerging need for institutions (especially small colleges) to re-define their core objectives and to establish viable parameters of operation. Most church leaders affirm that their schools are producing effective leaders, but this assessment is grounded on the traditional base of producing a theologically and biblically well informed graduate and not so much on the emerging need for the development of an engaging practitioner. The strengths of graduates are therefore approvingly cited as sound theological scholarship and biblical fidelity, with some (though not universal) acknowledgement of suitably developed ministry skills. The main focus of the theological and Bible colleges is training for ministry, with personal growth viewed as a secondary and supporting element of that training. This ministry focus is achieved by formal curriculum shaping (in the choice and arrangement of units offered), encouraged in the various extra-curricular programs and structures of colleges, and strongly influenced by the lecturers, whose personal examples, teaching methods, relations and attitudes do much to affect the shape of the ministry persona resulting from the study program. The lecturers are the most significant and pivotal agents in determining the shape of the graduate, as well as the shape of the curriculum.

However, among church leaders and more so among graduates, there is a growing recognition of the need for graduates to add more enhanced skills of appropriate leadership and social engagement to their knowledge base, with the minister of tomorrow (in an ordained or a lay situation) needing to manage people and society (both in and beyond the church) in a more dialogical manner. This will require more than a knowledgeable theologian and more than a skilled practitioner: it will also need an integrated person who has appropriated theological concepts and mastered principles of practice in a holistic expression of ministry in a variety of modern and often unpredictable contexts.

E6: What are the colleges' Strengths and Not-yet-strengths?

The institutions are all well regarded by their stakeholders, with some outstanding acknowledgements of consistent strengths. At the same time, there were many constructive suggestions in areas where further strengthening could be facilitated. This summary of strengths can be presented in terms of actual strengths (as reported by a consensus of respondents) and aspirational strengths (which are currently being worked on or are earnestly desired).

- **Actual Strengths**

Two dominant strengths stand out: the personal, professional and pastoral quality of the lecturers and the consistent focus on biblical orthodoxy and principles within a culture of breadth and depth of biblical and theological scholarship that is fostered in the colleges and universities alike. The lecturers are clearly the dominant influence in the entire educational process; the biblical scholarship is clearly the most eagerly sought component of that education. The universally strong affirmation of these elements by all stakeholder groups gives good ground for a positive evaluation of the theological sector.

As well as these dominant strengths, there are several others that were mentioned at various points, though without the same universal reference. The ability to read a missional context and confidence to lead in that context, based on the internalization of the basic principles of leadership, was one such item (especially noticeable in smaller and more innovative colleges). Another was the generation of a passion for ministry, with a clear and consistent sense of vocation (especially noticeable in colleges with a clearly defined focus on pastoral training). Also highly regarded was a widespread fostering of critical and adaptable theological thinking and attitudes of tolerance and respect in personal engagement, which developed an increased openness of theological and ecclesiastical perspectives, the observable development of independent and critical thinking, and a demonstrable growth in pastoral sensitivity (common in all forms of institutions). Reference was made to the positive aspect of small classes and small college communities as a facilitator of more personalised interaction with both lecturers and peers, which allowed for the practical outworking of theological understandings within a functioning peer community.

- **Aspirational Strengths**

The first set of aspirational strengths relates to curriculum. There is an oft-expressed desire for a greater sense of curriculum management and co-ordination, including more effective inter-relation of units in the course. The other area is in Supervised Field Education, where there is a growing move towards the establishment of more efficient and more accountable supervisor training and development and coordination of authentic field experiences, critical reflection and practical improvement processes. These elements are associated with the acknowledgement of the need for learning to constitute an authentic experience for the student, for theological teaching to connect with the real life of the students in some genuine way, and for students to discover rather than merely to receive theological truths.

The second related category of desired strengths is the enhancement of functional ministry capacity. This was expressed most particularly by graduates and church leaders responsible for the placement and oversight of graduates in ministry: a significant destination of theological graduates. This includes the desire for better leadership development, to include effective experience in a wider range of ministerial duties, learning how to master not only time and program management but also people management, and the ability to assess ministry and personal practices in terms of biblical and theological processes. It also includes the call for the more intentional and cohesive integration of college and local church in the overall training program, with more work done in and with the churches and more experimental and creative approaches to liturgy to facilitate a more contemporary expression of church worship. Beyond the church, there is a desire to broaden the educational horizons of both staff and students, to expand their world view and capacity for effectual dialogue with the broader society, beyond the narrow biblical and theological agenda of many schools. This is aimed at the integration of a theological world view and contemporary social action.

The third aspirational area is the need for theological education to be holistic and integrated rather than teaching just theological data. This need is commonly expressed in more innovative colleges, is emerging in universities, and remains somewhat cautiously approached in more traditional colleges. This requires the personal and strategic integration of cognitive, practical and affective elements of the theological development of the students, including those students who are not specifically ordination candidates. This involves the development of character and values as well as knowledge.

Appendix F: NCLS Leaders Survey 2011 Analysis

Profile of the Survey

The project participated in the NCLS Leaders Survey 2011 with a customised module on the experience of theological training received by ministers currently in positions of church leadership. The module contained items designed to match those in other surveys among current students and recent graduates. Questions asked respondents to indicate the degree to which their theological training had influenced the development of their doctrinal understanding, the promotion of inclusiveness in attitudes to other concepts and social relations, their vocational role and their denominational affiliation. The focus was on the transformative dimension of the theological education received. The purpose was to gain a larger picture of such experience as a supplement to the current field research undertaken within the project.

There were 2613 responses received to this module, with responses categorized into Anglican (41.4%), Catholic (7.2%), Uniting Church (9.4%), Baptist (13.9%), Pentecostal (7.7%) and Other Protestant (20.4%). While the age range of respondents was from 21 to 91, the majority (54.2%) of respondents were aged over 50, with a further 23.1% being over 40. The gender ratio of female to male respondents was 23:77. Some 35% of respondents had completed their initial theological training in the period since 2000, with a further 50% having done so in the period 1980-2000. Of the 65 theological training institutions cited for this training, the most widely represented were Moore Theological College (20.2% of respondents), Australian Lutheran College (5.7%), Morling Baptist College (5.1%), Salvation Army Training College (5.1%), Ridley Melbourne (4.5%) and Sydney Missionary and Bible College (4.4%). All other institutions had fewer than 100 respondents associated with them.

Analysis of the Responses

In the areas of major doctrinal concepts (understanding of God and attitude to the Bible, other people and the Church), most reported that existing understandings had been confirmed (46%) or modified but not radically changed (40%). Fewer than 0.5% reported the negation of previously held doctrinal concepts. There was not a high degree of variation across denominational or institutional types, although a slightly greater degree of change was noted in Catholic, Uniting Church and University bodies than in Anglican and Other Protestant colleges.

In relating how they viewed the differing claims of others both prior to and after their theological education, some respondents reported prior attitudes of lack of interest or awareness (18%), while most (66%) reported an attitude of respect for the right of others to hold different views. There was a slightly increased awareness in such prior views after 1990. In charting their personal development of greater or lesser inclusivity of such ideas as a result of their theological training, most reported having become more exclusive in their positions (11%) or having undergone no change (42%), but a significant minority (38%) reported some though not major growth in greater inclusivity. While there were limited variations across denominations, Anglican respondents reported a lower incidence of inclusivity, especially with regard to the understanding of creation and salvation, while slightly greater inclusivity was reported in areas such as worship and church. The overall incidence of inclusivity decreased slightly in those trained since 2000.

There was no significant effect of theological education reported in matters of family relations or other social networks. There was noted a slightly greater enhancement of family relations since 2000, and less impact among university-trained respondents, but the differences were minimal.

The "before and after" dimensions of social engagement were investigated with respect to topics such as social service, justice, welfare, environmental and political issues. Prior to theological study, some 75% reported having had no or rare involvement in such areas, although there was a very slight increase among those trained after 1990. Uniting Church and Catholic respondents reported the greatest prior involvement, with Anglicans and Baptists reporting the lowest level of involvement. As a result of their study, while 41% reported no change in interest in social engagement, 57% reported an increased or greatly increased interest. Again, Catholic and Uniting Church respondents reported the greatest levels of increased interest, with Anglicans and Pentecostals the lowest levels. There was no discernible difference between universities and theological colleges or in different periods of training. When it came to active involvement in such areas as distinct from merely increased interest, there was little increase reported, with most indicating no change or reduced activity (57%) or some but not major change in involvement (39%). Fewer than 4% indicated a greatly increased engagement. The greatest increase in activity was reported among Catholic, Uniting Church and Baptist respondents, with least increase reported by Anglican and Pentecostal respondents.

Respondents were asked to report on the impact of their theological study on such personal elements as vocational expectations, church affiliation and the connection of their study with their personal life experience. There was limited impact on vocational expectations, with most respondents having had their initial expectations confirmed (53%) or modified but not radically changed (35%). This was quite consistent across all denominations, institutional types and periods of training. Similarly, there was little impact of theological study on denominational affiliation, with an overall tendency to strengthen such affiliation (57%) or to make no change (31%). Catholics showed a slightly higher level of denominational strengthening during their study and Pentecostals showed a slight loosening of denominational affiliation, but over all, there was minimal change in the *status quo*. Connections drawn between theological studies and individual students' life experience were reported as non-existent (22%), occasional but not regular (32%), often and useful (35%), or consistent and intentional (12%). While there was no significant difference across denominations or institutional types, there was a steadily progressive increase in such connectedness in the decades from pre-1980s to post-2000, although even in the later periods, it remained "occasional but helpful."

Conclusions

The main impact of theological study has been consistently to confirm or slightly broaden the pre-existent conceptual understandings of students. The degree to which a greater inclusivity of conceptual thinking, attitudinal perspectives and social relations has been fostered by theological study seems positive, yet somewhat limited. Reports consistently indicate a broadening of intellectual horizons as a result of theological education and a softening of exclusivity in thinking about worship and church. Yet the degree of growth experienced seems to be indirectly proportional to the degree of prior awareness of wider concepts and social activity rather than attributable to the educational program itself. Those who reported a general lack of awareness of other thought or action worlds prior to theological study understandably tended to undergo greater growth in inclusivity, while conversely, those with more inclusive backgrounds or social engagement experience seemed not to experience the same challenges. While degree of change reported was generally minimal, the greatest degree of change in theological concepts and attitudes to others was reported by Catholic and Uniting Church respondents, although Catholics tended to do so concurrently with a strengthening of denominational identification. Conversely, Anglican and Pentecostal respondents indicated the least change in these areas. In no systems or denominations or periods of training was there significant evidence of radically transformative experience. On the contrary, there was rather a strong suggestion of conservatism in the confirmation rather than critical change of held views and practices. This is perhaps most concretely seen in the limited correlation between the reportedly high growth in interest in social engagement and the relatively limited increase in active participation or change in social relations. This perceived disjunction between growth in inclusivity in conceptual thinking and active impact on social relations, vocational outcomes and social engagement is a common element in all categories of responses.

INDEX

accommodation, 13, 23, 50, 96, 126, 134
accreditation, 29, 34, 36, 38, 39, 82, 88, 89, 114, 132
Adelaide College of Divinity, 7, 8, 33, 39, 104, 110, 147
Alphacrucis College, 8, 104, 105, 111, 113, 147
aspirations, 64, 106, 118
assessment, 9, 24, 28, 37, 38, 43, 47, 58, 59, 62, 64, 65, 73, 74, 82, 84, 86, 87, 96, 101, 103, 106, 108, 112, 116, 132, 136, 157, 162, 165, 166, 167
    evaluation, 6, 14, 16, 55, 58, 73, 76, 82, 85, 99, 114, 116, 130, 131, 132, 133, 135, 157, 166, 168
assimilation, 23, 50, 96, 126
Australian Catholic University, 7, 8, 34, 36, 40, 48, 104, 106, 115, 119, 147, 148
Australian College of Theology, 7, 8, 33, 37, 105, 108, 115, 147, 150
Australian Lutheran College, 7, 109, 113, 147, 170
Bible College of South Australia, 115, 147
Billett, Stephen, 20, 23, 34, 148
Brisbane College of Theology, 7, 8, 33, 39, 106, 113, 147
Catholic Theological College, 105, 107, 115, 147, 148
character, 1, 47, 76, 98, 102, 119, 121, 122, 124, 125, 136, 143, 169
Christian Community Experience, 40

Christian Heritage College, 8, 33, 39, 103, 107, 147
church leaders, 2, 7, 8, 9, 50, 66, 81, 83, 88, 90, 92, 96, 99, 114, 135, 163, 164, 167, 168
Clines, David, 21, 22, 29, 42, 43, 148
community, 16, 23, 25, 29, 30, 43, 59, 60, 61, 62, 68, 69, 73, 74, 77, 78, 80, 83, 84, 85, 87, 91, 97, 98, 100, 103, 110, 115, 119, 122, 123, 128, 131, 132, 145, 146, 149, 159, 161, 162, 164, 165, 168
    community engagement, 2, 62, 64, 65, 104, 105, 119, 132, 133, 165
    social engagement, 14, 84, 92, 93, 105, 124, 167, 171, 172
compartmentalisation, 1, 14, 21, 42, 46, 47, 48, 77, 85, 102, 123, 140, 141, 166
courses, 1, 2, 15, 16, 20, 22, 26, 28, 29, 30, 31, 33, 34, 35, 36, 38, 39, 41, 43, 44, 45, 46, 47, 48, 49, 52, 55, 57, 59, 61, 64, 65, 67, 71, 72, 73, 74, 75, 76, 77, 78, 79, 80, 85, 87, 88, 89, 90, 92, 93, 94, 95, 96, 97, 99, 100, 101, 103, 107, 109, 110, 111, 112, 114, 119, 120, 129, 131, 134, 135, 136, 137, 140, 141, 142, 145, 146, 147, 157, 158, 159, 165, 166, 168
    aims, 1, 18, 34, 139
    outcomes, 1, 28, 53, 78, 80, 93, 94, 139, 146, 167

curriculum
- content-centred, 2, 14, 92, 126, 140
- curriculum design, 2, 3, 6, 7, 8, 23, 30, 33, 44, 46, 62, 63, 77, 80, 87, 88, 90, 91, 92, 93, 94, 96, 97, 98, 103, 106, 107, 110, 111, 114, 118, 125, 136, 142, 145, 146, 161, 163, 164
- curriculum development, 6, 31, 34, 44, 50, 61, 76, 88, 89, 90, 91, 105, 164
- curriculum sequencing, 16, 42, 110, 137
- curriculum structure, 2, 3, 100, 136, 140, 141
- learner-centred, 36, 48, 92, 126
- student-centred, 2, 21, 26, 49, 94, 98, 126, 140, 142

deep learning, 2, 28, 106, 107, 145, 157
educational level, 8
faculty, 2, 7, 8, 9, 30, 39, 50, 56, 57, 59, 60, 61, 62, 64, 65, 66, 73, 76, 77, 78, 80, 81, 82, 88, 89, 90, 91, 93, 94, 96, 97, 99, 103, 104, 105, 106, 109, 112, 114, 115, 116, 118, 120, 125, 131, 132, 133, 134, 135, 140, 141, 144, 146, 147, 163, 164, 165
field education, 17, 55, 59, 114, 148, 149, 158, 159
- field placements, 1, 23, 39, 50, 76, 131, 132, 162
- supervised field education, 39, 40, 41, 42, 49, 60, 61, 64, 78, 80, 85, 113, 114, 132, 165, 166, 168

Forge Mission Training Network, 29, 113
formation, 5, 12, 13, 18, 19, 20, 23, 29, 30, 36, 40, 42, 46, 56, 61, 63, 74, 75, 78, 81, 85, 88, 92, 94, 98, 100, 108, 115, 121, 122, 123, 133, 136, 145, 146, 150, 160, 161, 164, 165, 166, 167
- ministerial formation, 40, 42, 43
- personal formation, 75, 82, 101, 108, 121, 134

Foster, Charles, 19, 20, 29, 149
foundationalism, 1, 22, 42, 43, 46, 47, 48

graduates, 2, 7, 8, 9, 20, 31, 50, 54, 56, 57, 59, 60, 61, 63, 64, 66, 73, 75, 76, 77, 81, 82, 83, 84, 85, 88, 90, 91, 92, 94, 96, 98, 99, 103, 104, 105, 110, 116, 118, 124, 133, 144, 147, 156, 163, 164, 166, 167, 168, 170
Grattan Institute, 14
Haar, Stephen, 18, 21, 22, 29, 42, 143, 149
institutional purpose, 2, 35, 104, 109
integration, 3, 23, 42, 46, 47, 49, 50, 54, 58, 59, 60, 61, 63, 75, 76, 77, 78, 80, 81, 82, 84, 85, 91, 93, 94, 95, 96, 97, 100, 101, 102, 103, 108, 109, 113, 114, 115, 116, 122, 124, 125, 130, 132, 133, 134, 135, 136, 140, 142, 145, 146, 156, 157, 158, 161, 166, 168, 169
- holistic learning, 24
- integrative learning, 5, 12, 18, 26, 100, 101, 102, 111, 116, 123, 136, 141, 142
- Integrative Ministry Practice, 110
- integrative teaching, 25
- personal integration, 2, 47, 80, 83, 84, 109, 134, 137, 140

learning styles, 1, 24, 25, 60, 93, 94, 95, 100, 134
- experiential learning, 1, 50, 61, 62, 64, 65, 84, 104, 105, 114, 115, 132, 141, 145, 164, 165

life experience
- current life experience, 58, 59, 60, 158
- prior life experience, 42, 50, 55, 56, 57, 58, 59, 60, 63, 64, 88, 116, 136, 158, 162

Malyon College, 106, 113, 114, 147, 148
Melbourne College of Divinity, 1, 6, 7, 8, 33, 37, 38, 147
- MCD University of Divinity, 1, 6, 7

Mezirow, Jack, 11, 12, 13, 14, 17, 18, 121, 142, 149, 150
Moore Theological College, 7, 8, 33, 39, 103, 147, 170
Murdoch University, 8, 40, 104, 107, 111, 114, 147

INDEX

Nazarene Theological College, 103, 110, 113, 114, 115, 147
online education, 110
   online learning, 24, 93, 100, 110, 130
ordination, 12, 61, 79, 164
   ordained ministry, 5, 6, 8, 30, 33, 53, 54, 121, 122, 156, 157, 160, 167
   ordination candidates, 45, 57, 59, 61, 62, 63, 64, 75, 76, 78, 80, 102, 109, 115, 120, 121, 160, 161, 164, 165, 169
   ordination requirements, 40, 44, 54, 90, 156, 163
outcomes
   graduate attributes, 2, 20, 56, 136, 137
   graduate outcomes, 20, 82, 84, 89, 91, 160
   learning outcomes, 2, 20, 34, 103, 136
pedagogy, 13, 14, 15, 17, 19, 20, 21, 34, 36, 42, 44, 46, 47, 88, 105, 106, 110, 125, 126, 128, 130, 133, 136, 140, 162
peer learning, 24, 25, 112, 129, 157
   collaborative learning, 62, 85, 113, 135, 166
Pentecostal, 33, 121, 160, 170, 171, 172
   Pentecostal colleges, 39, 45, 69, 108
perspectives, 8, 9, 11, 12, 21, 22, 23, 26, 28, 34, 58, 64, 67, 69, 74, 76, 87, 93, 94, 100, 101, 106, 110, 111, 113, 121, 134, 135, 145, 157, 168, 171
philosophy, 37, 38, 39, 40, 41, 96, 107, 140, 149, 158
   philosophical coherence, 2, 103
   philosophical ethos, 77, 103
practices, 2, 3, 8, 10, 12, 17, 20, 23, 24, 29, 47, 50, 54, 57, 70, 71, 72, 73, 78, 79, 84, 91, 100, 102, 103, 106, 108, 111, 112, 113, 114, 116, 118, 120, 122, 123, 124, 125, 126, 131, 134, 136, 142, 144, 156, 168, 172
principles, 1, 2, 3, 10, 13, 15, 18, 22, 24, 25, 27, 28, 54, 61, 67, 76, 83, 84, 85, 96, 100, 102, 103, 106, 108, 114, 116, 118, 123, 124, 125, 126, 130, 131, 133, 136, 142, 156, 162, 167, 168

Queensland Theological College, 113, 116, 147
Queensland University of Technology, 46, 147, 148
reflection, 5, 11, 23, 25, 26, 47, 48, 57, 58, 59, 60, 62, 76, 83, 84, 95, 97, 100, 101, 108, 109, 111, 113, 114, 115, 116, 121, 133, 134, 141, 145, 157, 160, 168
Ridley Melbourne, 33, 104, 109, 112, 113, 115, 147, 170
Sadler, D Royce, 15, 150
skills
   learning skills, 2, 14
   ministry skills, 35, 36, 39, 42, 50, 54, 67, 75, 76, 77, 81, 82, 83, 84, 97, 157, 158, 162, 164, 167
   vocational skills, 20, 35, 46, 47, 102, 121, 131
stakeholders, 1, 2, 5, 6, 8, 10, 50, 56, 58, 66, 76, 88, 89, 90, 91, 92, 96, 98, 101, 104, 105, 118, 122, 123, 125, 144, 163, 164, 167
Sydney College of Divinity, 7, 8, 33, 38, 147
Tabor Adelaide, 7, 8, 107, 108, 113, 147
Tabor Victoria, 7, 8, 106, 108, 111, 113, 147
teaching
   facilitator, 21, 24, 25, 30, 31, 98, 99, 112, 135, 168
   methods, 1, 7, 23, 100, 110
   roles, 26, 62, 79, 84, 98, 102, 131
team teaching, 102, 135, 157
terminology, 2, 14, 30, 41, 78, 85, 118, 145, 165
transformation
   personal transformation, 5, 34, 43, 66, 67, 79, 143, 160
   transformative experience, 1, 18, 22, 24, 74, 85, 122, 126, 133, 145, 166, 172
   transformative learning, 1, 2, 5, 6, 7, 8, 11, 12, 13, 14, 16, 17, 18, 19, 20, 21, 22, 23, 24, 25, 26, 27, 28, 29, 30, 31, 33, 42, 50, 66, 73, 77,

80, 81, 85, 86, 87, 88, 89, 92, 94, 95, 96, 97, 98, 99, 100, 101, 106, 109, 110, 111, 112, 116, 118, 121, 122, 123, 137, 141, 142, 145, 149, 150, 165, 166
    transformative units, 2, 80, 85, 108, 109, 166
UNESCO, 14, 46, 87, 150
Uniting College fo Leadership & Theology, 104, 105, 109, 147
units
    advanced units, 93, 111
    capstone units, 80, 97, 109
    integrative units, 93, 109
    introductory units, 1, 41, 43, 46, 47, 48, 80, 107, 141, 157

University of Queensland, 46, 47, 147
values, 11, 13, 20, 25, 27, 35, 67, 76, 83, 102, 110, 115, 121, 123, 124, 125, 144, 145, 157, 169
Vose Seminary, 108, 112, 116, 147
    Vose Mission, 115
Whitley College, 18, 104, 105, 107, 113
Williams, Rowan (Archbishop), 19, 20, 30, 150
Winkelmes, Mary-Ann, 23, 29, 150
Work Integrated Learning, 59, 104
work load, 1, 26, 42, 43, 73, 95, 96, 105, 111

www.ingramcontent.com/pod-product-compliance
Lightning Source LLC
Chambersburg PA
CBHW051333110526
44591CB00026B/2985